Thomas Wolfe
A Checklist

THE SERIF SERIES: BIBLIOGRAPHIES AND CHECKLISTS

GENERAL EDITOR: William White, Wayne State University

Thomas Wolfe

A Checklist

By Elmer D. Johnson

Radford College

The Kent State University Press

The Serif Series: Number 12
Bibliographies and Checklists

William White, General Editor
Wayne State University

Copyright © 1970 by Elmer D. Johnson
All rights reserved
Standard Book Number 87338-050-9
Library of Congress Card Catalogue Number 74-626233
Manufactured in the United States of America
at the Press of The Oberlin Printing Company
Designed by Merald E. Wrolstad

First Edition

Contents

Abbreviations

Avon *SS*: *Short Stories*. Avon Book Company, 1944.

Avon *THB*: *The Hills Beyond*. Avon Book Company, 1944.

FDTM: *From Death To Morning*. Charles Scribner's Sons, 1935.

Field: Leslie A. Field, ed. *Thomas Wolfe: Three Decades of Criticism*. New York University Press, 1968.

FOAN: *The Face of a Nation*. Charles Scribner's Sons, 1939.

Frings: *Look Homeward, Angel. A Play by Ketti Frings*. Charles Scribner's Sons, 1958.

Holman: C. Hugh Holman, ed. *The World of Thomas Wolfe*. Charles Scribner's Sons, 1962.

Letters: *The Letters of Thomas Wolfe*. Charles Scribner's Sons, 1956.

LHA: *Look Homeward, Angel*. Charles Scribner's Sons, 1929.

Lion *THB*: *The Hills Beyond*. Lion Books, 1955.

LTHM: *Letters to His Mother*. Charles Scribner's Sons, 1943.

OTDKB: *Only the Dead Know Brooklyn*. New American Library, 1952.

OTATR: *Of Time and the River*. Charles Scribner's Sons, 1935.

Penguin *SS*: *Short Stories*. Penguin Books, 1947.

Perennial *THB*: *The Hills Beyond*. Harper & Row, 1964.

Pollock: Thomas C. Pollock and Oscar Cargill, eds., *Thomas Wolfe at Washington Square*. New York University Press, 1954.

PTW:　*The Portable Thomas Wolfe*. Viking Press, 1946.

Short Novels:　C. Hugh Holman, ed. *The Short Novels of Thomas Wolfe*. Charles Scribner's Sons, 1961.

SLD:　*A Stone, A Leaf, A Door*. Charles Scribner's Sons, 1945.

SOAN:　*The Story of a Novel*. Charles Scribner's Sons, 1935.

THB:　*The Hills Beyond*. Harper and Brothers, 1941.

TWATR:　*The Web and The Rock*. Harper and Brothers, 1939.

TWR:　C. Hugh Holman, ed. *The Thomas Wolfe Reader*. Scribners, 1962.

Walser:　Richard Walser, ed. *The Enigma of Thomas Wolfe*. Harvard University Press, 1953.

YCGHA:　*You Can't Go Home Again*. Harper, 1940.

Introduction

Before he died in 1938 at the age of 37, Thomas Wolfe
was already a controversial figure on the American literary scene.
At that time he had published two novels, or only one
according to some of his critics, a book of short stories,
and an *apologia* that he called *The Story of a Novel*.
But his works were already being translated into several
European languages, and his critics were already legion.
Whereas some said he was a genius, others said genius was
not enough, and called his works merely formless effusions
of words. Today, three decades later, the critics still
debate his qualities as a writer and his place in
twentieth century literature.

But despite his questionable position as a writer—or perhaps
because of it—Thomas Wolfe has been one of the most
written-about authors in American literature. For every page he
wrote, at least ten have been written about him. He has been
compared to Joyce and Proust, and also to Whitman and
Melville. He has been accused of being pro-Communist
and pro-German, and of being anti-Semitic and anti-Negro;
yet his love for America is constantly apparent in his writings.
A dozen or more major books have been written about him,
along with scores of theses and dissertations, and hundreds
of articles. His posthumous publications included two additional
novels, culled by editors from his voluminous files, plus two

volumes of letters, and several other miscellaneous works. Some of his prose passages have been published as poetry, and even his notebooks were recently edited for publication. If his American audience is not enough, his works have been translated into at least fifteen foreign languages, and reviews and critical articles have appeared in just as many countries. Most important for posterity, his writings continue to command attention, and as much has been written about him in the sixties as in the thirties. It seems that each college-age generation discovers him and claims him for its own. Consequently, although bibliographies of Wolfe appeared in 1943 and in 1959, enough new material has appeared to warrant still another attempt at an exhaustive bibliography.

No bibliography is, of course, ever complete, and this one makes no claim to definitiveness. However, it is an attempt at a reasonably complete and essentially useful one. It is doubtful that any significant work by Wolfe has been overlooked, but it is possible that a few worthwhile articles about him have been omitted. For example, newspaper articles have been included only if they contained information or opinions not readily available elsewhere. Some, but not all, articles about Wolfe from undergraduate college publications have been included as examples of the type. The same is true of book reviews. Coverage of foreign material about Wolfe is representative rather than complete. Occasionally short references to Wolfe have been included because of the significance of the author, while similar items by relatively unknown writers are omitted. Such then is the nature of this Wolfe bibliography: not perfect, but hopefully complete enough to be useful for a long time.

Words of appreciation are due to many friends who have aided from time to time in the donations of Wolfeana or bibliographical references. Librarians, particularly those at

Harvard University and at the University of North Carolina,
have been most helpful. T. V. Theobald of Syracuse, N. Y.,
has shared numerous bibliographical finds on Wolfe
from his own files, and for this I am most grateful.
To all who have had a share in bringing these hundreds of items
together, I extend my heartiest appreciation. And for all
errors, I accept the responsibility.

ELMER D. JOHNSON

Radford, Virginia
March, 1969

A. Books

I. *Look Homeward, Angel.*

A1 First Edition:
Look Homeward, Angel / A Story of the Buried Life / by / Thomas Wolfe

"At one time the earth was probably a white-hot sphere like the sun."—Tarr and McMurry.*

Charles Scribner's Sons / New York / 1929

vii, 1 l., 3-626 p., 2 leaves. 19.5 by 14 cm.
Published October 18, 1929

*The quotation is from p. 1 of *A Complete Geography*, by Ralph S. Tarr and Frank M. McMurry (Macmillan, 1902). The title *Look Homeward, Angel* comes from John Milton's "Lycidas," line 163.

A2 First English Edition:
Look Homeward, / Angel / A Story of the Buried Life / by / Thomas Wolfe

(Quotation as above)

London / William Heinemann Ltd.

vii, 3-613 p., 3 blank pages. 17 by 13 cm. Published July 14, 1930.

This edition has several minor textual variations from the American edition. A new printing in 1932 and another in 1958.

A3 English Paperback Edition:

> A Four-Square Book / Look Homeward, Angel /
> Thomas Wolfe / (printer's device) / Four Square Books
> Limited / 173 New Bond Street, London, W. 1
>
> 2 l., 5-447 p., 1 unnumbered page. 11.5 by 18.5 cm.
> Published in 1960.

A4 Canadian Edition:

> Same as American first edition, except for imprint:
> Toronto, Macmillan, 1934

A5 Modern Library Reprint:

> Look Homeward, / Angel / A Story of the Buried Life /
> by / Thomas Wolfe
>
> (Quotation as in first edition, followed by Modern
> Library device)
>
> 5 l., 3-626 p., 4 l. 21 by 14.5 cm. Published in 1934.

A6 Grosset and Dunlap Reprint:

> Look Homeward, Angel / A Story of the Buried Life /
> (rule) / by /Thomas Wolfe / (Quotation as in first
> edition) / Grossett & Dunlap / Publishers New York /
> By special arrangement with Charles Scribner's
> Sons / (rule)
>
> 6 l., 3-626 p., 2 blank leaves. 14 by 20 cm.
> Published October 19, 1939.

A7 Garden City Reprint:

> Similar to first edition except for imprint: Garden City
> Publishing Company, Garden City, N. Y.
> Published November 7, 1940.

A8 Armed Services Edition:

Look Homeward, / Angel / A Novel by / Thomas
Wolfe. / Armed Services Edition
0-31

2 l., 5-512 p., 1 leaf; two columns to page;
oblong, 14.5 x 17.5 cm.

Published in 1943 in paperback, this version is slightly
condensed.

A9 Illustrated Edition:

A Story of the Buried Life / Look Homeward / Angel /
By Thomas Wolfe / Illustrated by Douglas W. Gorsline /
(picture of stone angel) / (quotation as in first
edition) / Charles Scribner's Sons New York / 1947

5 l., 1-662 p., 1 leaf. 24 by 16.5 cm. Reissued in 1956 and
1963. There are over 100 illustrations by Gorsline,
including 12 full page drawings.

A10 Canadian Illustrated Edition:

Similar to above, except for imprint: S. J. R. Saunders,
Toronto.

A11 Modern Standard Authors Edition:

A Story of the Buried Life / Look Homeward / Angel /
By / Thomas Wolfe / Illustrated by Douglas W.
Gorsline / With an Introduction by Maxwell E. Perkins /
Charles Scribner's Sons / New York

3 l., vii-xvi, 2 l., 1-662 p., 3 blank leaves. 21.5 by 15 cm.

Published in 1952 and re-issued in 1957, this is the same
as the Illustrated Edition, except for smaller format,
no full page illustrations, and the addition of
Perkins' "Introduction."

A12 Abridged Edition:

> Look Homeward, Angel / II. The Adventures of Young
> Gant / by Thomas Wolfe / With an Introduction by /
> Edward C. Aswell / (Quotation as in First Edition) /
> (Publisher's device) / A Signet Book / Published
> by the New American Library
>
> 3 l., vii-xiv, 15-192 p. 18 x 11 cm. Paperback. This is taken
> from pp. 180-370 of the original edition.

A13 Scribner Library Edition:

> Look Homeward, / Angel / A Story of the Buried Life /
> by / Thomas Wolfe / With an Introduction /
> by Maxwell E. Perkins / Charles Scribner's Sons /
> New York.
>
> 3 l., vii-xiv, 3 l., 3-522 p. 20.5 by 13.5 cm. Published in
> 1960, this is SL-9 in the Scribner Library Series.

A14 Ketti Fring's Play:

> Ketti Frings / Look / Homeward, / Angel / A Play /
> Based on the Novel by Thomas Wolfe / With an
> Introduction by Edward C. Aswell / Charles
> Scribner's Sons, New York.
>
> 12 l., 19-186 p., 2 blank leaves. 21 by 14 cm. Published
> in 1958, this has a double-paged illustration of the
> stage setting as frontispiece.

A15 Samuel French Edition:

> Look Homeward, / Angel / A Comedy-Drama / in
> Three Acts / by Ketti Frings / Based on the Novel /
> by Thomas Wolfe / Winner, Pulitzer Prize, 1958; /
> New York Critics' Award, 1958 / (publisher's device) /

Samuel French, Inc. / 25 West 45th Street
New York 36 / London Toronto

2 l., 3-99 p., 3 unnumbered pages. 18.5 by 13 cm. Paperback.

A16 First German Edition:

Thomas Wolfe / Schau Heimwärts, Engel! /
Eine Geschichte vom begrabnen / Leben / Roman /

Einst war die Erde wahrschein- /
lich ein Weissglühender Ball wie /
die Sonne. Tarr and McMurry /

1932 / Rowohlt / Berlin

6 l., 11-556 p., 1 leaf. 20.5 by 13 cm. Re-issued in Berlin,
1936, and in Hamburg, 1947 and 1951.
The translator was Hans Schiebelhuth.

A17 German Book-Club Edition:

Thomas Wolfe / Schau Heimwärts, Engel! / Eine
Geschichte vom begrabnen / Leben / Roman /
(Quotation as above) / Berlin / Deutsche
Buch-Gemeinschaft / G.m.b.H.

6 l., 11-583 p., 2 leaves. 19 by 13 cm. Published in 1937
and re-issued in 1948 and 1956, this is the
Schiebelhuth translation.

A18 Rowohlt Reprint Edition:

Similar to first German edition, except for imprint:
Hamburg, Rowohlt, 1954; and collation:

3 l., 3-446 p., 1 leaf. 19.5 by 13 cm.

A19 German Paperback Edition:

Thomas Wolfe / Schau Heimwärts, Engel ! / Eine
Geschichte vom begrabnen Leben / (Quotation as in

first German edition) / (publisher's device) /
Rowohlt

4 l., 9-452 p., 10 p. advertisements. 19 by 11.5 cm.
Paperback. Published in 1958, this is No. 275-276 in
Rowohlt's Rotations Romane series.

Other German Editions:

Other German editions of *LHA*, noticed in bibliographies
but unexamined, include ones with the following imprints:

A20 Halle, Mitteldeutscher Verlag, 1955. 508 p.

A21 Gutersloh, Bertelsmann Lesering, 1960. 476 p.

A22 Berlin, Darmstadt, Wien, Deutsche Buch-Gemeinschaft,
1959. 546 p.

A23 Swedish Edition:

Se Hemåt, Ängel ! / av / Thomas Wolfe / Med Inledning
av / Anders Österling / Till Svenska av / Elsa Af
Trolle / (publisher's device) / Stockholm /
Albert Bonniers Förlag

xii, 3-515 p. 19.5 by 13 cm. Published in 1932 and
translated by Elsa af Trolle.

A24 Norwegian Edition:

Thomas Wolfe / Finn Veien, Engel ! / (publisher's
device) / Steenske Forlag. Oslo

2 v. v.1: 3 l., 5-244 p., 1 leaf; v.2: 3 l., 245-544 p.,
1 leaf. 19.5 by 13 cm. Also in a one-volume cloth edition,
this was translated by Hans Heiberg and published in 1933.

A25 Norwegian Reprint Edition:

Thomas Wolfe / Finn Veien, Engel! / Til norsk ved / Hans Heiberg / J. W. Cappelens Forlag / Oslo 1963

2 l., 5-452 p., 1 leaf. 20.5 by 12.5 cm. Paperback.

A26 Czechoslovak Edition:

Thomas Wolfe / K Domovu Se Dívej, Andele / Evropský Literární Klub Praha

4 l., 9-508 p., 2 l. 22 by 14.5 cm. Published in 1936 and translated by Zdenek Vançura and Vladimir Vendys. Reprinted in 1958 under the imprint of "B. Janda, Praha."

A27 Czechoslovak Reprint Edition:

K Domovu Pohled', / Andele! / Pribeh zawuteho zivota / Praha, Statni Nakladatelstvi / Krasne Literatury a Umeni / 1961.

662 p. 21 by 14 cm. (Soudoba Svetova Proza, 115) This is the Vançura-Vendys translation with some revisions.

A28 Danish Edition:

Thomas Wolfe / Englen Paa Torvet / (Publisher's device) / Nyt Nordisk Forlag Arnold Busck / Kjobenhavn MCMXLI

2 v. v. 1: 4 l., 9-336 p.; v. 2: 3 l., 342-522 p., 1 leaf. 21.5 by 15.5 cm. Also available in one volume edition. Published in 1941, this was translated by Ulrich Knigge and Eva Mortensen.

A29 Danish Edition of the Frings Play:

Englen paa Torvet / Skuespil af Ketti Frings / Kobenhavn / Nyt Nordisk Forlag

2 l., 3-123 p. Translated by Holger Bech and published in 1959.

A30 Italian Edition:

Thomas Wolfe / Angelo, / guarda il passato / Traduzione di Jole Jannelli Pintor / Einaudi 4 l., 9-670 p., 1 leaf. 22 by 13.5 cm. Published in Turin, 1949.

A31 French Edition:

Thomas Wolfe / Aux Sources / Du Fleuve / Roman / Traduit de l'américain par / Pierre Singer / Preface de / Maurice Nadeau / 1956 / (double rule) / Librairie Stock / Delamain et Boutelleau / 6, rue Casimir Delavigne, / Paris

3 l., 7-542 p., 1 leaf. 20.5 by 14 cm.

A32 Serbian Edition:

Tomac Bylf / Pogledaj Dom Cboj Ahdjele / Prebeo / Lyka Semenovik / 1954 / Novo Pokolenje-Beograd

2 v. v. 1: 3 l., 5-340 p., 1 leaf; v.2: 4 l., 7-344 p., 3 leaves. Translated by Luka Semenovich, with an introduction by Vera Ilyich, this was published in Belgrade as v. 11-12 of Biblioteka Epoka.

A33 Croatian Edition:

Ozri se / proti domu, / angel / Thomas Wolfe / Cankarjeva Zalozba v Ljubljani 1964

2 v. v.1: 2 l., 5-366 p., 1 leaf; v.2: 2 l., 5-342 p., 1 leaf. 17.5 by 11.5 cm. This was translated by Mira Mihelich, with an introduction by Rapa Suklje.
An earlier edition may have been issued in 1957.

A34 Japanese Edition:

The title: / "Look Homeward, Angel!" / The Author: / Thomas Wolfe / The date: / 1929.

(This is followed by a portrait of Wolfe and a title-page in Japanese. The Japanese title is: *Tenshi yo kokyo o miyo*).

2 v. v.1: 3 l., 3-302 p., 1 leaf; v.2: 3 l., 1-300 p., 2 leaves. This was translated by Mamoru Osawa and published by Mikasa Shobo in Tokyo, 1954.

A35 Bosnian Edition:

Thomas Wolfe: Pogledaj dom svoj, Andjele. Sarajevo, Svjetlost, 1963.

2 v. v.1: 375 p.; v.2: 421 p.

A36 Polish Edition:

Thomas Wolfe: Spojre ku domowi, Aniele. Warsaw, Czytelnik, 1962.

582 p. Translated by Krystyna Tarnowska.

A37 Hungarian Edition:

Thomas Wolfe: Nézz vissza, Angyal; Az eltémetett élet tortenéte.

Budapest, Europa, 1962. 584 p. Translated by Lajos P. Horvath, with note on Wolfe by Peter Nagy.

A38 Egyptian Edition of Frings' Play:

Ila al-bayt ya Malaki. Cairo, Matba at Misr, 1962.

174 p., translated by Hilmi Jurji.

II. *Of Time and the River*

A39 First Edition:

> Of Time and the River / A Legend of Man's Hunger /
> in his Youth / by / Thomas Wolfe
>
> "Who knoweth the spirit of man that goeth upward, /
> and the spirit of the beast that goeth downward to /
> the Earth?" * /
>
> (Publisher's device) / Charles Scribner's Sons /
> New York / 1935.
>
> 7 l., 3-912 p., 2 l. 21.5 by 15 cm. Published March 8, 1935.
>
> *The quotation is *Ecclesiastes* 3:21.
>
> *OTATR* is divided into eight books: I. Orestes: Flight
> before Fury; II. Young Faustus; III. Telemachus;
> IV. Proteus: The City; V. Jason's Voyage; VI. Antaeus:
> Earth Again; VII. Kronos and Rhea: The Dream of Time;
> VIII. Faust and Helen.

A40 English Edition:

> Same as above except for publisher's device and imprint:
> William Heinemann Ltd.; London / 1935.
>
> Published August 19, 1935. Reprint edition issued in 1937.

A41 Grosset and Dunlap Reprint Edition:

> Identical with first edition except for imprint, and a
> slightly larger format: 23 by 15 cm. Published in 1939.

A42 Sun Dial Press Reprint Edition:

> Identical with first edition except for imprint and a
> smaller format: 21 by 14 cm. Published in 1944
> and issued simultaneously in Toronto by the
> Blue Ribbon Press.

A43 Armed Services Edition:

Of Time and / The River / by / Thomas Wolfe /
Editions for the Armed Services, Inc. / A non-profit
organization established by / the Council on Books
in Wartime. New York

2 l., 5-512 p., Oblong, 11.5 by 17 cm., 2 columns per page.
Considerably condensed, this includes "Orestes,"
"Young Faustus," "Telemachus," "Jason's Voyage,"
"Kronos and Rhea," and "Faust and Helen."
It is Armed Services Edition No. 1013.

A44 Scribner Library Edition:

Of Time and the River: / Young Faustus / Telemachus /
by / Thomas Wolfe / With an introduction by C. Hugh
Holman / (Quotation as in first edition) /
Charles Scribner's Sons / New York.

5 l., xi-xvii, 1 unnumbered page, 1 leaf, 3-318 p., 20.5 by
13.5 cm. Published in 1965. This is Scribner Library SL 106.

A45 German First Edition:

Thomas Wolfe / Von Zeit und Strom / Eine Legende
vom Hunger des Menschen / in der Jugend / Roman /
Erster Band (or Zweiter Band) / (Quotation in
German) / 1936 / Rowohlt / Berlin

2 v. v. 1: 5 l., 11-461 p., 1 blank page, 1 leaf; v.2: 4 l.,
9-622 p., 1 leaf. Published in 1936 and translated
by Hans Schiebelhuth.

A46 German Reprint Edition:

Thomas Wolfe / Von Zeit und Strom / Eine Legende /
vom Hunger des Menschen / in der Jugend / Roman /
(Quotation in German) / Rowohlt Verlag Hamburg

4 l., 9-976 p., 2 leaves. 20.5 by 13 cm. Published in 1952, this is the Hans Schiebelhuth translation.

A47 German Book-Club Edition:

Thomas Wolfe: Von Zeit und Strom. Darmstadt, Moderner Buch-Club, 1960. 972 p.

A48 Norwegian Edition:

Thomas Wolfe / I Drift / På Livets Elv / 2. Oplag / (Publisher's device) / Steenske Forlag / Oslo

4 l., 9-386 p., 1 leaf. 23 by 17 cm. Translated by Trygve Width and published in 1937, this volume contains the first three books of *OTATR*.

Thomas Wolfe / Byen, Reisen / og Drommen / (Publisher's device) Steenske / Forlag

3 l., 7-416 p. 23 by 17 cm. Translated by Trygve Width and published in 1938, this volume contains the last five books of *OTATR*.

A49 Dutch Edition:

Thomas Wolfe / Het Leven Schroeit / Vertaling van J. P. Maschmeijer-Buekers / Eerste Druk / (Quotation in Dutch) / N. V. Servire Den Haag

1-437 p., 1 blank page, 1 leaf. 22 by 16.5 cm. Published in 1935, this volume contains the first three books of *OTATR*. The remaining parts were to be published under the title *Een Mensch Keert Weer*, but were never issued.

A50 Argentine Edition:

Thomas Wolfe / Del Tiempo / y del Rio / Una Leyenda de la Ansiedad del / Hombre en su Juventud /

Tomo I (or II) / (Publisher's device) /
Emecé Editores, S. A. / Buenos Aires

2 v. v.1: 7 l., 15-604 p., 2 leaves; v.2: 5 l., 11-624 p.,
2 leaves. 20.5 by 13 cm. Published in 1948, this was
translated by Sara Kurlat de Lajmanovich.

A51 French Edition:

Thomas Wolfe / Au Fil du Temps / (Of Time and the
River) / Roman / Traduction / R. N. Raimbault /
Manoel Faucher / et / Charles P. Vorce / 1951 /
Librairie Stock / Delamain et Boutelleau /
6, rue Casimir Delavigne / Paris

3 l., 7-602 p., 3 leaves. 20 by 14.5 cm. Published in 1951,
this volume contains only the first four parts of *OTATR*.
There is an introduction by R. N. Raimbault.

A52 German Partial Edition:

A short group of selections from *OTATR*, illustrated
with woodcuts by Hans Orlowski, was published in Berlin
in 1939, by the Meister Schule des Deutschen Handwerks.
The title was: *So Beginnt Thomas Wolfes Von Zeit
und Strom*. It contained only 15 unnumbered pages,
and was 26 by 17 cm.

A53 Italian Edition:

Il Fiume / e il Tempo / Storia / dell' insaziabile fame
dell' uomo / nella giovinezza / di / Thomas Wolfe /
(Quotation in Italian) / Arnoldo Mondadori Editore /
(rule) / 1.9.5.8

5 l., 11-1015 p., 1 blank page, 1 leaf, 3 leaves advertising.
The translation is by Cesare Vivante.

A54 Hungarian Edition:

Thomas Wolfe / Az Idöröl és a Folyóról / Legenda /
az ember ifjúkori éhségéröl / Elsö Kötet (or Második
Kötet) / Európa Könyvkiadó / 1968

2 v. v.1: 7 l., 15-495 p., 1 unnumbered page; v.2: 3 l.,
7-611 p., 1 unnumbered page. Translated by Arpad Goncz.

A55 Czechoslovak Edition:

Thomas Wolfe: O Casu a Rěce; Vyprávění o Hladu
Mládi. Prague, 1961.

1108 p. Translated by Vladimir Vendys and
Jarmila Urbanková.

III. *From Death To Morning*

A56 First Edition:

From Death to Morning / By / Thomas Wolfe /
Vigil strange I kept on the field one night.* /
Charles Scribner's Sons / New York / 1935

7 l., 1-304 p., 1 leaf. 19.5 by 13.5 cm.

This is a collection of short stories, all of which had
appeared previously in periodicals. They are: "No Door,"
"Death the Proud Brother," "The Face of the War,"
"Only the Dead Know Brooklyn," "Dark in the Forest,
Strange as Time," "The Four Lost Men," "Gulliver,"
"The Bums at Sunset," "One of the Girls in Our Party,"
"The Far and the Near," "In the Park," "The Men
of Old Catawba," "Circus at Dawn," and "The Web of
Earth."

*From the "Drum Taps" sequence of Walt Whitman's
Leaves of Grass.

A57 English Edition:

From Death to Morning / by / Thomas Wolfe /
(Quotation as above) / (Publisher's device) / London /
William Heinemann, Ltd.

4 l., 1-280 p. 19 by 13 cm. Published in 1936.

A58 Grosset and Dunlap Edition:

Thomas Wolfe / From Death / to / Morning /
(Publisher's device) / Grosset & Dunlap, Publishers /
New York

6 l., 1-304 p., 1 leaf. 19.5 by 13.5 cm. Published in 1948.

A59 Scribner's Reprint Edition:

From Death / to Morning / by / Thomas Wolfe /
(Quotation as in first edition) / Charles Scribner's Sons /
New York.

6 l., 1-304 p., 1 leaf. 21 by 14 cm. Published in 1958.

A60 Penguin Paperback Edition:

Thomas Wolfe / Short / Stories / (Quotation as above) /
(Publisher's device) / Penguin Books, Inc. New York

4 l., 1-150 p., 1 leaf. 18 by 11 cm. Published in 1947;
reprinted 1949.

This edition contains seven stories from *FDTM*,
with "The Story of a Novel" added. They are:
"The Men of Old Catawba," "The Four Lost Men,"
"Circus at Dawn," "The Bums at Sunset," "Only the Dead
Know Brooklyn," and "Gulliver."

16

A61 Signet Paperback Edition:

Thomas Wolfe Short Stories / Only the Dead Know
Brooklyn / Selections from / From Death to Morning /
plus / The Story of a Novel / (Publisher's device) /
A Signet Book / Published by The New American Library

Except for cover and title page, this is a reprint of the
Penguin Edition, published in 1952.

A62 Scribner Library Edition:

Except for being in a paperback edition, and slightly
smaller (20.5 by 13.5 cm.), this is identical to the
Scribner's Reprint Edition. It is Scribner Library No. 117.

A63 German Edition:

Thomas Wolfe / Vom Tod Zum Morgen / (Quotation
in German) / 1937 / Rowohlt / Berlin

4 l., 9-308 p., 2 leaves. 20.5 by 13 cm. Translated by
Hans Schiebelhuth, this is complete.

A64 German Partial Editions:

Thomas Wolfe / Das Geweb aus Erde / Eine Erzählung /
Rowohlt / Stuttgart Hamburg

3 l., 7-134 p., 1 leaf. 22.5 by 14.5 cm. Published in 1948.

This is "The Web of Earth," from *FDTM*, translated
by Hans Schiebelhuth, and illustrated by Wilhelm Geyer.

A65 Thomas Wolfe / Das Geweb aus Erde / (rule) / 1954 /
(rule) / Albert Langen Georg Müller / München

2 l., 5-103 p., 1 p. ad. 18.5 by 11 cm. This is the
Schiebelhuth Translation.

A66 Thomas Wolfe / Tod / Der Stolze Bruder /
Erzählung / R. Piper & Co Verlag / München

2 l., 5-62 p., 1 leaf. 19 by 12.5 cm. Published in 1953.

This is "Death, the Proud Brother," from *FDTM*,
translated by Hans Schiebelhuth. There is a "Nachwort,"
pp. 61-62, by Hans Egon Holthusen. This is
Piper-Bücherei No. 57.

A67 Thomas Wolfe: Tod, der Stolze Bruder. Bielefeld /
Hannover, Velhagen und Klasing, 1950. 48 p.
Deutsche Lesebogen No. 25.

A68 Thomas Wolfe / Die Leute / von Alt-Catawba /
Erzählungen / Übersetzung von / Hans Schiebelhuth /
Nachwort von / Albert Haueis / Reclam-Verlag
Stuttgart

1 l., 3-85, 3 unnumbered pages. 15.5 by 9.5 cm.
Published in 1954.

This small paperback includes "Only the Dead Know
Brooklyn," "Dark in the Forest, Strange as Time,"
"In the Park," "The Men of Old Catawba," and
"Circus at Dawn."

A69 Thomas Wolfe / Mein Onkel Bascom / und / Das Geweb
aus Erde / Zwei Erzählungen / mit Dokumenten zu
ihrer / Vorgeschichte / (Publisher's device) / Rowohlt.

3 l., 7-153, 2 unnumbered pages, 5 p. ads. Published in 1962.

Besides "A Portrait of Bascom Hawke," and "The
Web of Earth," translated by Hans Schiebelhuth and
Susanna Rademacher, this paperback contains excerpts
from Nowell and Norwood, and two letters from
LTHM, pp. 145-154.

A70 French Edition:

Thomas Wolfe / De la Mort / au Matin / Traduit de
l'américain par / R. N. Raimbault et Ch. P. Vorce /
Preface d'André Bay / (Quotation in English) / 1948 /
Éditions Stock / Delamain et Boutelleau / 6, rue
Casimir Delavigne, 6 / Paris

3 l., 7-293 p., 3 blank pages. 19 by 12 cm. *FDTM* complete.

A71 Japanese Partial Edition:

Thomas Wolfe: Daichi o Ou Kumo No Su (The Web of
Earth). Tokyo, Eiho-sha, 1957.

3 l., 5-214, 10 p. ads. 17 by 11 cm. Translated by
Totaro Hosoiri.

This paperback contains "The Web of Earth," "The Far
and the Near," "Circus at Dawn," and "Dark in the
Forest, Strange as Time," all from *FDTM*. There
is a note on Wolfe, pp. 187-214.

A72 Italian Partial Edition:

Thomas Wolfe / Morte / orgogliosa sorella /
Traduzione / di Laurana Palombi Berra / Il Saggiatore

3 l., 7-70, 1 unnumbered page, 9 p. ads. 19 by 12.5 cm.
Hardboard. Published in 1959, in Milan.

This is "Death the Proud Brother," from *FDTM*.
There is a note on Wolfe, pp. 7-8. Biblioteca delle
Silerchie XXVIII.

A73 Polish Partial Edition:

Thomas Wolfe / Włóczedzy / O Zachodzie Słońca /
i inne opowiadánia / Przelózyla / Zofia Kierszys /
Państwowy / Instytut Wydawniczy

3 l., 7-303, 3 unnumbered pages. 19.5 by 12.5 cm.
Published in 1961.

This includes five stories from *FDTM* and six from *THB*.
From *FDTM*: "The Men of Old Catawba," "The Four
Lost Men," "Circus at Dawn," "The Bums at Sunset,"
and "Death the Proud Brother." From *THB*: "The Lost
Boy," "No Cure for It," "A Kinsman of His Blood,"
"Chickamauga," "The Return of the Prodigal,"
and "The Lion at Morning."

A74 Serbian Partial Editions:

Tomac Bylf / Tkanje Zhibota / Prilobetke /
(Publisher's device) / Nolit / Beograd / 1959

5 l., 9-315, 3 unnumbered pages. 17 by 12 cm. Translated
by Vera Ilyich.

This contains "The Web of Earth," "Death the Proud
Brother," "In the Park," "One of the Girls in Our Party,"
"The Near and the Far," "Circus at Dawn," and
"Four Lost Men," all from *FDTM*, plus "The Story of
a Novel." There is a note on Wolfe by the translator,
305-316.

A75 Tomac Bylf / Y Mpačhnoj Shymi / Tajahstbehoj /
Kao Bpeme / Prilobetke / (Publisher's device) /
Nolit / Beograd / 1962

3 l., 5-232, 3 unnumbered pages. 17 by 12 cm. Translated
by Vera Ilyich, This is Mala Knjiga, no. 69.

This contains "No Door," "The Face of the War,"
"The Bums at Sunset," "Dark in the Forest, Strange as
Time," "Only the Dead Know Brooklyn," "The Men
of Old Catawba," and "Gulliver" from *FDTM*,
plus "Chickamauga" from *THB*, and "A Portrait
of Bascom Hawke."

IV. *The Story of a Novel*

A76 First Edition:

The Story / of a / Novel / (double rule) / By /
Thomas Wolfe / (Printer's device) / Charles Scribner's
Sons. New York / Charles Scribner's Sons. Ltd.
London / 1936

4.l., 1-93 p., 1 blank page. 20 by 13 cm. Re-issued in 1949
and 1958, this first appeared in the *Saturday Review
of Literature*, December 14, 21, and 28, 1935.

A77 English Edition:

The Story / of a / Novel / (double rule) / By /
Thomas Wolfe / (Printer's device) /
London / William Heinemann / 1936

3 l., 1-93 p., 1 blank page. 20.5 by 13 cm.

A78 German Editions:

Thomas Wolfe / Uns Bleibt die / Erde / Die
"Geschichte eines Romans" / mit Briefen / und 4
Abbildungen / (Publisher's device) / Im Verlag der
Arche. Zürich.

2 l., 5-160 p., 19.5 by 12 cm. Published in 1951 and
translated by Hans Schiebelhuth.

"The Story of a Novel," pp. 11-86, is followed by
"Something Has Spoken to Me in the Night," in poem
form, English and German, pp. 86-87; seven letters
to his mother from *LTHM*; a letter to H. M.
Ledig-Rowohlt (June 10, 1936); memories of Wolfe by
his mother, pp. 119-127; and by Ledig-Rowohlt, pp.
127-158. There are four pages of illustrations between
pp. 144 and 145, and a brief bibliography, pp. 159-160.

A79 Thomas Wolfe: Uns Bleibt die Erde. Munich, Nymphenburger Verlagshandlung, 1952. Reprint of the Swiss edition.

A80 Thomas Wolfe / Die Geschichte / eines Romans / (Publisher's device) / im Verlag der Arche. Zürich

3 l., 7-80 p., 19.5 by 11.5 cm. Published in 1957 in the Hans Schiebelhuth translation, this reprints only "The Story of a Novel."

A81 *Danish Edition*:

Thomas Wolfe / Historien om en / Roman / (Publisher's device) / Nyt Nordisk Forlag Arnold Busck / Kjøbenhavn 1948

2 l., 5-89 p., 1 blank page, 2 p. ads. 19.5 by 13 cm. Translated by Eva Mortensen and Knud Bruun-Rasmussen

A82 Italian Edition:

Thomas Wolfe / Storia / di un romanzo / Autobiografia / Traduzione di Laurana Palombi Berra / Il Saggiatore

3 l., 7-70 p., 1 leaf. 19.5 by 12 cm. Published in 1958 in Milan, this is Biblioteca delle Silerchie II.

A83 Japanese Edition in English:

Thomas Wolfe: Out of My Life and Literature, ed. with introduction and notes by Minoru Nishida and Nagaloshi Miyawaki. Tokyo, Tsurumi Shoten, 1966. 81 p.

This is largely from *SOAN*, with English text and Japanese notes.

V. *The Web and the Rock*

A84 First Edition:

> Thomas Wolfe / (rule) / The Web / and / The Rock /
> (rule) / (Publisher's device) / Harper & Brothers.
> Publishers / New York and London
>
> 3 l., vii-viii, 1 leaf, 3-695 p., 1 unnumbered page.
> 21.5 by 14.5 cm. Published in 1939.
>
> This is divided into 7 books: "The Web and the Root,"
> "The Hound of Darkness," "The Web and the World,"
> "The Magic Year," "Life and Letters," "Love's
> Bitter Mystery," and "Oktoberfest."

A85 English Edition:

> The Web / and / The Rock / by / Thomas Wolfe /
> (Publisher's device) / William Heinemann Ltd. /
> London . Toronto
>
> 3 l., vii-xii, 1-642 p., 1 leaf. 20 by 13.5 cm.
>
> There is an introduction by J. B. Priestley, pp. ix-xii.
> Published in 1947.

A86 Sun Dial Reprint Edition:

> Published in 1940, this is identical to the first edition,
> except for the imprint: The Sun Dial Press /
> Garden City, New York

A87 Grosset and Dunlap Reprint Edition.

> Thomas Wolfe / The Web / and / The Rock /
> Grosset & Dunlap . New York
>
> 3 l., vii-viii, 1 leaf, 3-695 p., 1 unnumbered page.
> 21 by 15 cm. Published in 1960.

A88 Grosset and Dunlap Universal Library Edition.

Identical to Reprint Edition, except in paperback
and designated Grosset's Universal Library UL-12.

A89 Dell Edition:

Thomas / Wolfe / The Web / and the Rock /
with an introduction by Richard Chase /
(Publisher's device) / The Laurel Thomas Wolfe.

3 l., 1 unnumbered page, 8-736 p. 18 by 10.5 cm.
Published in 1960. Paperback.

The introduction by Richard Chase is on pp. 7-19.

A90 New American Library Edition.

Thomas Wolfe / The Web and the Rock / A Signet Book /
New American Library / 1966

640 p. paperback.

A91 French Edition:

Thomas Wolfe / La Toile / Et Le Roc / Traduit de
l'anglais par José Ravita / Roman / Marguerat

5 l., 11-590 p., 2 unnumbered pages. 21.5 by 14.5 cm.
Published in Lausanne, Switzerland, in 1948.

A92 Danish Edition:

Thomas Wolfe / Spindelvaev og Klippe / Roman /
(Publisher's device) / Nyt Nordisk Forlag Arnold Busck /
Kjøbenhavn MCMXL

2 v. v.1: 4 l., 9-243 p., 1 blank page; v.2: 4 l., 253-554 p.,
1 blank leaf. Translated by Ulrich Knigge and Eva
Mortensen, this is somewhat shortened.

A93 German Editions:

Thomas Wolfe / Strom des Lebens / Roman /
(Publisher's device) / Alfred Scherz Verlag

5 l., 11-743 p., 5 unnumbered pages. 21.5 by 15 cm.
Published in Bern, Switzerland, in 1941, no translator
is named. In other sources the translator is given as
Ernst Reinhard.

A94 Thomas Wolfe / Geweb und Fels / Roman / Rowohlt
Verlag Hamburg

5 l., 11-690 p., 6 unnumbered pages. 20.5 by 13.5 cm.
Translated by Susanna Rademacher and published in 1953

A95 Italian Edition:

Thomas Wolfe / La Ragnatela / e la Roccia / con un'
introduzione di / J. B. Priestley / e quindici illustrazioni
di / Angela Motti / (Publisher's device) /
Arnoldo Mondadori / Editore

3 l., 1 unnumbered page, 8-707 p., 5 unnumbered pages
of ads. 21 by 15 cm.

Translated by Cesare Vivante and published in 1955,
available in a boxed edition and illustrated with line
drawings, this is one of the most beautiful of the
Wolfe translations.

A96 Slovak Edition:

Thomas Wolfe / Pavučina / a Bralo / 1961 / Slovenske
é Vydavatel'stvo / Krásne j Literatúry / Bratislava

5 l., 11-763 p., 5 unnumbered pages. 21 by 14 cm.

This is translated by Josef Simo and has a note on Wolfe
by Zora Studena, pp. 751-764.

A97 German Book-Club Editions.

> Thomas Wolfe: Geweb und Fels. Zurich, Buch-Club
> Ex Libris, 1962. 628 p. This is the Susanna
> Rademacher translation.

A98 Thomas Wolfe: Geweb und Fels. Stuttgart, Europäischer
> Buch-Klub, 1962. 626 p. Also the Rademacher translation.

VI. *You Can't Go Home Again*

A99 First Edition:

> Thomas Wolfe / (rule) / You Can't / Go Home /
> Again / (rule) / (Publisher's device) / Harper &
> Brothers . Publishers / New York and London

> 3 l., vii-viii, 1 leaf, 3-743, 1 unnumbered page. 21 by 14.5
> cm. Published in 1940 and re-issued in 1944, 1951
> and 1968. A Canadian edition was published
> simultaneously by Musson in Toronto.
> *YCGHA* is divided into 7 books and 48 chapters.
> The books are entitled "The Native's Return,"
> "The World that Jack Built," "An End and a Beginning,"
> "The Quest of the Fair Medusa," "Exile and Discovery,"
> "I Have a Thing to Tell You," and "A Wind is Rising,
> And the Rivers Flow."

A100 British Edition:

> You Can't Go / Home Again / by / Thomas Wolfe /
> (Publisher's device) / William Heinemann Ltd. /
> London . Toronto

> 3 l., 1-600 p., 1 leaf. 20 by 13.5 cm. Published in 1947,
> re-issued in 1968.

A101 Sun Dial Edition:

Identical with first edition except for imprint: The Sun
Dial Press Garden City New York.
Published in 1942.

A102 Harper's Modern Classics Edition:

You Can't / Go Home Again / By / Thomas Wolfe /
With an Introduction by / Edward C. Aswell /
(Publisher's device) / New York / Harper & Brothers
Publishers

2 l., v-xix, blank page, 3 l., 3-743 p., blank page.
20 by 13.5 cm. Published in 1949, Aswell's "Introduction"
is on pp. v-xix.

A103 Harper Library Edition:

Identical with first edition, except slightly larger format,
22 by 15 cm. Issued in 1963.

A104 Grosset and Dunlap Edition:

Thomas Wolfe / You Can't / Go Home / Again /
Grosset's Universal Library / Grosset & Dunlap.
New York

5 l., 3-743 p., 1 blank page. 20.5 by 13.5 cm. This is
Grosset's Universal Library UL-16, paperback. Published
in 1957. A hardback reprint by Grosset and Dunlap,
identical but without the Universal Library designation,
issued in 1959.

A105 Dell Edition:

Thomas / Wolfe / You Can't / Go Home Again /
with an introduction by Richard Chase / (Publisher's
device) / The Laurel / Thomas Wolfe

9 p., 10-671 p., 1 unnumbered page. 18 by 10.5 cm.
The introduction is the same as that in the Dell edition
of *TWATR*, pp. 9-21. Published in 1960.

A106 German Editions:

Thomas Wolfe / Es Führt Kein Weg Zurück / Roman /
(Publisher's device) / Alfred Scherz Verlag

4 l., 9-747 p., 1 blank page. 21.5 by 15 cm. Translated
by Ernst Reinhard and published in Bern, Switzerland,
in 1942.

A107 Thomas Wolfe / Es Führt Weg Zurück / Roman /
Rowohlt Verlag. Hamburg

4 l., 9-622 p., 1 leaf. 20 by 13 cm. Translated by
Susanna Rademacher, this was published in 1950.

A108 Thomas Wolfe: Es Führt Kein Weg Zurück. Halle,
Mitteldeutscher Verlag, 1955.

A109 Thomas Wolfe: Es Führt Kein Weg Zurück. Hamburg,
Im Bertelsmann Lesering, 1957. 767 p.

A110 Thomas Wolfe: Es Führt Kein Weg Zurück. East Berlin,
Verlag Volk und Welt, 1963.

729 p. 21 cm.

A111 Italian Edition:

Thomas Wolfe / Non Puoi Tornare / A Casa / Romanzo /
Traduzione di Ettore Capriolo / Volume primo
(or secondo) / Arnoldo Mondadori Editore

2 v. v.1: 15 unnumbered pages, 16-470 p., 1 leaf;
v.2: 9 unnumbered pages, 10-423 p., 9 unnumbered pages.
19.5 by 12 cm. Published in Verona in 1962, this is v.470
of the Medusa series.

A112 Polish Edition:

Thomas Wolfe / Nie Ma / Powrotu / Tlumaczyla / Maria Skibniewska / Czytelnik

4 l., 9-735 p., 1 unnumbered page. 21 by 15 cm. Published in 1959, in Warsaw.

A113 Turkish Edition

Yuvaya / Dönemezsin / Thomas Wolfe / Ceviren: Kayhan Kargili / (Printer's device to left)

7 p., 8-415 p., 1 blank page. 20.5 by 14.5 cm. Published in Istanbul in 1958. This is greatly condensed.

A114 Japanese Edition:

Thomas Wolfe: Nanji Futatahi Kokyo Ni Kaerezu. Tokyo, Kochi Suppan-Sha, 1960

2 l., 5-526 p., 1 leaf. 19.5 by 13.5 cm. Boxed. Translated by Yukio Suzuki, this is No. 20 in the "Collection of Contemporary American Literature" series.
There is a "commentary" on Wolfe, pp. 520-526.

A115 Slovak Edition:

Thomas Wolfe: Domov Sa Vrátiť Nemôžeš. Bratislava, **Spalocnost Priatelon Krasnych Knih,** 1962.

644 p., 21 cm. Translated by Jan Vilikovsky.

A116 South Korean Edition:

Thomas Wolfe: Ceudae Dasineun Gonyang-e Mosgari. Seoul, Jeong-Eumsa, 1962. 507 p. Translated by Wang-la Jang.

A117 German Partial Editions:

Thomas Wolfe / Verbannung und Entdeckung /
aus dem Roman / "Es Führt Kein Weg Zurück" /
Besorgt von Wolfgang Klimke / Verlag Ferdinand
Schoningh. Paderborn.

1 leaf, 3-124 p., 2 p. ads. 18 by 12 cm. Paperback.

This is *YCGHA*, Book 5, "Exile and Discovery,"
in the Susanna Rademacher translation. There is a
"Vorwort" by Wolfgang Klimke, pp. 3-7.

A118 Thomas Wolfe / I Have a Thing / To Tell You /
(From *You Can't Go Home Again*) / Edited by
Wolfgang Klimke / Studienrat / Verlag Ferdinand
Schoningh. Paderborn.

3 p., 4-79, 1 blank page. 18 by 12 cm. Paperback.

This is *YCGHA*, Books 6 and 7, Chapters 38, 41, 42, 43, 44,
and 48, in English with notes in German. There is a
note by Klimke "About the Author," pp. 4-6.

VII. *The Hills Beyond.*

A119 First Edition:

Thomas Wolfe / The Hills / Beyond / With A Note
on Thomas Wolfe / by Edward C. Aswell /
(Publisher's device) / Harper & Brothers Publishers /
New York and London

4 l., 1-386 p., 3 leaves. 21 by 15 cm. Published in 1941,
with a simultaneous Canadian edition issued by
Musson in Toronto. Re-issued in 1944, 1950 and 1964.

THB contains a total of twenty stories, most of which had

previously appeared in periodical form. The first ten are:
"The Lost Boy," "No Cure for It," "Gentlemen of
the Press" (actually a short play), "A Kinsman of His
Blood," "Chickamauga," "The Return of the
Prodigal," "On Leprechauns," "Portrait of a Literary
Critic," "The Lion at Morning," and "God's Lonely Man."
The last ten stories are related and form *The Hills Beyond*
sequence, from which the volume takes its name.
They are: "The Quick and the Dead," "Old Man of
the Tribe," "The Great Schism," "How Certain Joyners
Went to Town," "The Plumed Knight," "The Battle
of Hogwart Heights," "A Stranger Whose Sermon
Was Brick," "The Dead World Relived," "The Bell
Strikes Three," and "The Lost Day." There is also
included "A Note on Thomas Wolfe," by Edward C.
Aswell, pp. 349-386.

A120 Sun Dial Press Edition:

Thomas Wolfe / The Hills / Beyond / With a Note on
Thomas Wolfe / by Edward C. Aswell / (Publisher's
device) / The Sun Dial Press / Garden City, New York

3 l., 1-386 p. 20.5 by 14.5 cm. Published 1943, and
issued simultaneously by Blue Ribbon in Toronto, Canada.

A121 Avon Editions:

Thomas Wolfe / The Hills Beyond / With a Note on
Thomas Wolfe / by Edward C. Aswell / (Publisher's
device) / New Avon Library / Jo Meyers E. B.
Williams / 432 Fourth Avenue, New York 16, N. Y. /
Published by special arrangement with / Harper
& Brothers.

2 l., 11-227 p., 3 p. ads. 16.5 by 11.5 cm. Published in 1944.

This volume includes the ten stories of the *THB* sequence, plus "On Leprechauns," "Portrait of a Literary Critic" and "God's Lonely Man" along with Aswell's "Note on Thomas Wolfe."

A122 Stories / by / Thomas Wolfe / (Publisher's device) / Avon Book Company / Jo Meyers E. B. Williams / 432 Fourth Avenue, New York 16, N. Y. / Published by special arrangement with / Harper & Brothers.

1 leaf, 11-135 p., 1 p. ad. 19.5 by 13.5 cm. Published in 1944, this is "Avon Modern Short Story Monthly No. 17."

This volume includes the remaining seven stories from *THB*, plus 'The Battle of Hogwart Heights," which was included in the other volume.

A123 Lion Books Edition:

The / Hills / Beyond / (Publisher's device) / Lion Books, Inc. / 655 Madison Avenue New York City

3 l., 7-288 p. 18 x 10.5 cm. Published in 1955, this includes all of *THB* except the Aswell "Note on Thomas Wolfe."

A124 Pyramid Books Edition:

By Thomas Wolfe / author of Look Homeward, Angel / Of Time and the River / From Death to Morning / The Web and the Rock / You Can't Go Home Again / (rule) / The Hills Beyond / (rule) / (Publisher's device) / Pyramid Books / 444 Madison Avenue, New York 22, New York

3 l., 7-288 p. 18 by 11 cm. Otherwise identical with Lion Books Edition. Published in 1958 and re-issued with a different cover in 1961.

A125 Perennial Library Editions:

> Thomas Wolfe / (device) / The Hills / Beyond /
> With a Note on Thomas Wolfe by / Edward C. Aswell /
> (device) / Perennial Library / Harper & Row,
> Publishers / New York, Evanston, and London
>
> 4 l., 1-181p., 1 blank page. 18 by 10.5 cm. Published in 1964.
>
> This volume contains the ten stories of the *THB*
> sequence, plus Aswell's "Note."

A126 Thomas Wolfe / (device) / The Lost Boy / With a
> Note on Thomas Wolfe / by Edward C. Aswell /
> (device) / Perennial Library / Harper & Row, Publishers /
> New York and Evanston
>
> 4 l., 3-247 p., 3 blank pages. 18 by 10.5 cm.
> Published in 1965.
>
> This volume contains the first ten stories of *THB*,
> plus Aswell's "Note."

A127 Partial Edition:

> Gentlemen of the / Press. . . A Play / by Thomas /
> Wolfe / William Targ: / The Black Archer Press /
> Chicago, Illinois
>
> 7 unnumbered pages, 8-27 p., 5 blank pages. 20.5 by 14 cm.
> Published in 1942; bound in cloth in limited edition
> of 350 copies.

A128 German Edition:

> Thomas Wolfe / Hinter jenen Bergen / Erzählungen /
> Mit einem Nachwort von / Edward C. Aswell /
> (Publisher's device) / Rowohlt
>
> 2 l., 5-279 p., 1 unnumbered page, 6 p. ads.
> Published in 1956.

This is the complete *THB*, published in 1956; translated by Susanna Rademacher as "Ro ro ro Taschenbuch No. 200."

A129 East German Edition:

Thomas Wolfe: Der zerstorte Tag; Erzählungen. Berlin, Verlag Volk und Welt, 1964.
400 p. 21 cm.
Includes stories from both THB and FDTM.

A130 East German Partial Edition:

Thomas Wolfe / Der verlorene Knabe / und andere Erzählungen / Herausgegeben von / Prof. Dr. Karl-Heinz Schönfelder / Verlag Phillipp Reclam Jun. Leipzig

1 leaf, 3-258 p., 3 leaves. 15 by 10 cm. Published in 1961.

This contains six stories from *THB* and three from *FDTM*, in the Schiebelhuth and Rademacher translations.
From *THB*: "The Lost Boy," "The Lion at Morning," "On Leprechauns," "Portrait of a Literary Critic," "The Gentlemen of the Press," and "Chickamauga."
From *FDTM*: "No Door," "Far and Near," and "Death the Proud Brother." There is a "Nachwort" by Schönfelder, pp. 249-259.

A131 Danish Editions:

Thomas Wolfe / De Fjerne Bjerge / (Publisher's device) / Nyt Nordisk Forlag. Arnold Busck / Kjøbenhavn MCMIL

2 l., 5-240 p., 21 by 14 cm. Published in 1949; the translators are Eva Mortensen, and Knud Bruun-Rasmussen.

This volume contains the ten stories of the *THB* sequence, plus Aswell's "Note."

A132 Thomas Wolfe / Den Tabte Tid / (Publisher's device) /
Nyt Nordisk Forlag. Arnold Busck / Kjøbenhavn 1950

3 l., 7-263 p., 21 by 14 cm. Published in 1950; the
translators are Eva Mortensen, and Knud
Bruun-Rasmussen.

This volume contains the first ten stories of *THB*, plus a
shorter "Note" by Aswell, pp. 257-263.

VIII. *Letters*

A134 First Edition:

Thomas Wolfe's / Letters to his Mother / Julia Elizabeth
Wolfe / (rule) / Edited with an Introduction / by /
John Skally Terry / Department of English /
Washington Square College / New York University /
New York / Charles Scribner's Sons / 1943

4 l., vii-xxv, 1 blank page, 1-368 p., Index. 20.5 by 15 cm.

There is a portrait of Mrs. Wolfe as a frontispiece,
and the end papers reproduce samples of Tom's writing.
Terry's "Introduction." pp. vii-xxv, include's some
reminiscences of Mrs. Wolfe concerning Tom.
The letters date from 1909 to 1938, but most of them
are after 1920.

A135 German Edition:

Thomas Wolfe / Briefe / an die Mutter / Übertragen
von Ina Seidel / (rule) / Nymphenburger
Verlagshandlung

3 l., 7-471, 5 unnumbered pages, inc. ads. 19.5 by 11.5 cm.

There is a "Geleitwort" by Ina Seidel, pp. 7-14,
and Terry's "Introduction." Mrs. Wolfe's reminiscences
come last, pp. 427-465, with notes by the translator,
pp. 467-472.

A136 German Reprint Edition:

Thomas Wolfe: / Briefe an die Mutter / Übersetzt und
eingeleitet von Ina Seidel / Deutscher Taschenbuch
Verlag / dtv

2 l., 5-319, 2 unnumbered p., 6 pages ads. 18 by 10.5 cm.
Published in Munich in 1961; this is identical in contents
to the original edition in German.

A137 *Letters to Homer Andrew Watt*:

The Correspondence of / Thomas Wolfe / and /
Homer Andrew Watt / Edited by Oscar Cargill / and /
Thomas Clark Pollock / New York University Press /
Washington Square. New York / (rule) / London:
Geoffrey Cumberlege Oxford University Press / 1954

4 l., vii-xi, 1 blank page, 1 leaf, 3-53 p., 1 blank page.
24 by 16 cm.

This correspondence between 1924 and 1930 includes
nine letters by Wolfe and thirteen by Watt. There is also
an exchange of letters between Wolfe and Harry
Woodburn Chase. Pollock has an "Introductory Note,"
pp. ix-xi, and the frontispiece is a portrait of Homer
Andrew Watt, 1926. Watt was Chairman of the
Department of English, New York University,
when Wolfe taught there.

A138 Nowell Edition of Letters:

> The Letters of / Thomas / Wolfe / Collected and
> Edited, / with an Introduction and / Explanatory Text,
> by / Elizabeth Nowell / New York / Charles
> Scribner's Sons

> 3 l., vii-xviii, 1 leaf, 1-797, 1 blank page, Index.
> 24 by 16.5 cm. Published in 1956.

> Letters from 1908 to 1938, to every correspondent except
> his mother. There is an introduction by Miss Nowell,
> pp. xiii-xviii, and a photograph of Wolfe as a
> frontispiece.

A139 English Edition:

> Selected Letters of / Thomas Wolfe / * / Edited,
> with an Introduction / and explanatory text by / Elizabeth
> Nowell / and selected by / Daniel George / (Publisher's
> device) / Heinemann / London Melbourne Toronto

> 4 l., vii-xxii, 1 leaf, 1-326 p., 1 leaf, Index. 21.5 by 15.5 cm.
> Published in 1958.

> This collection includes about half of the original volume.
> Its contents were selected, according to Mr. George,
> as those letters of most interest to the English reader.
> There is another Wolfe photograph as frontispiece.

A140 German Edition:

> Thomas Wolfe / Briefe / Herausgegeben von / Elizabeth
> Nowell / Rowohlt Verlag

> 3 l., 7-623, 1 unnumbered page, Index. 20.5 by 13 cm.
> Published in 1961. Translated by Susanna Rademacher.
> The frontispiece photograph of Wolfe is again
> different from that in the American edition.

A141 Revised Letters to His Mother:

The Letters of / Thomas Wolfe / To His Mother /
(device) / Newly edited from the original manuscripts /
by C. Hugh Holman / and Sue Fields Ross

5 l., 1 unnumbered page, x-xxxi, 4 unnumbered pages,
4-320 p., Index. 23.5 by 15.5 cm. Published in Chapel Hill,
North Carolina, by the University of North Carolina
Press, in 1968.

This corrected edition contains an introduction by the
editors, plus additional notes on Wolfe's life and on his
family. The frontispiece photograph is of Wolfe
and his mother.

IX. *Selections.*

A142 (Woodcut) / The Face / of a / Nation / Poetical
Passages / From the Writings / of / Thomas Wolfe /
(decoration) / Decorations by / Edward Shenton /
(rule) / Charles Scribner's Sons. New York / 1939

2 l., v-xii, 1 leaf, 1-321, 1 unnumbered page.
23.5 by 16 cm.

Selections, mostly brief, from *LHA, OTATR, FDTM,*
and *SOAN.* There is an introduction by John Hall
Wheelock, pp. v-vi. A Literary Guild edition, identical
except for imprint, was issued at the same time.

A143 A Stone, A Leaf, A Door / Poems / By Thomas Wolfe /
Selected and Arranged in Verse by / John S. Barnes /
(Device) / With a Foreword by / Louis Untermeyer /
New York / Charles Scribner's Sons / 1945.

2 l., v-ix, 1 blank page, 1-166 p. 21 by 14 cm.
Re-issued 1961.

These are brief excerpts from *LHA*, *OTATR*, *TWATR*,
YCGHA, and *THB*, arranged in blank verse form.
Exact sources are not given.

A144 The Portable / Thomas Wolfe / Edited by
Maxwell Geismar / (Publisher's device) / New York:
The Viking Press / 1946

2 l., v-vi, 1-712 p., 2 p., ads. 17 by 11 cm.

This includes lengthy excerpts from *LHA*, *OTATR*,
TWATR, *YCGHA*, plus *SOAN* complete, and the
short stories "The Face of the War," "Only the Dead
Know Brooklyn," "Dark in the Forest, Strange as Time,"
"Circus at Dawn," and "In the Park," from *FDTM*,
and "Chickamauga" from *THB*. Geismar's "Introduction"
is on pp. 1-27.

A145 The Indispensable / Thomas / Wolfe / Edited by /
Maxwell Geismar / (Device) / New York,
The Book Society, 1950.

2 l., v-vi, 1-712 p., 1 blank leaf. 18 by 12 cm.

The contents are the same as those of *PTW*.

A146 Selections from the Works of / Thomas Wolfe /
Edited by Maxwell Geismar / (Publisher's device) /
William Heinemann Ltd / Melbourne; London; Toronto

3 l., vii-viii, 1-712 p., 1 blank leaf. 19 by 13 cm.
Published in 1952

The contents are the same as those of *PTW*

A147 The / (rule) / Thomas Wolfe / (rule) / Reader /
Edited, with an Introduction and Notes, by /
C. Hugh Holman / New York / (rule) /
Charles Scribner's Sons

2 l., v-vi, 2 l., 3-690 p., 3 blank leaves. 21.5 by 14.5 cm.
Published in 1962.

This volume contains selections from *LHA*, *OTATR*,
TWATR and *YCGHA*, plus *SOAN* complete. There are
also five stories from *FDTM*, "The Face of the War,"
"Only the Dead Know Brooklyn," "Dark in the Forest,
Strange as Time," "The Far and the Near," and
"In the Park," and two from *THB*, "The Lost Boy,"
and "God's Lonely Man." Holman's "Introduction" is
on pp. 2-10, and the volume ends with an excerpt
from Wolfe's last letter to Maxwell Perkins.

A148 The Short Novels of / (device) Thomas Wolfe /
Edited, / with an Introduction / and Notes by /
C. Hugh Holman / Charles Scribner's Sons
(device) New York

2 l., v-xx, 2 leaves, 3-323, 5 blank pages. Published in 1961.

This volume contains "A Portrait of Bascom Hawke,"
"The Web of Earth," "No Door," "I Have a Thing
to Tell You," and "The Party at Jack's," usually in the
form in which they originally appeared in magazines
rather than in the forms used in the later volumes.
Holman's "Introduction" is on pp. vii-xx, and there is a
separate brief introduction to each story.

A149 Spanish Edition:

Thomas Wolfe / Tengo Algo / Que Deciros / (line
drawing) / Luis de Caralt / Editor / Barcelona

7 unnumbered pages, 8-189, 3 unnumbered pages.
20 by 14 cm. Published in 1964; the translator is
F. Santos Fontenla.

This volume includes only three of the above stories:
"I Have a Thing to Tell You," "The Party at
Jack's," and "No Door."

A150 German Edition:

Thomas Wolfe: Sämtliche Erzählungen. Hamburg,
Rowohlt, 1967. 445 p.

X. *Miscellaneous Publications*:

A151 *The Crisis in Industry*:

University of North Carolina / Department of
Philosophy / The Crisis in Industry / (Crowned with
the Worth Prize) / Thomas Wolfe / Chapel Hill /
Published by the University / 1919.

2 l., 5-14 p., 1 leaf. 22.5 by 15 cm.

This was Wolfe's first separate publication, in an edition
of two hundred copies. There was a brief introduction
by Dr. Horace H. Williams.

A152 *A Note on Experts*:

A Note on Experts: / Dexter Vespasian Joyner /
Thomas Wolfe / (Publisher's device) / House of Books,
Ltd. / New York, 1939

16 unnumbered leaves; text on pages that would be
numbered 9-28. 19 by 12.5 cm. Published in 1939
in an edition of three hundred copies;
not published elsewhere.

A153 *America*:

From Of Time and the River / America / By Thomas
Wolfe / Privately Printed Chicago / 1942.

4 l., 9-26 p., 2 l., blank leaf, Illustrations. 18 by 13.5 cm.

According to the colophon, this excerpt, taken from
OTATR, pp. 155-160, was designed by a class in
typography at Harrison Commercial Art Institute, and
printed at the Norman Press in Chicago, April, 1942.

A154 America. . . / The Greenwood Press / San Mateo,
California / 1942

2 l., 1-11 p., 1 blank page. Paper pamphlet, 20.5 by 14 cm.
in folder 22 by 15 cm.

This excerpt from *OTATR* was handset and printed by
Jack Werner Stauffacher in an edition of one hundred
and fifty copies.

A155 *What Is Man?*:

Thomas Wolfe: What is man? Chicago, James T. Mangan,
1942. 8 p.

This pamphlet, taken from *YCGHA*, was issued in
one hundred copies by planograph in the handwriting
of Robert Hunter Middleton.

A156 *To Rupert Brooke*:

Thomas Wolfe: To Rupert Brooke. Paris, Lecram Press,
1948. 4 p. leaflet .

Privately printed for Richard Jean Picard, in one hundred
copies, this poem originally appeared in the *University
of North Carolina Magazine*, May, 1918.

A157 *The Years of Wandering*:

". . . The Years of Wandering / in Many Lands and
Cities" / Thomas Wolfe / (Publisher's device) /
Charles S. Boesen, Publisher / 145 West 57th Street,
New York 19, N. Y.

5 l., printed, 6 l. with reproductions of Wolfe's notebook
pages tipped in, 2 blank leaves. 32 by 25.5 cm. Boxed.
Published in 1949, six hundred copies.

There is a foreword, probably by Boesen.

A158 *Mannerhouse*:

First Edition:

Mannerhouse / A Play / in a Prologue and Three Acts /
by / Thomas Wolfe / (Publisher's device) / New
York / Harper & Brothers Publishers / 1948

3 l., 1-183, 3 blank pages. 21 by 14.5 cm.

A159 A special collector's edition was also issued in five
hundred copies at the time of publication. It was boxed
and included a portrait of Wolfe and a twelve-page
facsimile of a Wolfe holograph letter not contained in
the regular edition. *Mannerhouse* was written in the 1920's.

A160 English Edition:

Mannerhouse / A Play / in a Prologue and Three Acts /
by / Thomas Wolfe / (Publisher's device) /
William Heinemann Ltd / Melbourne London Toronto

10 unnumbered leaves, 1-86 p., 1 blank leaf. 19 by 12.5 cm.
Published in 1950.

This edition includes, in the unnumbered pages, the
facsimile letter mentioned above.

A161 Swedish Edition:

Ny Amerikansk Dramatik / Thomas Wolfe / Huset I
Den Gamla / Stilen / Översättning av Börje Lindell /
Radioversion av Henrik Dyfverman / Inledning av
Gunnar Ollén / (rule) / Radiotjänsts
Teaterbibliotek 92

1 leaf, 3-79, 1 unnumbered page. 18.5 by 12 cm.
Published in Stockholm, 1949.

A162 German Edition:

Thomas Wolfe / Herrenhaus / Schauspiel in drei Akten /
und einem Vorspiel / Rowohlt Verlag Hamburg

3 l., 7-83, 1 unnumbered page. 20.5 by 13 cm. Translated
by Peter Sandberg and published in 1953.

A163 Danish Edition:

Thomas Wolfe / Mannerhouse / Et Skuespil / I En
Prolog Og Tre Akter / Paa Dansk ved / Ole Storm /
(Publisher's device) / Kobenhavn / Steen
Hasselbalchs Forlag / MCMLII

2 l., 5-65, 3 unnumbered pages. 18 by 12.5 cm.
In two-column pages.

A164 *A Western Journal*:

A Western Journal / (rule) / A Daily Log / of /
The Great Parks Trip / (rule) / June 20—July 2, 1938 /
by / Thomas Wolfe / 1951 / University of Pittsburgh Press

2 l., v-x, 1 unnumbered page, 2-3, two-seventy, 71-72 p.,
1 leaf. 23.5 by 16 cm.

In addition to the journal, this includes Edward C. Aswell's "Note on 'A Western Journey,'" and editorial notes by Agnes Lynch Starrett. There is a map of the trip on the end papers.

A165 Thomas Wolfe / A / Western / Journal / A Daily Log of the Great Parks Trip / June 20—July 2, 1938 / University of Pittsburgh Press

2 l., v-x, 1 unnumbered page, 2-76 p., 1 leaf. 20.5 by 14 cm. The map appears as a frontispiece in this 1967 paperback reprint.

A166 *Welcome to Our City*:

Thomas Wolfe / Willkommen / in Altamont! / Herrenhaus / Zwei Dramen / (rule) / Die Herren von der Presse / Eine Szene / Im Anhang / Horst Frenz "Thomas Wolfe / als Dramatiker" / und Briefe zur Entstehungsgeschichte / der Dramen / (Publisher's device) / Rowohlt

4 l., 9-170, 2 l., 184, 1 leaf, 6 p. ads. 19 by 11.5 cm. Published in 1962 and translated by Peter Sandberg and Susan Rademacher.

This is the only book appearance of "Welcome to Our City," which first appeared in *Esquire*, October, 1957.

A167 *Purdue Speech*:

Thomas Wolfe's Purdue Speech / "Writing and Living" / edited from the dictated and revised / typescript with an introduction and notes by / William Braswell / and Leslie A. Field / (Publisher's device) / 1964 / Purdue University Studies

2 l., 5-133 p., 1 unnumbered page, 1 leaf. 23.5 by 16 cm.

The editors provide an "Introduction," pp. 9-17;
"Notes," pp. 21-23; and "Textual Notes," pp. 79-83.
The appendices contain "Passages of the Dictated Speech
Revised for Use in *YCGHA*," pp. 85-116; and
William Braswell's article "Thomas Wolfe Lectures
and Takes a Holiday" reprinted from
College English, October, 1939.

B. Articles By Wolfe

B1 "Alles war so ganz anders," *Der Monat*, I (October 1948), 67-68. This is an excerpt from a letter of Wolfe's to Heinz Ledig-Rowohlt, June 10, 1936.

B2 "American October," *Reader's Digest*, LVII (October 1950), 41-42. From *OTATR*, 329-331.

B3 "America's Promise," *This Week Magazine*, November 2, 1958, p. 3. From *YCGHA*, 505-508.

B4 "The Anatomy of Loneliness," *American Mercury*, LIII (October 1941), 467-475. This is the same as "God's Lonely Man," *THB*, 186-197.

B5 "An Angel on the Porch," *Scribner's Magazine*, LXXXVI (August 1929), 205-210. Reprinted in *Scribner's Magazine*, CV (May 1939), 17-18, 62. This was Wolfe's first appearance in a major magazine. Similar to *LHA*, 99-100, 262-269.

B6 "An Appreciation," *University of North Carolina Magazine*, XLIX (May 1919), 79.

B7 "April, Late April," *American Mercury*, XLII (September 1937), 87-97. Similar to *TWATR*, 441-452.

48

B8 "Arnold Pentland," *Esquire*, June, 1935, pp. 26-28.
Similar to "A Kinsman of His Blood," *THB*, 66-76.

B9 "Autobiographical Sketch," *The Book Digest of Best Sellers*,
November, 1937. Originally appeared in Georges
Schreiber, ed., *Portraits and Self-Portraits*.

B10 "Begegnung mit Rowohlt," *Der Kurier* [Berlin],
March 19, 1950.

B11 "Baseball," *New York Times Magazine*, April 19, 1964,
p. 94-95 From *OTATR*, 202.

B12 "The Bell Remembered," *American Mercury*, XXXVIII
(August 1936), 457-466. Similar to "The Bell Strikes
Three," and "The Lost Day," in *THB*, 327-348.

B13 "Biographical Fragment," *Carolina Quarterly*, XI
(Spring 1960), 9-10. Previously unpublished.

B14 "The Birthday," *Harper's Magazine*, CLXXIX (June
1939), 19-26. Similar to *TWATR*, 346-358.

B15 "Boom Town," *American Mercury*, XXXII (May 1934),
21-39; reprinted, LXIV (January 1947), 81-103.
Similar to *YCGHA*, 88, 120, 142-146.

B16 "Briefe an Mrs. Roberts," *Prisma*, I (August 1947).
German translation of "Writing is My Life,"
Atlantic Monthly, December, 1946.

B17 "The Bums at Sunset." *Vanity Fair*, October, 1935,
pp. 30, 62. Similar to *FDTM*, 150-154.

B18 "The Challenge," *University of North Carolina Magazine*,
XLVIII (March 1918), 223-224.

B19 "Chickamauga," *Yale Review*, XXVII (Winter 1938), 274-298. Also *Saga*, April, 1961, pp. 30-33, 68, 70-73. From *THB*, 77-107.

B20 "The Child by Tiger," *Saturday Evening Post*, CCX (September 11, 1937), 10-11, 92-102. Similar to *TWATR*, 132-136.

B21 "Circus at Dawn," *Modern Monthly*, IX (March 1935), 19-21, 52. Also appears in *FDTM*, 205-211. Translated into German, *Story* [Stuttgart], III (March 1947), 30-33.

B22 "The Company," *New Masses*, January 11, 1938, pp. 33-35. Similar to *YCGHA*, 129-140.

B23 "Concerning Honest Bob," *University of North Carolina Magazine*, L (May 1920), 251-261.

B24 "Cottage by the Tracks," *Cosmopolitan*, July, 1935, pp. 48-50. Reprinted in *Cosmopolitan*, CL (March 1961), 100-103. Similar to *FDTM*, 164-168.

B25 "The Creative Movement in Writing," *Tar Heel* [University of North Carolina], XXVII (June 14, 1919), 2. Wolfe wrote numerous articles for this student newspaper, most of them unsigned. This is given as an example.

B26 "A Cullenden of Virginia," *University of North Carolina Magazine*, XLVIII (March 1918), 234-239. A short play.

B27 "Dark in the Forest, Strange as Time," *Scribner's Magazine*, XCVI (November 1934), 273-278. Included in *FDTM*, 98-113. German translation, *Die Monat*, XI (October 1958), 56-63.

B28 "Dark Messiah," *Current History*, LI (August 1940), 29-32. Similar to *YCGHA*, 621-633.

B29 " 'Dear Mabel,' Letters of Thomas Wolfe to His Sister, Mabel Wolfe Wheaton," *South Atlantic Quarterly*, LX (August 1961), 469-483. Edited by Mary Lindsay Thornton.

B30 "Death the Proud Brother," *Scribner's Magazine*, XCIII (June 1933), 333-338, 378-388. Also appears in *FDTM*, 15-70. German translation, *Story* [Stuttgart], V (1948), 3-17.

B31 "Deferred Payment," *University of North Carolina Magazine*, XLIX (June 1919), 139-153. A short play.

B32 "The Drammer," *University of North Carolina Magazine*, XLIX (April 1919), 72-74. A poem.

B33 "'E, a Recollection," *New Yorker*, July 17, 1937, pp. 13-15. Similar to *YCGHA*, 513-527.

B34 "Enchanted City," *Reader's Digest*, XXV (October 1939), 132-135. Similar to *TWATR*, 220-232; also to "The Golden City," below.

B35 "Even Two Angels not Enough," *Andean Quarterly*, Summer, 1945, pp. 67-71. Originally appeared in *YCGHA*, 723-730. Translation into Spanish follows on pp. 72-76.

B36 "The Face of the War," *Modern Monthly*, IX (June 1935), 223-231, 247. Similar to *FDTM*, 71-90.

B37 "Fame and the Poet," *American Mercury*, XXXIX (October 1936), 149-154.

B38 "The Far and the Near," *Der Bücherwurm*, XXII (February 1937), 150-153. In German translation. Originally in *FDTM*, 164-168.

B39 "A Field in Flanders," *University of North Carolina Magazine*, XLVIII (November 1917), 77. A poem.

B40 "For Professional Appearance," *Modern Monthly*, VIII (December 1934), 660-666. Similar to *OTATR*, 861-870.

B41 "The Four Lost Men," *Scribner's Magazine*, XCV (February 1934), 101-108. Also appears in *FDTM*, 114-133.

B42 "Franco Prepares for Tourists," *Nation*, CXLVI (May 21, 1938), 598. Letter to the editor.

B43 "From the Letters of Thomas Wolfe," *Writer's Digest*, XXXVII (December 1956), 13-17.

B44 "From Thomas Wolfe in College . . . ," *Motive*, October, 1947, p. 3. Originally in *LTHM*, 48-53. See also p. 4 for related note.

B45 "The Golden City," *Harper's Bazaar*, June, 1939, pp. 42-43. Similar to *TWATR*, pp. 220-232, and to "The Enchanted City," above.

B46 "Good Reading," *New York Herald Tribune*, August 17, 1935. A short note by Wolfe, included in Lewis Gannett's column "Books and Other Things," on the books he considered the best he had ever read.

B47 "God's Lonely Man," *Texte und Zeichen*, I (July 1955), 355-364. In German translation. Excerpts in *Midstream*, IV (Autumn 1958), 49-56. Originally in *THB*, 186-197.

B48 "The Grass Roof," *New York Evening Post*, April 4,
1931. This is a review by Wolfe of a book written
by Younghill Kang.

B49 "The Gowanus Canal," *Life*, July 7, 1952, p. 71. From
YCGHA, 399-401.

B50 "Gulliver, the Story of a Tall Man," *Scribner's Magazine*,
XCVII (June 1935), 328-333. Also appears in *FDTM*,
134-139.

B51 "The Hills Beyond," *Omnibook*, IV (January 1942),
129-160. Excerpts from *THB*, 201-217, 222-234, 240-252,
264-280, 287-297, 299-309, 327-348.

B52 "His Father's Earth," *Modern Monthly*, IX (March 1935),
99-104. Similar to *TWATR*, 86-90.

B53 "The Hollow Men," *Esquire*, October, 1940, pp. 37-39.
Similar to *YCGHA*, 460-479

B54 "The Hollyhock Sowers," *American Mercury*, L (August
1940), 401-405. Similar to *YCGHA,* 605-611.

B55 "The House of the Far and Lost," *Scribner's Magazine*,
XCVI (August 1934), 71-81. Similar to *OTATR*,
619-627, 637-652.

B56 "How to Keep Out of War," *Nation*, CXLVI (April 2,
1938), 13. A brief contribution by Wolfe to a symposium
under this title.

B57 "I Have a Thing to Tell You," *New Republic*, XC
(March 10, 17, and 24, 1937), 132-136, 159-164, 202-207.
Similar to *YCGHA*, 634-704.

B58 "In the Park," *Harper's Bazaar*, June, 1935, p. 54-57. German translation in *Europäische Revue*, XII (June 1936), 389-398. Similar to FDTM, 169-184.

B59 "The Isle of Quisay," *Comparative Literature*, IX (Winter 1957), 41-42.

B60 "Katamoto," *Harper's Bazaar*, October, 1937, 74-76. Similar to *YCGHA*, 28-36.

B61 "Land of Smoke and Dreams," *Coronet*, XLVI (October 1959), 142-151. Brief excerpts from *TWATR* and *LHA*, accompanying photographs.

B62 "The Last Letter of Thomas Wolfe," *Carolina Play-Book*, XV (September 1941), reprinted, XVI (March-June 1943), 12. Dated August 13, 1938, this letter was addressed to Maxwell Perkins.

B63 "The Last Letter of Thomas Wolfe and the Reply to It," *Harvard Library Bulletin*, I (August 1947), 278-279.

B64 "Letter," *National Institute News Bulletin*, IV (1938), 12.

B65 "A Letter from Thomas Wolfe," *Story*, XIX (September-October 1941), 68-69. To Sherwood Anderson, dated September 22, 1937.

B66 "Letter to Prof. Koch," *Carolina Play-Book*, XVI (March-June 1943), 23-26. To Frederick Koch, at the University of North Carolina, dated November 26, 1920.

B67 (Letter to the Editor), *Asheville Times*, May 4, 1930.

B68 (Letters to Henry T. Volkening), *Virginia Quarterly Review*, XV (Spring 1939), 196-215.

B69 "The Lion at Morning," *Harper's Bazaar*, October, 1941, pp. 47-50. Also appears in *THB*, 264-276.

B70 "Look Homeward, Angel," *Omnibook*, I (December 1938), 193-320. An abridgment of *LHA*.

B71 "London Tower," *Asheville Citizen*, July 19, 1925.

B72 "The Lonely Giant Self-Revealed," *Saturday Review*, XXXIX (October 13, 1956), 14. Excerpts from *Letters*.

B73 "The Lost Boy," *Nagyvilag* [Budapest], IV (1958), 467-490. Hungarian translation. Also in *Redbook Magazine*, November, 1937, pp. 37-41. Similar to *THB*, 1-42.

B74 "The Man Who Lives with His Idea," *Carolina Play-Book*, XVI (March-June 1943), 15-22. A tribute to Frederick Koch and the Carolina Playmakers, written about 1923.

B75 "La Marquise de Mornaye," *Encore*, V (May 1944), 531-535.

B76 "Mr. Malone," *New Yorker*, XIII (May 29, 1937), 22-27. Similar to *TWATR*, 525-536.

B77 "The Names of the Nation," *Modern Monthly*, VIII (December 1934), 521-525. Similar to *OTATR*, 861-870.

B78 "More Poems," *University of North Carolina Magazine*, LXVI (December 1936), 30.

B79 "Nebraska Crane," *Harper's Magazine*, CLXXXI (August 1940), 279-285. Similar to *YCGHA*, 55-69.

B80 "Night Stop in the South," *Scholastic*, XLV (January 22, 1945), 15-16. Excerpt from *OTATR* 30-33.

B81 "No Door, a Story of Time and the Wanderer," *Scribner's Magazine*, XCIV (July 1933), 7-12, 46-56. Similar to *FDTM*, 1-14; *OTATR*, 2, 90-93, 327-334, 601-608, 611-613; and *YCGHA*, 37-44. French translation in *L'Arbalète*, Autumn, 1944, pp. 219-234.

B82 "Notes from *A Western Journal*," *Holiday*, X (July 1951), 102-107. Excerpts from *A Western Journal*, illustrated with photographs.

B83 "Observe the Whole of It," *Life*, July 4, 1950, pp. 49-52. From *YCGHA*, 505-506. Also included in a folder entitled *American Words*, distributed by *Life*.

B84 "October," *University of North Carolina Magazine*, LXVIII (October 1938), 8-10. Excerpt from *OTATR*.

B85 "October Has Come Again," *Encore*, II (October 1942), 473-477.

B86 "Oktoberfest," *Scribner's Magazine*, CI (June 1937), 27-31. Similar to *TWATR*, 662-672.

B87 "Old Catawba," *Virginia Quarterly Review*, XI (April 1935), 191-197. Similar to *FDTM*, 185-187, 195-204.

B88 "Old Man Rivers," *Atlantic Monthly*, CLXXX (December 1947), 92-104.

B89 "One of the Girls in Our Party," *Scribner's Magazine*, XCVII (January 1935), 6-8. Similar to *FDTM*, 155-163.

B90 "Only the Dead Know Brooklyn," *New Yorker*, XI (June 15, 1935), 13-14. Similar to *FDTM*, 91-97. Translated into German, *Story* [Stuttgart], I (December 1946), 31-35.

B91 "The Party at Jack's," *Scribner's Magazine*, CV (May 1939), 14-16, 40-49, 58-62. Parts of this appear in *YCGHA*, scattered from pp. 196-322.

B92 "Polyphemus," *North American Review*, CCXL (June 1935), 20-26. Reprinted in *Fiction Parade*, (October 1935). Similar to *FDTM*, 187-195.

B93 "Portrait of a Literary Critic: A Satire," *American Mercury*, XLVI (April 1939), 429-437. Also in *THB*, 152-161.

B94 "A Portrait of Bascom Hawke," *Scribner's Magazine*, XCI (April 1932), 193-198, 239-256. Similar to *OTATR*, 104-150. Translated into German, *Story*, V (January 1950), 39-100.

B95 "The Plumed Knight," *Town and Country*, XCVII (October 1941). Similar to *THB*, 264-276.

B96 "A Prologue to America," *Vogue*, CXI (February 1, 1938), 63-66, 150-152, 161.

B97 "The Promise of America," *Coronet*, VIII (September 1940), 9-12. Similar to *YCGHA*, 505-508.

B98 "Return," *Asheville Citizen-Times*, May 16, 1937; reprinted as "Thomas Wolfe Describes His Feelings at Being Home Again," *Asheville Ciitzen-Times*, March 26, 1950.

B99 "Russian Folk Song," *University of North Carolina Magazine*, XLIX (June 1919), 191. A poem.

B100 "So This Is Man," *Town and Country*, XCV (August 1940), 28, 69-70. Similar to *YCGHA*, 432-440, 501-505.

B101 "Something of My Life," *Saturday Review of Literature*, XXI (February 7, 1948), 6-8. This is the original sketch submitted for use in Georges Schreiber's *Portraits and Self-portraits*, 1936.

B102 "The Story of a Novel," *Saturday Review of Literature*, XIII (December 14, 1935), 3-4, 12-16; (December 21, 1935), 3-4, 15; (December 28, 1935), 3-4, 14-16. Condensed in *Writer's Digest* (February, 1936). Translated into German in *Der Neue Rundschau*, XLVII (November 1936), 1121-1142.

B103 "The Streets of Durham, or, Dirty Work at the Crossroads," *Tar Baby*, I (1919), 4-5. This is an example of Wolfe's writing in the University of North Carolina student humor magazine.

B104 "The Sun and the Rain," *Scribner's Magazine*, XCV (May 1934), 358-360. Also in *Scholastic*, XXVII (November 1935), 4-6. Similar to *OTATR*, 797-802.

B105 "The Third Night: A Play of the Carolina Mountains," *Carolina Play-Book*, XII (September 1938), 70-75. Originally produced at the University of North Carolina, October 12, 1919.

B106 "Three O'Clock," *North American Review*, CCXLVII (Summer 1939), 219-224. Similar to *TWATR*, 17-21.

B107 "To France, a Poem," *University of North Carolina Magazine*, XLVII (December 1917), 165.

B108 "To Rupert Brooke," *University of North Carolina Magazine*, XLVII (May 1918), 314-315. A poem.

B109 "Tom Wolfe's Purpose," *Saturday Review*, XXXIX
(October 6, 1956), 16. Extract from a letter to M. E.
Perkins, dated 1936.

B110 "The Train and the City," *Scribner's Magazine*, XCIII
(May 1933), 285-294. Similar to *TWATR*, 441-449;
OTATR, 407-419; *YCGHA*, 3-4.

B111 "The Web of Earth: a Complete Short Novel," *Scribner's
Magazine*, XCII (July 1932), 1-5, 43-64. Similar to
FDTM, 212-304.

B112 "A Western Journey," *Virginia Quarterly Review*, XV
(Summer 1939), 335-357. Excerpts from the notes
later published as *A Western Journal*.

B113 "Welcome to Our City," *Esquire*, XLVIII (October
1957), 58-83. First publication of this play, written while
Wolfe was at Harvard.

B114 "What a Writer Reads," *Book Buyer*, I (December
1935), 13-14.

B115 "The Winter of Our Discontent," *Atlantic Monthly*,
CLXIII (June 1939), 817-823. Similar to *TWATR*,
414-426.

B116 "Writing Is My Life: Letters of Thomas Wolfe,"
Atlantic Monthly, CLXXVIII (December, 1946), 60-66;
CLXXIX (January 1947), 39-45; CLXXIX (February
1947), 55-61. Letters, 1920-1938, to Mrs. J. M.
Roberts, Asheville, N. C.

B117 "Ye Who Have Been There Only Know," *Tar Heel*
[University of North Carolina], December 13, 1919. Also
in *Modern Fiction Studies*, XI (Autumn 1965),
270-271.

B118 "You Can't Escape Autobiography: New Letters of Thomas Wolfe," *Atlantic Monthly*, CLXXXVI (November 1950), 80-83. Written in 1932 to Julian R. Meade, Danville, Va.

B119 "You Can't Go Home Again," *Scholastic*, XLVII (November 26, 1945), 26-27, 36-37, 42. Brief excerpt from *THB*, 108-120.

B120 "You Can't Go Home Again," *Life*, July 7, 1952, p. 71. A brief excerpt from *YCGHA*, 399-401.

C. Parts of Books by Wolfe

C1 "Alone," *TWATR*, 273-294: *TWR,* 526-546. Also in
   Charles Laughton, ed., *Tell Me A Story* (1957), 95-110.

C2 "America," *FOAN*, 1-9; from *OTATR*, 155-160.

C3 "America Is the Place," in L. N. Richardson, ed., *The
   Heritage of American Literature* (1951), 815-818.

C4 "American Landscape," in Sharon Brown, ed., *Portrait of a
   World* (1941), 7-10; Marjorie Barrow, ed., *One Thousand
   Beautiful Things* (1947), 30-31; Clayton E. Wheat, ed.,
   The Democratic Tradition in America (1943),
   112-114. From *OTATR*, 155-160.

C5 "American October," in Lionel Crocker, ed., *Interpretative
   Speech* (1952), 298-299. From *OTATR*, 329-331.

C6 "The Anatomy of Loneliness," in *American Mercury
   Reader* (1943), 35-41. Same as "God's Lonely Man,"
   THB, 186-197.

C7 "The Angel on the Porch," *TWR*, 77-84; from *LHA*,
   262-269.

C8 "The Anodyne," *YCGHA*, 483-498.

C9 "Antaeus: Earth Again," *OTATR*, 795-850.

61

C10 "April in Altamont," *TWR*, 104-127; from *LHA*, 324-348.
Excerpt in Norman Kiell, ed. *The Adolescent Through
Fiction* (1959) 115-120.

C11 "April, Late April," *TWATR*, 441-452.

C12 "Arnold Pentland," in Arnold Gingrich, ed., *The Armchair
Esquire* (1958), 60-68. Similar to "A Kinsman of His
Blood," *THB*, 66-76.

C13 "Artemidorus, Farewell," *SLD*, 8-9, *PTW*, 34-234; from
LHA, 391-551.

C14 "Aunt Mag and Uncle Mark," *TWATR*, 97-100.

C15 "Aunt Maw's Funeral," in Robert Terrall, ed., *Great
Scenes from Great Novels* (1956), 499-512.
From *YCGHA*, 95-108.

C16 (Autobiographical sketch), in Georges Schreiber, ed.,
Portraits and Self-Portraits (1936), 163-167. See also
"Something of My Life."

C17 "Awakening," in Claude M. Fuess, ed., *Unseen Harvests*
(1947), 436-437. From *LHA*, 318-319.

C18 "Bank Failure in Libya Hill," in Harvey Swados, ed.,
The American Writer and the Great Depression (1966),
503-509. From *YCGHA*, 366-372.

C19 "The Battle of Hogwart Heights," *THB*, 277-293; Avon
SS, 96-107; Lion *THB*, 230-243; Avon *THB*, 82-98;
and Perennial *THB*, 72-87. In German, *Hinter
Jenen Bergen*, 200-211. In Danish, *De Fjerne Bjerge*,
100-121.

C20 "The Bells Strike Three," *THB*, 327-341; Avon *THB*,
131-145; Lion *THB*, 271-282; Perennial *THB*, 119-133.
In German, *Hinter Jenen Bergen*, 235-245. In Danish,
De Fjerne Bjerge, 164-182.

C21 "The Birthday," *TWATR*, 346-358.

C22 "Boom Town," *TWR*, 588-614. Also in Harry Hansen, ed.,
O. Henry Memorial Award Prize Stories of 1934,
243-279; and in Charles Grayson, ed., *Stories for Men*
(1936), 555-583. Similar to *YCGHA* 109-140.

C23 "A Boy's Reverie," in Ann Watkins, ed., *Taken at the
Flood* (1946), 75-82. From *TWATR*, 21-29.

C24 "The Bums at Sunset," *FDTM*, 150-154; Penguin *SS*,
37-41; *OTDKB*, 37-41. Also in Cleveland Amory,
ed., *Vanity Fair Cavalcade* (1960), 310-312. In Serbian, *U
Mrachnoi Shumi Tajanstvenoi Kao Vreme*, 78-83. In
Polish, *Wloczedzy o Zachodzie Słońca*, 237-242. In French,
De la Mort au Matin, 152-156. In German, *Vom Tod
zum Morgen*, 175-182.

C25 "The Butcher," *TWATR*, 118-131.
"Burning in the Night," *SLD*, 158-165; also in Frank
Brookhouse, ed., *These Were Our Years* (1959), 17-23.
From *YCGHA*, 499-508.

C26 "Chickamauga," *THB*, 77-107; Avon *SS*, 35-55; Lion *THB*,
68-92; *PTW*, 681-712; *The Lost Boy*, 81-112. Also in
Charles Grayson, ed., *The Golden Argosy* (1947), 636-656;
and in Orville Prescott, ed., *The Undying Past* (1961),
601-623. In German, *Hinter Jenen Bergen*, 59-79. In
Polish, *Wloczedzy o Zachodzie Słońca*, 76-112. In Serbian,

U Mrachnoi Shumi Tajanstvenoi Kao Vreme, 5-41. In
German, *Der Verlorene Knabe*, 146-180. In Danish
Den Tabte Tid, 103-141.

C27 "The Capture," *YCGHA*, 691-699.

C28 "The Catastrophe," *YCGHA*, 359-372.

C29 "The Child by Tiger," *TWATR*, 132-156; *TWR*, 500-525.
Also in Roger Butterfield, ed., *The Saturday Evening
Post Treasury* (1954), 243-265; Guy A. Cardwell, ed.,
Readings from the Americas (1947), 611-636; Earl Davis,
ed., *Readings for Enjoyment* (1959), 32-46; *Post Stories
of 1937* (1938), 243-265; and Jessie C. Rehder, ed.,
The Story at Work (1963), 345-372.

C30 "The Child Caliban," *TWATR*, 3-12.

C31 "The Circus at Dawn," *FDTM*, 205-211; *PTW*, 659-665;
Penguin *SS*, 32-37; *OTDKB*, 32-37. Also in Walter
Havighurst, ed., *Selection: A Reader for College Writing*
(1955), 8-10; Hiram Haydn, ed., *A World of Great Stories*
(1947), 76-80; Rewey Belle Inglis, ed., *Adventures in
American Literature* (1950), 153-156; Robert C. Pooley,
ed., *The United States in Literature* (1952),
253-257; and Stark Young, ed., *Southern Treasury of Life
and Literature* (1937), 594-598. In German, Norbert
Krejcik, ed., *Amerikanisches Literaturbrevier*
(1954), 262-268; in *Vom Tod zum Morgen*, 243-252; and
in *Die Leute von Alt-Catawba*, 73-81. In Serbian, *Tkanje
Zhivota*, 216-223. In Polish, *Wloczedzy o Zachodzie
Slońca*, 230-236. In Japanese, *Daichi o Ou Kumo No Su*,
177-186. In French, *De la Mort au Matin*, 203-206.

C32 "The City of Lost Men," *YCGHA*, 141-146.

C33 "The City Patriots," *TWATR*, 233-249.

C34 "The Company," *YCGHA*, 129-140. Also in Joseph Gaer, ed., *Our Lives: American Labor Stories* (1948); and in Lillian B. Gilkes, ed., *Short Story Craft* (1949), 192-202.

C35 "Conversation by Moonlight," *FOAN*, 28-42; from *LHA*, 617-629.

C36 "Credo," *YCGHA*, 739-743; *TWR*, 637-640. Also in *The Britannica Library of Great American Writing* (1960), v.2, pp. 1615-1618; L. S. Brown, ed., *Literature For Our Time* (1947), 829-832; Stuart G. Brown, ed., *We Hold These Truths* (1941), 324-326; Norman Cousins, ed., *A Treasury of Democracy* (1942); Alexander Cowie, ed., *American Writers Today* (1956), 55-58; David Hoffman, ed., *Readings in Democracy* (1952), 106-109; Clara Molendyk, ed., *Thus Be It Ever* (1942), 364-366; George Seldes, ed., *The Great Quotations* (1960), 754-755; Bernard Smith, ed., *The Democratic Spirit* (1941), 867-869; and Harvey Swados, ed., *The American Writer and the Great Depression* (1966), 513-515.

C37 "Dark in the Forest, Strange as Time," *FDTM*, 98-113; *PTW*, 643-658; *TWR*, 470-480. Also in Joshua McClennen, ed., *Masters and Masterpieces of Short Stories* (1957); and in Edward Wagenknecht, ed., *The Fireside Book of Romance* (1948), 542-553. In French, *De la Mort au Matin*, 105-119. In German, *Vom Tod zum Morgen*, 117-134; and *Die Leute von Alt-Catawba*, 10-29. In Japanese, *Daichi o Ou Kumo No Su*, 145-168. In Serbian, *U Mrachnoi Shumi Tajanstvenoi Kao Vreme*, 84-99.

C38 "Dark Interlude," *TWATR*, 485-486.

C39 "Dark Messiah," *YCGHA*, 621-633.

C40 "Dark October," *TWATR*, 680-688.

C41 "The Dead World Relived," *THB*, 310-326; Avon *THB*, 115-130; Lion *THB*, 257-270; Perennial *THB*, 103-118. In German, *Hinter Jenen Bergen*, 223-234. In Danish, *De Fjerne Bjerge*, 142-163.

C42 "The Death of Ben Gant," *TWR*, 171-213. Also excerpt in Alexander Cowie, ed., *American Writers Today* (1956), 53-54. From *LHA*, 536-583.

C43 "The Death of Stoneman Gant," in William R. Benet, ed., *Oxford Anthology of American Literature* (1938), 1537-1553. From *OTATR*, 246-273.

C44 "The Death of W. O. Gant," *TWR*, 240-303. From *OTATR*, 210-268.

C45 "Death in the City," in S. S. Basket, ed., *The American Identity* (1962), 387-389. From *FDTM*, 18-22.

C46 "Death the Proud Brother," *FDTM*, 15-70; Penguin *SS*, 47-93; *OTDKB*, 47-93. Also in James D. Hart, ed., *America's Literature* (1955), 912-933, and in Harry A. Warfel, ed., *The American Mind*, (1937), v.2, 1462-1474. In German, *Der Verlorene Knabe*, 181-248; also published separately as *Tod, Der Stolze Bruder.*; *Vom Tod zum Morgen*, 23-84. In French, *De la Mort au Matin*, 30-79. In Serbian, *Tkanje Zhivota*, 117-180. In Polish, *Wloczedzy o Zachodzie Słońca*, 243-304.

C47 "Depression in New York City," in Harvey Swados, ed., *The American Writer and the Great Depression* (1966), 511-513. From *YCGHA*, 412-414.

C48 "Downtown," *YCGHA*, 187-195.

C49 "The Dream of Time," *TWR*, 415-446; *FOAN, 162-105.* From *OTATR*, 853-870, 880-886, 892-893.

C50 "The Drunken Beggar on Horseback," *YCGHA*, 3-14.

C51 "Ecclesiasticus," *YCGHA*, 731-738.

C52 "Economic Views of the Depression," in *Man in Contemporary Society: A Source Book* (1956), 179-194. From *YCGHA*, 359-373, 391-396, 412-414.

C53 "Enchanted City," in Alex Klein, ed., *Empire City: A Treasury of New York,* (1955), 437-442. From *TWATR*, 222-232.

C54 "An End and a Beginning," *YCGHA*, 232-396.

C55 "Enter Mr. Lloyd McHarg," *YCGHA*, 537-552.

C56 "Esther's Farewell," *TWATR*, 616-620.

C57 "Esther's House," *TWATR*, 362-383.

C58 "Even Two Angels Not Enough," *YCGHA*, 723-730.

C59 "Eugene and Laura," in George Mayberry, ed., *A Little Treasury of American Prose* (1949), 791-799. Excerpts from *LHA*, 427-456.

C60 "Eugene Gant's Harvard," in William Bentinck-Smith, ed., *The Harvard Book* (1953), 261-266. From *OTATR*.

68

C61 "Evening in Brooklyn," in Pearl Hogrefe, ed.,
The Process of Creative Writing (1956), 62-65. An excerpt
from "No Door."

C62 "Exile and Discovery," *YCGHA*, 509-618. In German,
published separately as *Verbannung und Entdeckung*
(1959).

C63 "The Face of the War," *FDTM*, 71-90; *PTW*, 617-636;
TWR, 450-464. Also in Willard Thorp, ed., *A Southern
Reader* (1953), 702-709. In German, *Vom Tod zum
Morgen*, 85-108. In French, *De la Mort au Matin*, 80-97.
In Serbian, *U Mrachnoi Shumi Tajanstvenoi Kao
Vreme*, 57-77; and in Jaroslav Schejhal, ed. *Dni a Noci
Ameriky* (1964), 424-441.

C64 "The Face of America," in William A. Bacher, ed.,
The Treasury Star Parade (1942), 143-150. Adaptation, in
play form, of *OTATR*, 155-160.

C65 "Fame's First Wooing," *YCGHA*, 15-28.

C66 "The Family of Earth," *YCGHA*, 680-690.

C67 "The Far and the Near," *FDTM*, 164-168; *TWR*,
481-484. Also in Walter Blair, ed., *The United States in
Literature* (1963), 474-476; Cleanth Brooks, ed., *The Scope
of Fiction* (1960), 292-295; Cleanth Brooks, ed.,
Understanding Fiction (1959), 422-425;
Samuel Moskowitz, ed., *Great Railroad Stories of the
World* (1954). In French, *De la Mort au Matin*, 166-170.
In German, *Vom Tod zum Morgen*, 195-202; *Der
Verlorene Knabe*, 68-73. In Japanese, *Daichi o Ou Kumo
No Su*, 169-176. In Serbian, *Tkanje Zhivota*, 210-215.

C68 "Farewell to Altamont," in Joseph Liss, ed., *Radio's Best Plays* (1947). A radio play by Elizabeth Lomax, adapted from parts of *LHA*.

C69 "Faust and Helen," *OTATR*, 901-912. Also in Bennett Cerf, ed., *Reading for Pleasure* (1957), 133-141.

C70 "First Party," *TWATR*, 468-484.

C71 "Five Passengers for Paris," *YCGHA*, 665-679.

C72 "Flight before Fury," *TWR*, 266-234; from *OTATR*, 68-76.

C73 "The Four Lost Men," *FOAN*, 267-281; *FDTM*, 114-133; Penguin *SS*, 16-32. Also in Bernard Duffey, ed., *Modern American Literature* (1951), 158-174; and in A. P. Hudson, ed., *Nelson's College Caravan* (1940), v. 3, 209-218. In French, *De la Mort au Matin*, 120-137. In German, *Vom Tod zum Morgen*, 135-156. In Polish, *Wloczedzy o Zachodzie Słońca*, 207-229. In Serbian, *Tkanje Zhivota*, 224-249.

C74 "The Fox," *YCGHA*, 438-459.

C75 "Freshman Year," in Walter Havighurst, ed., *Selection: A Reader for College Writing*, (1955), 32-36. From *LHA*.

C76 "From Thomas Wolfe's Purdue Speech," in Field, 123-129.

C77 "Gentlemen of the Press," *THB*, 49-65; Avon *SS*, 15-26; Lion THB, 45-58; *The Lost Boy*, 52-69. In German, *Hinter Jenen Bergen*, 39-50; *Der Verlorene Knabe*, 127-145; *Willkommen in Altamont*, 159-171. In Danish, *Den Tabte Tid*, 68-88.

70

C78 "Go, Seeker," in Harold H. Wagenheim, ed., *Our Reading Heritage: This Is America* (1956); Ralph L. Woods, ed., *The Family Reader of American Masterpieces* (1959), 1-2. From *YCGHA.*

C79 "God's Lonely Man," *THB*, 186-197; Avon *THB*, 172-183, *TWR*, 675-686; Lion *THB*, 156-165; *The Lost Boy*, 193-208. Also in Whit Burnett, ed., *The Seas of God* (1944), 60-69; Whit Burnett, ed., *The Spirit of Man* (1958), 19-30; and Nathan C. Starr, ed., *The Pursuit of Learning* (1956), 574-581. In Danish, *Den Tabte Tid*, 241-256. In German, *Hinter Jenen Bergen*, 135-143.

C80 "The Golden City," *TWATR*, 91-94.

C81 "The Golden World," *FOAN*, 10-13; also in Charlotte Lee, ed., *Oral Interpretation* (1952), 185, 188, 195-196; and in Jessie C. Rehder *The Young Writer at Work* (1962), 69-72. From *LHA*, 84-87.

C82 "The Golden Years at the University," in Norman Kiell, ed., *The Adolescent Through Fiction* (1959), 60-62. From *LHA*, 596-598.

C83 "A Good Idea for a Story," in Floyd Watkins, ed., *Writer to Writer* (1966), 7-15. From *SOAN.*

C84 "Götterdämmerung," *TWATR*, 250-272.

C85 "Glory Deferred," *TWATR*, 512-523.

C86 "The Great Schism," *THB*, 222-239; Avon *THB*, 31-47; Lion *THB*, 186-200; Perennial *THB*, 21-37. Also in R. C. Beatty, ed., *The Literature of the South* (1952),

1017-1027. In German, *Hinter Jenen Bergen*, 161-173. In Danish, *De Fjerne Bjerge*, 31-53.

C87 "Greeting and Farewell," *FOAN*, 14-16; also in Charlotte Lee, ed., *Oral Interpretation* (1952), 152-153.
From *OTATR*, 410-411.

C88 "A Guest in Spite of Himself," *YCGHA*, 568-594.

C89 "Gulliver," *FDTM*, 134-149; *OTDKB*, 93-105; Penguin *SS*, 93-105. In French *De la Mort au Matin*, 138-151. In German, *Vom Tod zum Morgen*, 157-174. In Serbian, *U Mrachnoi Shumi Tajanstvenoi Kao Vreme*, 129-145. In Hebrew, S. Skulsky, ed., *Mivchar Hasipur Ha Americai*.

C90 "He Remembered Yet. . . ," in R. A. Beals, ed., *Readings in Description and Narration* (1930). From *LHA*, 84-85. Probably the earliest use of an excerpt from Wolfe in a textbook.

C91 "The Hidden Terror," *YCGHA*, 45-89.

C92 "A High Pressure World, Its Heaven and Hell," in Edgar Johnson, ed., *A Treasury of Satire* (1945), 746-754. From *YCGHA*, 129-140. See also "The Company."

C93 "The Hills Beyond," *THB*, 201-348; Avon *THB*, 11-151; Lion *THB*, 169-288; Perennial *THB*, 1-142. In German, *Hinter Jenen Berge*n, 145-250. In Danish, *De Fjerne Bjerge*, 5-190.
This subsection of *THB* includes the ten stories; "The Quick and the Dead;" "Old Man of the Tribe;" "The Great Schism;" "How Certain Joyners Went to Town;" "The Plumed Knight;" "The Battle of Hogwart Heights;" "The Stranger Whose Sermon Was Brick;" "The Dead World Relived;" "The Bell Strikes Three;" and "The Lost Day."

C94 "His Father's Earth," in Erich A. Walter, ed., *1936 Essay Annual*, 104-114. Similar to *TWATR*, 86-90.

C95 "The Hollow Men," *YCGHA*, 460-482; *TWR*, 614-633. Also in Alex Austin, ed., *Great Tales of City Dwellers* (1955), 44-65; *The Esquire Treasury* (1953), 279-285; and J. H. Nelson and Oscar Cargill, eds., *Contempory Trends: American Literature Since 1900* (1949), 841-854.

C96 "The Home Coming," *YCGHA*, 90-108.

C97 "Home From the Mountain," *TWATR*, 157-170.

C98 "Hope Springs Eternal," *TWATR*, 424-436.

C99 "The Hospital," *TWATR*, 673-679.

C100 "The Hound of Darkness," *TWATR*, 95-170.

C101 "The House in the Country," *YCGHA*, 559-614.

C102 "The House of the Far and Lost," *TWR*, 386-409; *Short Novels*, 194-220. From *OTATR*, 619-627, 637-652. Also in R. C. Beatty, ed., *Contemporary Southern Prose* (1940), 325-349; R. C. Beatty, ed., *The Literature of the South* (1952), 995-1011; John T. Frederick, ed., *Present Day Stories* (1941), 450-480; and Robert Penn Warren, ed., *A Southern Harvest* (1937). See also *No Door*.

C104 "How Certain Joyners Went to Town," *THB*, 240-263; Avon *THB*, 48-69; Lion *THB*, 201-219; Perennial *THB*, 38-59. In German, *Hinter Jenen Bergen*, 174-190. In Danish, *De Fjerne Bjerge*, 54-83.

C105 "How to Tell a Major Poet from a Minor Poet," in James Kreuzer and Lee Cogan, eds., *Studies in Prose Writing* (1967). From a letter to his sister, Mabel Wheaton.

C106 "I Have a Thing to Tell You," *YCGHA*, 619-704; *Short Novels*, 236-278. In Spanish *Tengo Algo Que Deciros*, 5-53. Excerpt in Robert B. Luce, ed., *The Faces of Five Decades* (1965), 247-258.

C107 "In the Park," *FDTM*, 169-184; *PTW*, 665-680; *TWR*, 485-496. In French, *De la Mort au Matin*, 171-184. In German, *Vom Tod zum Morgen*, 203-220; *Die Leute von Alt-Catawba*, 30-48. In Serbian, *Tkanje Zhivota*, 181-198. Excerpt in Esther McCullough, ed., *As I Pass, O Manhattan* (1956), 143-145.

C108 "In the Sleeper," in Allen Tate, ed., *American Harvest* (1942), 154-163. From *OTATR*, 468-476.

C109 "Jack at Morn," *YCGHA*, 149-161.

C110 "Jason's Voyage," *OTATR*, 599-704; *PTW*, 237-395.

C111 "Journey to the North," *FOAN*, 55-70; from *OTATR*, 68-77.

C112 "Justice Is Blind," Walser, 91-100. First appearance in print.

C113 "A Kinsman of His Blood," *THB*, 66-76; Avon *SS*, 27-34; Lion *THB*, 59-68; *The Lost Boy*, 70-80. In German, *Hinter Jenen Bergen*, 51-58. In Danish, *Den Tabte Tid*, 89-102. In Polish, *Wloczedzy o Zachodzie Słońca*, 63-75. See also "Arnold Pentland."

C114 "Kronos and Rhea," *OTATR*, 851-900.

C115 "The Last Farewell," *YCGHA*, 654-664.

C116 "The Letter," *TWATR*, 315-319.

C117 "A Letter of Gratitude and Indebtedness," in Claude M. Fuess, ed., *Unseen Harvests* (1947), 437-438. To Mr. Frank Wells, Superintendent of Schools in Asheville, N. C. See *Letters*, 16-17.

C118 "Letter to J. G. Stikeleather, Jr.," in Charles Hurd, ed., *A Treasury of Great American Letters* (1962), 268-271. See *Letters*, 474-476.

C119 "Letter to Helen," Charles Hurd, ed., *A Treasury of Great American Letters*, (1962), 267-268. See *Letters*, 207-208.

C120 "Letter to Maxwell Perkins," *TWR*, 689-690. Also in Maxwell Perkins, *Editor to Author* (1950), 141. See *Letters*, 777-778.

C121 "Letter to His Mother," Holman, 6-8. Also in William Stafford, ed., *Twentieth Century American Writing* (1965), 492-494. From *LTHM*, 48-53, dated May, 1923.

C122 "Letter to His Mother," in Charles Van Doren, ed. *Letters to Mother, an Anthology* (1959), 346-350. See *LTHM*, 241-245, dated February 27, 1933.

C123 "Letter to Miss Lewisohn," in *Mannerhouse* (English edition, 1950), vii-xviii. Also in special, boxed edition of the first American edition, and in *Willkommen in Altamont*, 184-185. See *Letters*, 103-104.

C124 "Letter to Scott Fitzgerald," in F. Scott Fitzgerald, *The Crack-up* (1945), 312-316. See *Letters*, 641-645.

C125 "Letter to Sherwood Anderson," in James Schevill, *Sherwood Anderson* (1951), 325-326. See *Letters*, 654-656, dated September 22, 1937.

C126 "Letters to Henry T. Volkening," Walser, 33-50.
See *Letters*, 180-182, 226-228, 261-266, 289-293.

C127 (Letters on his plays), *Wilkommen in Altamont*,
180-185. Letters to George Pierce Baker, Mrs. Margaret
Roberts, and Alice Lewisohn.

C128 (Letters to his mother), *Uns Bleibt die Erde*, 91-110.
Excerpts from *LTHM*.

C129 (Letter to Heinz Ledig-Rowohlt), *Uns Bleibt die Erde*,
110-115. See *Letters*, 523-527.

C130 "Life as Seen From the Floor," in Donald Davidson, ed.,
American Composition and Rhetoric (1939), 329-332.
From *LHA*, 36-39.

C131 "Life and Letters," *TWATR*, 453-536.

C132 "The Lion at Morning," *THB*, 162-185; Avon *SS*, 79-95;
Lion *THB*, 137-155; *The Lost Boy*, 169-192. In
German, *Hinter Jenen Bergen*, 118-134; and *Der Verlorene
Knabe*, 74-102. In Danish, *Den Tabte Tid*, 210-240.
In Polish, *Wloczedzy o Zachodzie Slońca*, 152-182.

C133 "The Lion Hunters," *YCGHA*, 341-351.

C134 "The Locusts Have No King," *YCGHA*, 399-437.
Also in Joe Lee Davis, ed., *American Literature* (1949),
v.2, pp. 797-807.

C135 "A Lonely Year," in A. C. Spectorsky, ed., *The College
Years* (1958), 128-135. From *LHA*, 394-402.

C136 "Look Homeward, Angel," Excerpts from *LHA* in *PTW*,
33-234; *TWR*, 53-222. Also brief excerpts in John K.
Hutchens, ed., *The American Twenties* (1952), 257-269;

G. D. Sanders, ed., *Unified English Composition* (1945),
633-634; Caroline Schroder, ed., *Psychology Through
Literature* (1943), 18-33; and Stark Young, ed., *Southern
Treasury of Life and Letters* (1937), 598-602. Digests
of *LHA* are to be found in Hiram Haydn, ed., *Thesaurus
of Book Digests* (1949), 439-440; and in Frank N. Magill,
ed., *Masterpieces of World Literature in Digest Form*
(1949), 517-520.

C137 "Look Homeward, Angel," (Frings' adaption in play
form) in E. B. Watson and Benfield Pressey, eds.,
Contemporary Drama: Fifteen Plays (1959). Condensed
versions in Louis Kronenberger, ed., *The Best Plays
of 1957-1958* (1958), 136-160; John Gassner, ed., *Best
American Plays: Fifth Series*, 1957-1963.

C138 "The Looking Glass," *TWATR*, 689-695.

C139 "The Lost Boy," *THB*, 1-42; Avon *SS*, 108-135; Lion
THB, 7-39; *The Lost Boy*, 3-45; *TWR*, 643-674. Also in
Leonard S. Brown, ed., *Literature for Our Time*
(1947), 390-411; in Joe Lee Davis, ed., *American
Literature* (1949), v.2, 778-797; Wallace Stegner, ed., *The
Writer's Art* (1950), 146-178; Arlin Turner, ed.,
Southern Stories (1960), 221-256; Richard Walser, ed.,
North Carolina in the Short Story (1948), 145-158;
and Richard Walser, ed., *Short Stories from the Old North
State* (1959), 275-288. In German *Der Verlorene Knabe*,
3-50; *Hinter Jenen Bergen*, 5-34. In Danish, *Den
Tabte Tid*, 7-60. In Polish, *Wloczedzy o Zachodzie Słońca*,
7-56.

C140 "The Lost Day," *THB*, 342-348; Avon *THB*, 146-151; Lion *THB*, 283-288; Perennial *THB*, 134-139. In Danish, *De Fjerne Bjerge*, 183-190. In German, *Hinter Jenen Bergen*, 146-150.

C141 "Louise in Charleston," *TWR*, 127-138. From *LHA*, 357-369.

C142 "Love in the Enchanted Wood," *TWR*, 139-170. From *LHA*, 427-461.

C143 "Love is Not Enough," *YCGHA*, 312-322.

C144 "Love's Bitter Mystery," *TWATR*, 537-620; *PTW*, 399-503.

C145 "The Magic of Youth," in J. D. Adams, ed., *The New Treasure Chest* (1953), 371-372. From *OTATR*, 454.

C146 "The Magic Year," *TWATR*, 295-452.

C147 "Make America Your Garden, Seeker," in James I. Brown, ed., *Efficient Reading* (1952), 126-127; also in Erich A. Walter, ed., *Essay Annual, 1941* xi-xiii. From *YCGHA*, 505-508.

C148 "Man-Creating and Man-Alive," *YCGHA*, 352-358.

C149 "Mannerhouse," *Willkommen in Altamont*, 87-158.

C150 "May Morning in the Park," *FOAN*, 312-315; also in Esther M. McCullough, ed. *As I Pass, O Manhattan* (1958), 143-145. From "In the Park," *FDTM*, 182-184.

C151 "The Meadows of Sensation," in *TWR*, 71-77. From *LHA*, 81-87.

C152 "Memories," in Charles Lee, ed., *North, East, South, West: A Regional Anthology* (1945), 354-358. From *OTATR*, 411-415.

C153 "The Men of Old Catawba," *FDTM*, 185-205; Penguin *SS*, 1-15; *OTDKB*, 1-15. Excerpt in Hardnett Kane, ed., *The Romantic South* (1961), 30-32. In French, *De la Mort au Matin*, 185-202. In German, *Vom Tod zum Morgen*, 221-242; *Die Leute von Alt-Catawba*, 49-72. In Polish, *Wloczedzy o Zachodzie Słońca*, 185-206. In Serbian, *U Mrachnoi Shumi Tajanstvenoi Kao Vreme*, 108-128.

C154 "The Microscopic Gentleman from Japan," *YCGHA*, 28-36.

C155 "Mr. Hirsch Could Wait," *YCGHA*, 264-272.

C156 "Mrs. Jack Awake," *YCGHA*, 162-186.

C157 "A Moment of Decision," *YCGHA*, 255-263.

C158 "The Morning After," *YCGHA*, 615-618.

C159 "Mother and Daughter," in W. D. Templeman, ed., *Models and Motivations for Writing* (1941), 560-562. From *YCGHA*.

C160 "Names of the Nation," *FOAN*, 234-252; *TWR*, 429-433. Also in Clara Molendyk, ed., *Thus Be It Ever* (1942), 129-134; and Carl Van Doren, ed., *An Anthology of World Prose* (1935), 1558-1561. From *OTATR*, 861-870.

C161 "The Native's Return," *YCGHA*, 1-146.

C162 "Nebraska Crane," *TWR*, 576-587; also in Charles Einstein, ed., *The Fireside Book of Baseball* (1956), 376-380. From *YCGHA*, 55-69.

C163 "The New Principal," in Claude M. Fuess, ed., *Unseen Harvests* (1947), 432-435. From *LHA*, 205-209.

C164 "A New World," *TWATR*, 389-404.

C165 "No Cure for It," *THB*, 43-48; Avon *SS*, 11-14; Lion *THB*, 40-44; *The Lost Boy*, 46-51. In German, *Hinter Jenen Bergen*, 35-38. In Danish, *Den Tabte Tid*, 61-67. In Polish, *Wloczedzy o Zachodzie Slońca*, 57-62.

C166 "No Door," *FDTM*, 1-14; *Short Novels*, 155-232. The short version is also in Holman, 33-37; and Esther M. McCullough, ed., *As I Pass, O Manhattan* (1958), 464-473. In German, *Vom Tod zum Morgen*, 9-22; *Der Verlorene Knabe*, 51-67; and in Ernst Schnabel's *Thomas Wolfe* (1947), 23-36. In French, *De la Mort au Matin*, 17-29. In Serbian, *U Mrachnoi Shumi Tajanstvenoi Kao Vreme*, 42-56. In Spanish, th e longer version is in *Tengo Algo Que Deciros*, 105-189. The longer version consists of "No Door" plus "The House of the Far and Lost."

C167 "October," *SLD*, 143-151; also in Ben G. Henneke, ed., *Reading Aloud Effectively* (1954), 362-364; Barbara Webster, ed., *Country Matters, An Anthology* (1959). From *OTATR*, 327-332.

C168 "October Feast in Munich," in Carlos Baker, ed., *The American Looks at the World* (1944), 108-121. From *TWATR*, 662-672. See also "Oktoberfest."

C169 "October Had Come Again," *FOAN*, 156-168; also in Clifton Fadiman, ed., *Fireside Reader* (1961), 141-146. From *OTATR*, 327-332.

C170 "Octubre sombrio," in John Peale Bishop, ed., *Antologia de Escritores Contemporaneos de los Estados Unidos* (1944), 351-364. From *TWATR*, 680-688.

C171 "Of Time and the River," Excerpts from *OTATR* in *PTW*, 237-395, and *TWR*, 223-446. Brief excerpts are in Walter Blair, ed., *The Literature of the United States* (1946), 1086-1088; Leon Howard, ed., *American Heritage* (1954), v.2, 788-793; George Oppenheimer, ed., *The Passionate Playgoer* (1958), 58-67; and in Bernard Smith, ed., *The Democratic Spirit* (1941), 859-867. Digests of *OTATR* are in Frank N. Magill, ed., *Masterpieces of World Literature in Digest Form*, 674-676; and in Hiram Haydn, ed., *Thesaurus of Book Digests*.

C172 "Oktoberfest," *TWATR*, 621-695; *TWR*, 547-572.

C173 *"Old Man of the Tribe,"* *THB*, 211-221; Avon *THB*, 20-31; Lion *THB*, 177-185; Perennial *THB*, 10-21. Also in R. C. Beatty, ed., *The Literature of the South* (1952), 1011-1017. In German, *Hinter Jenen Bergen*, 153-160. In Danish, *De Fjerne Bjerge*, 17-30.

C174 "Oliver Gant and the Pentlands," in M. L. Rosenthal, ed., *Effective Reading* (1944), 446-453. From *LHA*, 3-15.

C175 "Olympus in Catawba," *TWATR*, 173-187; also in Earle Davis and W. C. Hummel, eds., *Readings for Opinion from Literary Ideas and Attitudes* (1952), 83-91. *Ibid.*, (1960), 316-327.

C176 "On Leprechauns," *THB*, 142-149; Avon *THB*, 152-159; Lion *THB*, 120-126; *The Lost Boy*, 148-156. In German, *Hinter Jenen Bergen*, 103-108; *Der Verlorene Knabe*, 103-112. In Danish, *Den Tabte Tid*, 185-194.

C177 "One Big Fool," *YCGHA*, 634-653. Also in Philip Rahv, ed., *Discovery of Europe* (1947), 645-662.

C178 "One of the Girls in Our Party," *FDTM*, 155-163. Also in Carlos Baker, ed., *The American Looks at the World* (1944), 48-54; and in Allen Churchill, ed., *A Treasury of Modern Humor* (1940). In French, *De la Mort au Matin*, 157-165. In German, *Vom Tod zum Morgen*, 183-194. In Serbian, *Tkanje Zhivota*, 199-209.

C179 "Only the Dead Know Brooklyn," *FDTM*, 91-97; *PTW*, 636-643; *TWR*, 465-469; Penguin *SS*, 42-47; *OTDKB*, 42-47. Also in Edward Bloom, ed., *The Order of Fiction* (1964), 137-146; Martha Foley, ed., *Fifty Best American Short Stories, 1915-1965* (1965), 148-153; Harry Hansen, ed., *O. Henry Memorial Award Prize Stories of 1935*; E. J. O'Brien, ed., *Best Short Stories of 1936*, 327-332; *Short Stories from the New Yorker* (1940), 123-128; John D. Kern, ed., *This America* (1942), 722-727; Milton Crane, ed., *Fifty Great Short Stories* (1952), 108-113; and in Theodore Morison, ed., *Five Kinds of Writing* (1939). In French, *De la Mort au Matin*, 98-104; R. Laffont, ed., *Anthologie des Contes Américains* (1947). In German, *Vom Tod zum Morge*n, 109-116; *Die Leute von Alt-Catawba*, 3-9. In Serbian, *U Mrachnoi Shumi Tajanstvenoi Kao Vreme*, 100-107.

C180 "Orestes: Flight Before Fury," *OTATR*, 1-86.

C181 "Out of Control," *YCGHA*, 303-311.

C182 "The Paper Route," *TWR*, 273-293; also in Charles Laughton, ed., *Tell Me a Story* (1957), 192-175. From *LHA*, 294-306.

C183 "Paris," *TWATR*, 634-649.

C184 "The Parting," *TWATR*, 600-615.

C185 "The Party at Jack's," *YCGHA*, 230-254; *Short Novels*, 282-323. Also in Marsden V. Dillenbeck, ed., *Seven Novellas* (1966). In Spanish, *Tengo Algo Que Deciros*, 55-104. The longer version comes from *YCGHA*, 196-322.

C186 "Penelope's Web," *TWATR*, 405-423.

C187 "The Pension in Munich," *TWATR*, 650-661.

C188 "The Philanthropists," *TWATR*, 487-496.

C189 "Piggy Logan's Circus," *YCGHA*, 273-283.

C190 "The Place of Deathless Moments," *TWR*, 234-240. From *OTATR*, 155-160.

C191 "Play Us a Tune on an Unbroken Spinet," *SLD,* 18-22; also in Walter Havighurst, ed., *Approach to America* (1942), 458-462. From *OTATR*, 853-855.

C192 "The Plumed Knight," *THB*, 264-276; Avon *THB*, 70-81; Lion *THB*, 220-229; Perennial *THB*, 60-71. In German, *Hinter Jenen Bergen*, 191-199. In Danish, *De Fjerne Berge*, 84-99.

C193 "Portrait of a Literary Critic," *THB*, 150-161; Avon *THB*, 70-81; Lion *THB*, 127-136; *The Lost Boy*, 157-168. In Danish, *Den Tabte Tid*, 195-209. In German, *Hinter Jenen Bergen*, 109-117; *Der Verlorene Knabe*, 113-126.

C194 "A Portrait of Abraham Jones," *TWR*, 357-385; also in John H. Nelson, ed., *Contemporary Trends: American Literature Since 1900* (1949), 798-840. From *OTATR*, 440-497.

C195 "Portrait of a Player," in *Theatre Annual* (1947), 43-54. From *TWATR*, 414-426. See also "The Winter of our Discontent."

C196 "A Portrait of Bascom Hawke," *Short Novels*, 4-71. Also in J. A. Burrell, ed., *Bedside Book of Famous American Stories* (1936), 1154-1206; M. C. Wegner, ed., *Albatross Book of American Short Stories* (1935), 364-439; Caroline Schroder, ed., *Approaches to Literature* (1959), 579-604; and Carl Van Doren, ed., *Modern American Prose* (1934), 743-795. In German, *Mein Onkel Bascom*, 5-64. In Italian, Elio Vittorini, ed., *Americana: Raccolta di Narratori Dalle Origini ai Nostri Giorni* (1941), 906-960. In Serbian, *U Mrachnoi Shumi Tajanstvenoi Kao Vreme*, 146- 233. Similar to *OTATR*, 104-192. In Spanish, Lenka Franulic, ed., *Antologia del Cuento Norteamericano* (1943).

C197 "The Priestly One," *TWATR*, 188-201.

C198 "Professor Hatcher's Celebrated Course," *TWR*, 303-357. Also excerpt in George Oppenheimer, *Passionate Playgoer* (1958), 58-67. From *OTATR*, 130-135, 167-175, 282-304, 309-324.

C199 "A Prologue to America," in *Vogue's First Reader* (1942), 13-20; and in *Vogue's Fireside Book* (1944), 9-15. Similar to *TWATR*, 474-475; *YCGHA*, 429-431, 506-508.

C200 "The Promise of America," *YCGHA*, 499-508; *TWR*, 634-636. Also in Joseph M. Bachelor, ed., *American Thinking and Writing* (1942), 8-11; Arno L. Bader, ed., *Essays for Our Time* (1947), 261-264; Walter Blair, ed., *Literature of the United States* (1947), 1089-1093; Leonard S. Brown, ed., *Literature for Our Time*

(1947), 824-829; E. A. Cross, ed., *Heritage of World Literature* (1946), 3-5; O. J. Campbell, ed., *Patterns for Living* (1946), v.2, 1224-1226; Hugh Graham, ed., *An American Treasury* (1949), 383-385; Charles Laughton, ed., *Tell Me a Story* (1957), 389-392; Samuel Rapport, ed., *America Remembers* (1956), 667-669; and Ralph Woods, ed., *Family Reader of American Masterpieces* (1959), 1-2.

C201 "Proteus: The City," *OTATR*, 405-598.

C202 "Proud, Cruel City," *FOAN*, 120-122; also in Esther M. McCullough, ed., *As I Pass, O Manhattan* (1958), 1199-1201. From *OTATR*.

C203 "Pursuit and Capture," *TWATR*, 589-593.

C204 "Quality of the Spirit," in J. D. Adams, ed., *Treasure Chest* (1946), 369-370. From *YCGHA*.

C205 "The Quarrel," *TWATR*, 556-570.

C206 "The Quest of the Fair Medusa," *YCGHA*, 397-508; excerpts *PTW*, 507-557.

C207 "A Question of Guilt," *YCGHA*, 325-340.

C208 "The Quick and the Dead," *THB*, 201-210; Avon *THB*, 11-19; Lion *THB*, 169-176; Perennial *THB*, 1-9. In German, *Hinter Jenen Bergen*, 146-152. In Danish, *De Fjerne Bjerge*, 5-14.

C209 "Race and Occupation," in P. W. Souers, ed., *Writer's Reader* (1950), 26-33. From *YCGHA*, 553-559.

C210 "The Radiant Beauty of Heroic Souls," in R. A. Beals, ed., *Readings in Description and Narration* (1930). From *LHA*, 533-535.

C211 "Remembered Odors," in Reed Smith, *Learning to Write* (1937), 483. From *LHA*, 35.

C212 "Remorse," *TWATR*, 576-588.

C213 "Return," in Richard Walser, ed. *The North Carolina Miscellany* (1962), 168-173. From article by Wolfe in *Asheville Citizen-Times*, May 16, 1937.

C214 "The Return of Buck Gavin," in F. H. Koch, ed., *Carolina Folk-Plays*, Second Series (1924), 31-44; F. H. Koch, ed., *Carolina Folk-Plays* (1941), 113-123; Richard Walser, ed., *North Carolina Drama* (1956), 93-102.

A play first produced by the Carolina Playmakers at the University of North Carolina, March 15, 1919.

C215 "The Return of the Far Wanderer," *TWR*, 61-70. Also in William Stafford, ed., *Twentieth Century American Writing* (1965), 494-502. From *LHA*, 70-80.

C216 "The Return of the Prodigal," *THB*, 108-141; Avon *SS*, 56-78; Lion *THB*, 93-118; *The Lost Boy*, 113-147. In German, *Hinter Jenen Bergen*, 80-102. In Danish, *Den Tabte Tid*, 142-184. In Polish, *Wloczedzy o Zachodzie Słońca*, 113-151.

C217 "The Ride," *TWATR*, 320-326.

C218 "The Ring and the Book," *TWATR*, 455-467.

C219 "The Rock," *TWATR*, 219-232. Also in S. S. Basket, ed., *The American Identity* (1962), 383-396.

C220 (Selections), in Douglas Bement, ed., *The Fabric of Fiction* (1943), 16-17, 72-75, 128, 147-150, 216-218; Dwight L. Burton, ed., *Literature Study in High Schools* (1959), 68, 73, 77, 227; Alexander Cowie, ed., *American Writers Today* (1956), 52-58; Edward Pratt Dickson, ed., *The Shadows of Desire* (1956), 31, 36, 38, 41; Clifton Fadiman, ed., *The American Treasury* (1955), 18, 30, 73, 90, 109, 478, 965-966; Ben G. Henneke, ed., *Reading Aloud Effectively* (1954), 84, 106, 362-364, 368; J. K. Hutchens, ed., *The American Twenties* (1952), 257-269; Charles Laughton, ed., *The Fabulous Country* (1962), 2, 10-12, 23-24, 48-51, 67-71, 85-89, 119-121, 231, 242; Charles Laughton, ed., *Tell Me a Story* (1957), 95-110, 192-195, 389-392; J. A. S. McPeek, *Handbook of English* (1956), 236-237, 290-291, 295; Gladys E. Mansir, ed., *Life in America* (1941), 291-338; Raymond C. Palmer, *The Uncreative Mind* (1957), 414-421; Jessie C. Rehder, ed., *The Young Writer at Work* (1962), 40, 60, 72, 81, 250; Arthur Richmond, ed., *Modern Quotations for Ready References* (1947), 42, 97, 122, 123, 161, 162, 173, 176-178, 244, 265, 273, 297, 313, 329, 358, 365, 370, 388-390, 393, 397, 412, 433; Nellie S. Tillett, ed., *Image and Incident* (1933), 18-19, 22, 49-50; and C. H. Woolbert, ed., *The Art of Interpretative Speech* (1956), 112, 284-296, 320-321, 420-421.

C221 "Service Entrance," *YCGHA*, 196-210.

C222 "The Ship," *TWATR*, 297-314.

C223 "Something Has Spoken to Me in the Night," *TWR*, 689; *Uns Bleibt die Erde*, 86-87. Also in Rodman Selden, ed., *100 American Poems* (1948), 170. From *YCGHA*, 743.

C224 "Some Things Will Never Change," *YCGHA*, 37-44, *SLD*, 121-127. Also in Frank F. Bright, ed., *To Be an American* (1957), 530-537.

C225 "Something of My Life," Walser, 3-7. From *Saturday Review of Literature* (February 7, 1948), 6-8.

C226 "South Carolina," in George Bradshaw, ed., *A Collection of Travel in America* (1948), 139-153. From *OTATR*, 361-370.

C227 "Stein and Rosen's," *TWATR*, 434-440.

C228 "The Story of a Novel," *PTW*, 562-611; *TWR*, 11-52; Penguin *SS*, 109-150; *OTDKB*, 109-150; Holman, 9-32. Also excerpts in Norman Cousins, ed., *Writing for Love or Money* (1949), 79-94; Brewster Ghiselin, ed., *The Creative Process* (1952), 192-205; H. O. Waite, ed., *Literature for Our Time* (1958), 182-188; *Saturday Review Treasury* (1957), 54-80. In German, *Uns Bleibt die Erde*, 11-86. In Serbian, *Tkanje Zhivota*, 250-304.

C229 "The Stranger Whose Sermon Was Brick," *THB*, 294-309; Avon *THB*, 99-114; Lion *THB*, 244-256; Perennial *THB*, 88-102. In German, *Hinter Jenen Bergen*, 212-222. In Danish, *De Fjerne Bjerge*, 122-142.

C230 "The Street of the Day," *TWATR*, 101-117.

C231 "The Sun and the Rain," *TWR*, 409-415. Also in R. M. Mikels, ed., *Short Stories for English Courses* (1935), 461-470; E. J. O'Brien, ed., *Best Short Stories of 1935*, 313-318; Virginia C. Perkins, *The Writing of Modern Prose* (1936). In German, Kurt Ullrich, ed., *Neu Amerika* (1937), 412-420. From *OTATR*, 797-802.

C232 "Telemachus," *OTATR*, 325-404.

C233 "The Theatre," *TWATR*, 327-345.

C234 "Things That Will Never Change," in J. D. Adams, ed., *Treasure Chest* (1946), 368-369. From *TWATR*.

C235 "The Third Night," in F. H. Koch, ed., *Carolina Folk-Plays* (1941), 125-143. A one-act play originally written about 1919.

C236 "Thirst and Hunger for Life," in L. N. Richardson, ed., *The Heritage of American Literature* (1951), 812-818. From *OTATR*, 155-160.

C237 "This Thing Is Ours," *TWATR*, 384-388.

C238 "Throughout the Land," in Robert C. Pooley, ed., *Exploring Life through Literature* (1951), 540-542. From *YCGHA*, 505-506.

C239 "Three O'Clock," *TWATR*, 13-67.

C240 "Time Is a Fable," *TWATR*, 623-633.

C241 "Together," *TWATR*, 359-361.

C242 "The Torch," *TWATR*, 202-218.

C243 "Toward Which. . . ," *SLD*, 166; also in Halford E. Luccock, ed., *The Questing Spirit* (1947), 711. From *YCGHA*, 743.

C244 "Train Race," in Walter Havighurst, ed., *Approach to America* (1942), 205-212. From *OTATR*, 407-412.

C245 "The Two Visitors," *YCGHA*, 553-567.

C246 "Two Worlds Discrete," *TWATR*, 68-90.

C247 "The Universe of Daisy Purvis," *YCGHA*, 511-536. Also in Philip Rahv, ed., *Discovery of Europe* (1947), 623-644.

C248 "Unscheduled Climax," *YCGHA*, 284-302.

C249 "A Vast Aerial World," in Whit Burnett, ed., *Time to Be Young* (1945), 171-178, and the Armed Services Edition (1945), 190-199. From *LHA*, 36-44.

C250 "Veteran Ball Player," in R. S. Graber, ed., *The Baseball Reader* (1951), 56-66. From *YCGHA*.

C251 "The Vision in the Square," in *TWR*, 213-222. From *LHA*, 617-626.

C252 "A Vision of Death in April," *TWATR*, 539-555.

C253 "A Visit to the Fair," *TWATR*, 662-672.

C254 "Voices of the Books," *FOAN*, 211-218; from *OTATR*, 587-591.

C255 "Waiting for Glory," *TWATR*, 497-511.

C256 "The Way of No Return," *YCGHA*, 700-704.

C257 "We Are the Sons of America," in Tremaine McDowell, ed., *America in Literature* (1944), 5-8. From *OTATR*.

C258 "The Weaver at Work Again," *TWATR*, 594-599.

C259 "The Web and the Rock," Excerpts in *PTW*, 394-503; *TWR*, 497-572. Digests in Frank N. Magill, ed., *Masterpieces of World Literature in Digest Form* (1949), 1101-1103; and Hiram Haydn, ed., *Thesaurus of Book Digests* (1949).

C260 "The Web and the Root," *TWATR*, 1-94.

C261 "The Web and the World," *TWATR*, 171-294.

C262 "The Web of Earth," *FDTM*, 212-304; *Short Novels*, 75-154. Also in Leonard Brown, ed., *A Quarto of Modern Literature* (1935), and in Alfred Dashiell, ed., *Editor's Choice* (1934), 33-112. In French, *De la Mort au Matin*, 209-293. In German, *Vom Tod zum Morgen*, 253-354; *Mein Onkel Bascom*, 67-141. In Japanese, *Daichi o Ou Kumo No Su*, 3-144. In Serbian, *Tkanje Zhivota*, 9-116.

C263 "Welcome to Our City," *Willkommen in Altamont*, 5-85.

C264 "What Are We?" in Halford E. Luccock, ed., *The Questing Spirit* (1947), 618-619. From *LHA*.

C265 "What He Remembered," in Donald Davidson, ed., *American Composition and Rhetoric* (1939), 356-358. From *LHA*, 84-86.

C266 "Where Now?" in Leonard Brown, ed., *A Quarto of Modern Literature* (1940). From *SOAN*, 30-49. See also *FOAN*, 26-28.

C267 "A Wind Is Rising and the Rivers Flow," *YCGHA*, 705-743. An excerpt of this in O. J. Campbell, ed., *Patterns for Living* (1946), v.2, 1227-1247.

C268 "World's Series," in Winfield H. Rogers, ed., *Explorations in Living* (1941); also R. S. Graber, ed., *Baseball Reader* (1951). From *OTATR*, 200-207.

C269 "A Window on All Time," *TWR*, 56-60. From *LHA*, 2-8.

C270 "W. O. Gant," in Jerome W. Archer, ed., *A Reader for Writers* (1962), 402-405. From *LHA*.

C271 "The World of Books," *TWR*, 96-104. From *LHA*, 307-315.

C272 "The World That Jack Built," *YCGHA*, 147-322.

C273 "The Wounded Faun," *YCGHA*, 373-396.

C274 "A Writer's Creation and Vision of Life," in Homer A. Watt, ed., *Biography and Exposition* (1948), 103-104. From *LTHM*, letter dated November 6, 1929.

C275 "The Years That the Locusts Hath Eaten," *TWATR*, 571-575.

C276 "You Can't Go Home Again," *PTW*, 507-557; *TWR*, 573-640. Excerpts in Walter Blair, ed., *The Literature of the United States* (1946), 1089-1093; E. A. Cross, ed., *The Heritage of World Literature* (1946), 618-621; *Man in Contemporary Society: A Source Book* (1955), 179-194; Harvey Swados, ed., *The American Writer and the Great Depression* (1966), 502-515; and in French, Albert J. Guerard, ed., *Écrit aux U. S. A.* (1947), 315-327. Digest in Frank N. Magill, ed.,

Masterpieces of World Literature in Digest Form
(1949), 1142-1144.

C277 "Young Faustus," *OTATR*, 87-324. Excerpts in
Walter Blair, ed., *The Literature of the United States*
(1947), 1086-1088; also Leon Howard, ed.,
American Heritage (1955), v.2, 788-793.

C278 "Young Icarus," *YCGHA*, 707-722.

C279 "The Young Writer," in Oscar J. Campbell, ed.,
Patterns of Living (1946). From *SOAN*.

C280 "Zero Hour," *YCGHA*, 211-229.

D. Books and Pamphlets about Thomas Wolfe

D1 Adams, Agatha Boyd. *Thomas Wolfe: Carolina Student, A Brief Biography*. Chapel Hill: University of North Carolina Library, 1950. 92 p.

Available in both cloth and paper editions, this is the January, 1950, number of the University of North Carolina Library Extension Publications.

D2 ———. *Thomas Wolfe Letters Given to the Library of the University of North Carolina*, Chapel Hill: University of North Carolina Library, 1949. 4 p.

D3 Austin, Neal F. *A Biography of Thomas Wolfe*. Austin, Texas: Roger Beacham, Publisher, 1968. x, 212 p., illus., index.

D4 Bhattacharya, Lokenath. *Thomas Wolfe: A Tragic Giant*. New Delhi, India: United States Information Service, 1961. 8 p.

Leaflet distributed by U.S.I.S.; originally appeared in *Span*, (October 1961), 36-40.

D5 Botta, Guido. *Thomas Wolfe O Della Solitudine*. Naples: Fausto Fiorentino, Editore, 1964. 190 p. biblio., index.

94

D6 Brodin, Pierre. *Thomas Wolfe*. Asheville, N. C.: The
Stephens Press, 1949. 41 p.

Translated by Imogene Riddick, this is a chapter from
Brodin's *Les Écrivains Américains de l'Entre-Deux-Guerres*
(Paris, 1948). There is a preface by Richard Walser.

D7 Daniels, Jonathan. *Thomas Wolfe: October Recollections*.
Columbia, S. C.: Bostick and Thornley, Publishers,
1961. 26 p.

This was an address given before the Southeastern
Library Association in Asheville, N. C., October 14, 1960.
Edition limited to seven hundred and fifty copies.

D8 Delakas, Daniel L. *Thomas Wolfe, la France, et les
Romanciers Français*. Paris: Jouve & Cie., 1950.
xii, 154 p., biblio., index.

A doctoral dissertation, this was issued in a limited edition
of four hundred copies.

D9 Dewsnap, Terence. *Look Homeward, Angel; and Of
Time and the River: A Critical Commentary and Notes*.
New York: Monarch Notes and Study Guides, 1965. 55 p.

D10 ———. *The Web and the Rock; and You Can't Go
Home Again*. New York: Monarch Notes and
Study Guides, 1965. 68 p.

The cover has the titles in reverse order: *YCGHA*
and *TWATR*.

D11 Field, Leslie A., ed. *Thomas Wolfe: Three Decades
of Criticism*. New York: New York University Press, 1968.
xxv, 304 p., index.

Includes essays by Oscar Cargill, C. Hugh Holman,
J. Russell Reaver and Robert I. Strozier, Louis D. Rubin, Jr.,

Margaret Church, Robert C. Slack, Bernard De Voto, Maxwell E. Perkins, Edward C. Aswell, Martin Maloney, Floyd C. Watkins, Richard Walser, Bruce R. McElderry, Jr., Richard S. Kennedy, Robert Penn Warren, Irving Halpern, Paschal Reeves, Clyde D. Clements, Jr., Leslie A. Field, Wallace Stegner, Lois Hartley, and Edward A. Bloom, as well as Wolfe's "Purdue Speech," and a selected list of Wolfe criticism compiled by Field and Maurice Beebe. Published simultaneously in paper and cloth editions.

D12 Fisher, Vardis. *Thomas Wolfe As I Knew Him, And Other Essays*. Denver: Alan Swallow, 1963. 166 p.

Includes the essays "Thomas Wolfe as I Knew Him," and "Thomas Wolfe and Maxwell Perkins," which formerly appeared in the April and July, 1951, issues of *Tomorrow*. Other scattered references to Wolfe: 61, 63-66, 69, 80, 82, 91-92, 106, 108, 160.

D13 Gillan, Maria M. *Wolfe's Look Homeward, Angel and Of Time and the River: A Critical Commentary*. New York: Barrister Publishing Company, 1966. 64 p.

D14 Goethals, Thomas R. *A Critical Commentary*: *You Can't Go Home Again*. New York: American R. D. M. Corporation, 1964. 56 p.

D15 Heath, John R. *The Strange Case of Thomas Wolfe*. Chicago: Chicago Literary Club, 1949. 32 p.

Privately printed in an edition of three hundred and fifty copies.

D16 Helmcke, Hans. *Die Familie im Romanwerk von Thomas Wolfe: Studien zu Entstehung, Verformung und Eigenmächtigkeit eines Kernthemas seines Schaffens.* Heidelberg, Carl Winter Universitätsverlag, 1967. 352 p., biblio., index.

Beihefte 22, *Jahrbuch für Amerikastudien.*

D17 Holman, C. Hugh. *Thomas Wolfe.* Minneapolis: University of Minnesota Press, 1960. 47 p., biblio.

University of Minnesota Pamphlets on American Writers, No. 6. This is also included in William Van O'Connor, ed., *Seven Modern American Novelists* (Minneapolis, 1964). It is translated into Spanish in *Tres Escritores Norteamericanos* (Madrid, 1961), and published separately in Arabic, translated by Arris Zaki Hassan, Beirut, 1961.

D18 ———. *Three Modes of Modern Southern Fiction: Ellen Glasgow, William Faulkner, Thomas Wolfe.* Athens: University of Georgia Press, 1966. 95 p., index.

Includes "Thomas Wolfe: The epic of the national self," 49-72, and other Wolfe references, x, xii, 8, 9, 25, 74-82, 91-92.

D19 ———. *The World of Thomas Wolfe: A Scribner Research Anthology.* New York: Charles Scribner's Sons, 1962. xix, 187 p.

Includes a letter from Wolfe to his mother, "The Story of a Novel," and an excerpt from "No Door," a short story. Also essays or comments on Wolfe from Clifton Fadiman, Maxwell E. Perkins, Edward C. Aswell, Floyd C. Watkins, Basil Davenport, C. Hugh Holman, Pamela Hansford Johnson, W. M. Frohock, Bernard

De Voto, Maurice Natanson, John Peal Bishop,
Joseph Warren Beach, Bella Kussy, Edgar Johnson,
Edwin Berry Burgum, Herbert Muller, Maxwell Geismar,
Henry Steele Commager, Walter F. Taylor, William F.
Kennedy, Blanche Housman Gelfant, Louis D. Rubin, Jr.,
Robert E. Spiller, Malcolm Cowley, and J .B. Priestley.

D20 Johnson, Elmer D. *Of Time and Thomas Wolfe:
A Bibliography with a Character Index of His Works.*
New York: The Scarecrow Press, 1959. 226 p., index.

D21 Johnson, Pamela Hansford. *Thomas Wolfe: A Critical
Study.* London: William Heinemann, 1947. 138 p.

D22 ———. *Hungry Gulliver: An English Critical Appraisal
of Thomas Wolfe.* New York: Charles Scribner's Sons,
1948. 170 p.

The first American edition of the previous item.

D23 ———. *The Art of Thomas Wolfe.* New York: Charles
Scribner's Sons, 1963. 170 p.

A second American edition, identical except for the
addition of a five-page, unnumbered preface.

D24 Kennedy, Richard S. *The Window of Memory: The
Literary Career of Thomas Wolfe.* Chapel Hill:
University of North Carolina Press, 1962. xiv, 461 p.,
biblio., index.

Paperback edition, 1968.

D25 Lindroth, James, and Lindroth, Colette. *Wolfe's The Web
and the Rock and You Can't Go Home Again.*
New York: Barrister Publishing Company, 1966. 72 p.

D26 McCoy, Lola Love. *Tom Wolfe's Dixieland.* Asheville, N. C.: The Stephens Press, 1949. 16 p., illus.

D27 McElderry, Bruce R., Jr. *Thomas Wolfe.* New York: Twayne Publishers, Inc., 1964. 207 p., biblio., index.

D28 Muller, Herbert J. *Thomas Wolfe.* Norfolk, Conn.: New Directions Books, 1947. 196 p., biblio., index.

D29 ———. *Thomas Wolfe in Selbstzeugnissen und Bilddokumenten.* Hamburg: Rowohlt, 1962. 178 p., illus., biblio., index.

This is a slightly abridged translation of the item above, with the addition of numerous photographs of Wolfe and related subjects.

D30 Norwood, Hayden. *The Marble Man's Wife.* New York: Charles Scribner's Sons, 1947. 200 p.

This is a "conversational biography" of Mrs. Julia Elizabeth Wolfe.

D31 Nowell, Elizabeth. *Thomas Wolfe: A Biography.* Garden City, N. Y.: Doubleday & Company, 1960. 456 p., index.

A Book-of-the-Month Club edition was issued simultaneously.

D32 ———. *Thomas Wolfe: A Biography.* London: Heinemann, 1961. 456 p., index.

English edition, identical to the American, except slightly reduced in size and with a different binding and dust jacket.

D33 Osawa, Mamoru. *Thomas Wolfe*. Tokyo, Kenkyusha, 1966. 287 p., biblio., index.
In Japanese.

D34 Pfister, Karin, *Zeit und Wirklichkeit bei Thomas Wolfe*. Heidelberg: Carl Winter Universitätsverlag, 1954. 140 p., biblio.

Dissertation completed at the University of Marburg, and published as Heft 89 of *Anglistische Forschungen*.

D35 Pollock, Thomas Clark, and Cargill, Oscar. *Thomas Wolfe at Washington Square*. New York: New York University Press, 1954. xii, 163 p., biblio.

Pages 84-152 are given over to "Memorabilia" of Wolfe by his former students and friends, including A. Gerald Doyle, Bernard W. Kofsky, James Mandel, Robert Dow, Henry T. Volkening, Vardis Fisher, and Russell Krauss.

D36 Preston, George R., Jr. *Thomas Wolfe: A Bibliography*. New York: Charles S. Boesen, 1943. 127 p., index.

D37 Raynolds, Robert. *Thomas Wolfe: Memoir of a Friendship*. Austin, Texas: University of Texas Press, 1965. 154 p .

D38 ———. *Thomas Wolfe and Robert Raynolds: Memoir of a Friendship*. Newton, Conn., 1964. 76 p.

This was a preliminary edition of D37, mimeographed and distributed in only sixty copies.

D39 Reeves, George M., Jr. *Thomas Wolfe et l'Europe*. Paris: Librairie Marcel Didier, 1955. Biblio., index. Dissertation, University of Paris, 1953.

D40 Reeves, Paschal. *Thomas Wolfe's Albatross: Race and Nationality in America*. Athens, Ga.: University of Georgia Press, 1968. 160 p., biblio., index.

D41 Rubin, Louis D., Jr. *Thomas Wolfe: The Weather of His Youth*. Baton Rouge: Louisiana State University Press, 1955. xiii, 183 p., index.

D42 Ryssel, Fritz Heinrich. *Thomas Wolfe*. Berlin: Colloquium Verlag, 1963. 93 p.

Köpfe der XX. Jahrhunderts, Band 31.

D43 Schnabel, Ernst. *Thomas Wolfe*. Hamburg: Hansischer Gildenverlag, 1947. 36 p.

Dichter der Gegenwart, Heft 3. A German translation of Wolfe's short story "No Door" is included, 23-36.

D44 Turnbull, Andrew. *Thomas Wolfe*. New York: Charles Scribner's Sons, 1967. x, 374 p., notes and references, 325-347, illus., index.

D45 Voigt, Walter. *Die Bildersprache Thomas Wolfes: Mit Besonderer Berücksichtigung der Metaphorik des Amerikanischen Englisch*. Munich: Max Hueber Verlag, 1960. xi, 280 p., biblio.

Dissertation at the University of Tübingen, published in the *Mainzer Amerikanistische Beiträge*, Band 3.

D46 Walser, Richard, ed. *The Enigma of Thomas Wolfe: Biographical and Critical Selections*. Cambridge: Harvard University Press, 1953. xii, 313 p.

Includes two selections by Wolfe, "Something of My Life," and "Justice Is Blind," and essays or articles by Don Bishop, Richard S. Kennedy, Henry T. Volkening,

John Skally Terry, Maxwell Perkins, William Braswell, Jonathan Daniels, Edward C. Aswell, Maxwell Geismar, Robert Penn Warren, Henry S. Canby, Bernard De Voto, Clifton Fadiman, Stephen Vincent Benet, Thomas Lyle Collins, Edwin B. Burgum, Monroe M. Stearns, E. K. Brown, W. M. Frohock, W. P. Albrecht, Margaret Church, Nathan L. Rothman, Franz Schoenberner, and Betty Thompson.

D47 ———. *Thomas Wolfe: An Introduction and Interpretation.* New York: Barnes and Noble, 1961. viii, 152 p., illus., biblio., index.

D48 Watkins, Floyd C. *Thomas Wolfe's Characters: Portraits from Life.* Norman: University of Oklahoma Press, 1957. xiv, 194 p., illus., index.

D49 Wertheim, Stanley C. *A Critical Commentary: Look Homeward, Angel.* New York: American R. D. M. Corporation, 1964. 42 p.

D50 Wheaton, Mabel Wolfe, and Blythe, LeGette. *Thomas Wolfe and His Family.* Garden City, N. Y.: Doubleday, 1961. 336 p., illus.

These reminiscences by Thomas Wolfe's sister were edited after her death by LeGette Blythe. For a supplementary chapter, not included here, see "Papa Wolfe Takes Children to Fair," *Daily News* [Greensboro, N. C.], October 11, 1964, D1, D11.

D51 Yndurain, Francisco. *Thomas Wolfe: Novelista Americano.* Madrid: Langa y Cia., 1954. 43 p.

E. Theses and Dissertations about Wolfe

E1 Abbott, Arthur Travis. "Quest in Time: A Study of Thomas Wolfe." Honors essay, University of North Carolina, 1967.

E2 Adams, Richard Powell. "Thomas Wolfe and James T. Farrell, A Comparison in the Autobiographical Method." Master's thesis, University of Illinois, 1940.

E3 Aker, John Edwards. "Thomas Wolfe, A Study in Literary Conflict." Master's thesis, Vanderbilt University, 1946.

E4 Ballinger, Sara Elizabeth. "The Reception of the American Novel in German Periodicals, 1945-1957." Ph.D. dissertation, Indiana University, 1959.

E5 Barsch, Hans G. "Das Epos Thomas Wolfes." Ph.D. dissertation, Mainz, 1952.

E6 Baumser, Ruth. "The Dominant Themes in the Major American Novels between 1919 and 1929." Master's thesis, Columbia, 1947.

E7 Behrens, Robert H. "William Oliver Wolfe and Thomas Wolfe: A Study in Paternal Influence." Master's thesis, Haverford College, 1947.

E8 Beja, Morris. "Evanescent Moments: The Epiphany in the Modern Novel." Ph. D. dissertation, Cornell University, 1963.

E9 Blackwelder, James Ray. "The Dimensions of Literature in *Look Homeward Angel*." Ph.D. dissertation, Emory University, 1968.

E10 Boyle, Thomas E. "Thomas Wolfe's Myth of America." Ph.D. dissertation, University of Michigan, 1964.

E11 Bush, Charles K., III. "A Comparison of the Youths of Thomas Wolfe's Eugene Gant and George Webber." Master's thesis, University of North Carolina, 1962.

E12 Childers, Helen W. "American Novels about Adolescence, 1917-1953." Ph. D. dissertation, George Peabody College, 1958.

E13 Clemans, Edna W. "A Study of the Structure of the Narratives in the Short Novels of Thomas Wolfe." Master's thesis, University of North Carolina, 1964.

E14 Clements, Clyde C., Jr. "Symbolic Patterns in *You Can't Go Home Again*." Master's thesis, Bowling Green State University, 1961.

E15 Cleveland, Stuart H. "Thomas Wolfe as a Social Novelist: A Marxist Interpretation." Honors thesis, Harvard University, 1947.

E16 Crews, J. C. "The Treatment of Social Problems in Recent Southern Literature." Master's thesis, Baylor University, 1944.

E17 De Jovine, Felix A. "The Literature of the Youthful Hero
in American Fiction as the Basis for a Study Unit
in the Secondary School." Ph.D. dissertation,
Ohio State University, 1967.

E18 Delmare, Maxine L. "Thomas Wolfe: Another Estimate."
Master's thesis, Kansas State Teachers College
(Emporia), 1947.

E19 Deutschberger, Paul. "Man and Movements in Modern
Literature." Master's thesis, Columbia, 1941.

E20 Donno, Daniel J. "The Quest of Thomas Wolfe,"
Master's thesis, Miami University, Ohio, 1947.

E21 Doster, William Clark. "Wolfe and Whitman, a
Comparative Study." Master's thesis, University of
Florida. 1948.

E22 Eichelberger, Clayton L. "Thomas Wolfe's America:
An Expository Evaluation of the Wolfe Novels."
Ph.D. dissertation, University of Texas, 1956.

E23 Ellison, Francis E. "The Significance of Character
Development in Thomas Wolfe's Early Novels." Master's
thesis, University of Texas, 1954.

E24 Elmore, Cenieth Catherine. "To Keep Time with,
A Secular Cantata with Text from Thomas Wolfe."
Master's composition, University of North Carolina, 1962.

E25 Erstling, Julius H. "Thomas Wolfe's Knowledge and
Use of Milton." Master's thesis, University of Florida, 1941.

106

E26 Everett, Ruth Elizabeth. "The Brooklyn Novel and the Brooklyn Myth: Source Materials for the Teaching of the Urban Novel." Ph.D. dissertation, Columbia University, 1966.

E27 Fertig, Goldie M. "The Treatment of Adolescence in Contemporary American Literature," Master's thesis, University of Louisville, 1942.

E28 Fink, Charlotte A. "Methods and Devices of Characterization in the Novels of Thomas Wolfe." Master's thesis, University of Tennessee, 1945.

E29 Finney, Frank Florer, Jr. "A Critical Examination of the Transition From a Psychological Vision of Life to an Increasingly Christian Awareness of Evil in the Fiction of Thomas Wolfe." Ph.D. dissertation, University of Oklahoma, 1961.

E30 Fleming, Delmont Florrie. "Humor in the Works of Thomas Wolfe." Ph.D. dissertation, University of Pennsylvania, 1966.

E31 Foster, Ruel Elton. "Thomas Wolfe, A Critical Study." Master's thesis, University of Kentucky, 1939.

E32 ———. "Freudian Influences in the American Autobiographical Novel," Ph.D. dissertation, Vanderbilt University, 1941.

E33 Fowler, Herbert E. "Criticism of Education in Twentieth Century American Novels." Ed. D. dissertation, New York University, 1932.

E34 Foy, John Vail. "An Analysis of the Meaning and Structure of Symbolism in the Novels of Thomas Wolfe." Master's thesis, Cornell University, 1948.

E35 Gatlin, Jesse Cecil, Jr. "The Development of Thomas Wolfe as a Literary Artist," Ph.D. dissertation, University of Denver, 1961.

E36 Geddes, Leonard R. "An Analysis of Thomas Wolfe's *The Web of Earth.*" Master's thesis, University of North Carolina, 1962.

E37 Gelfant, Blanche. "Urbanization as an Influence on Dreiser, Dos Passos, and Wolfe." Ph.D. dissertation, University of Wisconsin, 1948.

E38 George, Marie. "Comparison of Modern Fiction with the Earlier Canons of Criticism." Master's thesis, Texas Technological College, 1941.

E39 Gibbs, Robert C. "Thomas Wolfe's Four Years at Chapel Hill: A Study of Biographical Source Material." Master's thesis, University of North Carolina, 1958.

E40 Gober, Ruth Bell. "The American Novelist Interprets the Student of Higher Education." Ph.D. dissertation, University of Oklahoma, 1956.

E41 Gobrecht, Eleanor A. "A Descriptive Study of the Value Commitments of the Principal Characters in Four Recent American Plays: *Picnic, Cat on a Hot Tin Roof, Long Day's Journey into Night,* and *Look Homeward, Angel.*" Ph.D. dissertation, University of Southern California, 1965.

108

E42 Gossett, Louise Young. "Violence in Recent Southern Fiction." Ph.D. dissertation, Duke University, 1961.

E43 Gregory, Hoosag K. "Lord Byron and Thomas Wolfe: A Comparison of Their Philosophical and Personal Problems." Master's thesis, University of Illinois, 1940.

E44 Halperin, Irving. "The Basis and Nature of Unity in the Novels of Thomas Wolfe." Ph.D. dissertation, Washington University (St. Louis), 1957.

E45 Hanig, David D. "The Comic Element in the Novels of Thomas Wolfe." Master's thesis, North Texas State College, 1957.

E46 Harnack-Fish, Mildred. "Die Entwicklung der amerikanischen Literatur der Gegenwärt." Ph.D. dissertation, Giessen, 1941.

E47 Harrington, Eva Ione. "Thomas Wolfe: The Theory and Practice of His Characterization," Master's thesis, University of Idaho, 1947.

E48 Harris, Arthur S., Jr. "Thomas Wolfe, Remembrance of Time." Master's thesis, Harvard University, 1942.

E49 Hart, Robert C. "Writers on Writing: Opinions of Six Modern American Novelists on the Craft of Fiction." Ph.D. dissertation, Northwestern University, 1954.

E50 Hartin, John S. "The Southeastern United States in the Novel Through 1950: A Bibliographic Review." Ph.D. dissertation, University of Michigan, 1956.

E51 Hewitt, Francis S. "Pessimism in the Modern American Novel." Master's thesis, Rutgers University, 1936.

E52 Hilfer, Anthony C. "The Revolt From the Village in American Literature, 1915-1930," Ph.D. dissertation, University of North Carolina, 1963.

E53 Hinson, Katherine W. "North Carolina Writers of Literary Prose, 1900-1940." Master's thesis, East Carolina College, 1942.

E54 Hipkiss, Robert A. "The Value of Expatriation for the Major American Novelists, 1914-1941." Ph.D. dissertation, University of California at Los Angeles, 1966.

E55 Hodge, Elizabeth Ann. "A Study of Thomas Wolfe's *Look Homeward, Angel.*" Master's thesis, University of Texas, 1949.

E56 Hoffman, Emily H. "A Bibliography of Thomas Wolfe." Master's thesis, Simmons University, 1939.

E57 Hogan, Frances Virginia. "Thomas Wolfe, Whale in a Strait-Jacket." Master's thesis, Columbia University, 1940.

E58 Hollingsworth, Marian E. "The Search for a Father in the Novels of Thomas Wolfe." Master's thesis, University of North Carolina, 1957.

E59 Howard, James K. "The American Proletarian Novel." Master's thesis, University of Texas, 1939.

E60 Howard, Shelley W. "By a Mountain Rock: Thomas Wolfe, Dramatist." Master's thesis, University of North Carolina, 1965.

E61 Hurt, Lester E. "A House Divided: A Study of Theme in Thomas Wolfe's Novels." Ph.D. dissertation, University of Minnesota, 1956.

110

E62 Idol, John Lane. "Thomas Wolfe's Satire: A Study of Objects, Motives, and Artistry," Ph.D. dissertation, University of Arkansas, 1965.

E63 Johnson, Stanley L. "A Critical Study of the Works of Thomas Wolfe." Ph. D. dissertation, University of Southern California, 1955.

E64 Keim, Miriam E. "The American Novel of 1931-1935 as Depression Literature." Master's thesis, Temple University, 1939.

E65 Kennedy, Richard S. "A Critical Biography of Thomas Wolfe to His Thirty-fourth Year." Ph.D. dissertation, Harvard University, 1953.

E66 Kilburn, Patrick E. "Ulysses in Catawba, A Study of the Influence of James Joyce on Thomas Wolfe." Ph.D. dissertation, New York University, 1954.

E67 Kimbrough, William E. "L'influence de Jean-Christophe sur le roman américain contemporain, et notamment sur Wolfe." Ph.D. dissertation, Strasbourg, 1954.

E68 King, George W. "The Concept of Time as Developed by Marcel Proust and Thomas Wolfe." Master's thesis, University of Denver, 1948.

E69 Kracht, Fritz "Die Thomas Wolfe Kritik in den Vereinigten Staaten und Deutschland." Ph.D. dissertation, Munich, 1953.

E70 Kytle, Juanita S. "Walt Whitman and Thomas Wolfe." Master's thesis, University of Oklahoma, 1946.

E71 Lantos, Carl. "Thomas Wolfe, the Struggle for Maturity." Master's thesis, University of Texas, 1948.

E72 Larass, Horst. 'Thomas Wolfe: zur Problematik des
     burgerlichen Dichters im Zeitalter des Imperialismus."
     Ph.D. dissertation, Greifswald, 1961.

E73 LaSalle, Claude William. "Thomas Wolfe: The Dramatic
     Apprenticeship." Ph.D. dissertation, University of
     Pennsylvania, 1964.

E74 Lawler, John J. "A Study of Some of the Relations between
     the Periodical and Book Publications of Thomas Wolfe."
     Master's thesis, University of North Carolina, 1949.

E75 Lawrence, Oliver Clare. "Thomas Wolfe: From Individual
     to Man-Swarm." Ph.D. dissertation, University of
     Washington, 1961.

E76 Lehnstuhl, A.B. "A Critical Comment on the Works of
     Thomas Wolfe." Master's thesis, New York
     University, 1938.

E77 Linder, Wolfgang. "Die epische Struktur des Romanwerkes
     von Thomas Wolfe." Ph.D. dissertation, Bonn, 1951.

E78 Logan, Susan H. "Concepts of Love in the Novel with an
     Emphasis on the Twentieth Century American Novel."
     Ph.D. dissertation, Florida State University, 1966.

E79 Lyons, John Ormsby. "The Novel of Academic Life in
     America." Ph.D. dissertation, University of Florida, 1960.

E80 McCormick, John O. "Thomas Wolfe, André Malraux,
     Hermann Hesse: A Study in Creative Vitality."
     Ph.D. dissertation, Harvard University, 1951.

E81 Maddock, Lawrence H. "The Critical Image of Thomas
     Wolfe." Ph. D. dissertation, George Peabody
     College, 1965.

112

E82 Magee, Annie T. "The Theory and Techniques of Thomas Wolfe." Master's thesis, Southwest Texas State College, 1951.

E83 Marley, Lena S. "A Study of the Structure of the Narrative in 'Proteus: the City.' " Master's thesis, University of North Carolina, 1966.

E84 Marshall, Marion C. "Thomas Wolfe's Conception of the South." Master's thesis, University of Virginia, 1955.

E85 Maxwell, Allen. "Thomas Wolfe, Dichtung and Wahrheit." Master's thesis, Southern Methodist University, 1940.

E86 Maxwell, Bert H. "Thomas Wolfe's You Can't Go Home Again: A Critical Study." Master's thesis, University of Texas, 1954.

E87 Melito, Ignatius M. "Themes of Adolescence: Studies in American Fiction of Adolescence." Ph.D. dissertation, University of Denver, 1965.

E88 Miller, John C. "Thomas Wolfe as a Novelist." Master's thesis, University of Virginia, 1947.

E89 Moore, Irene. "The Tradition of the College in the American Novel, 1895-1937." Master's thesis, University of Texas, 1940.

E90 Morris, Ann Roberson. "A Study of Rhythm in the Novel." Ph.D. dissertation, Florida State University, 1961.

E91 Moser, Thomas C. "The Characters of Thomas Wolfe: A Study in the Development of Technique." Honors thesis, Harvard University, 1948.

E92 Neuner, Thea. "Amerika und der amerikanische Mensch in den Werken von Thomas Wolfe." Ph.D. dissertation, Vienna, 1953.

E93 Newman, Carol M., Jr. "The Symbols of Thomas Wolfe." Master's thesis, University of Virginia, 1946.

E94 Nolte, William Henry. "The Satire of Thomas Wolfe." Master's thesis, University of Texas, 1952.

E95 Oertel, Ferdinand. "Die Europa-Erfahrung Thomas Wolfes." Ph.D. dissertation, Köln, 1954.

E96 Otterness, Lyle Amos. "The Methods of Character Development in the Novels of Thomas Wolfe." Bachelor's thesis, University of Illinois, 1940.

E97 Powell, Richard R. "Thomas Wolfe: Heritage and Destiny." Honors thesis, University of North Carolina, 1967.

E98 Proehl, Louise. "The Personality of Thomas Wolfe." Bachelor's thesis, University of Illinois, 1945.

E99 Pusey, W. W. "The Thomas Wolfe Vogue in Germany." Master's thesis, Washington and Lee University, 1948.

E100 Reeves, George M., Jr. "Thomas Wolfe et l'Europe." Ph.D. dissertation, University of Paris, 1955.

E101 Reeves, Walter Paschal. "Race and Nationality in the Works of Thomas Wolfe." Ph.D. dissertation, Duke University, 1963.

E102 Rice, Jerry. "Thomas Wolfe as a Dramatist." Master's thesis, Ohio State University, 1959.

E103 Robillard, Ambolena H. "Maxwell Evarts Perkins,
The Author's Editor." Ph.D. dissertation,
University of Florida, 1954.

E104 Rogers, Elizabeth Jane. "An Analysis of Thomas Wolfe's
Look Homeward, Angel, and *Of Time and the River*."
Master's thesis, Ohio State University, 1944.

E105 Ross, Sue Fields. "A Study of Terry's Edition of
Thomas Wolfe's Letters to His Mother, with Emphasis
on Dating Errors." Master's thesis, University of
North Carolina, 1965.

E106 Rubin, Larry J. "Image and Theme in the Tetralogy
of Thomas Wolfe." Ph.D. dissertation, Emory University,
1956.

E107 Schulte, Wolfgang. "Die romantischen und realistischen
Elemente im Werk Thomas Wolfes."
Ph.D. dissertation, Kiel, 1955.

E108 Shannon, Florine F. "Women in American Fiction
from 1920 to 1941." Master's thesis, University of
Tulsa, 1942.

E109 Shealy, Ann. "Thomas Wolfe, A Critical Study of
His Views of the American Scene." Master's
thesis, University of South Carolina, 1947.

E110 Shufford, Catherine B. "Thomas Wolfe and Walt
Whitman." Master's thesis, North Texas State College,
1941.

E111 Simons, Helen T. "The Pessimism of Thomas Wolfe."
Master's thesis, University of Pittsburgh, 1947.

E112 Skipp, Francis E. "Thomas Wolfe and His Scribner's Editors." Ph.D. dissertation, Duke University, 1962.

E113 Smith, Eleanor G. M. "Wolfe's Unfinished Symphony: A Study of Form in the Novels of Thomas Wolfe." Ph.D. dissertation, University of Wisconsin, 1948.

E114 Smitherman, Betty J. "Thomas Wolfe's Imagery." Master's thesis, University of Texas, 1953.

E115 Springer, Anne Marie. "The American Novel in Germany: A Study of Eight American Novelists between the Two World Wars." Ph.D. dissertation, University of Pennsylvania, 1959.

E116 Sprowles, Harry D., Jr. "The Search for Thomas Wolfe, With Particular Stress Upon the Meaning of the Amatory Theme." Ph.D. dissertation, University of Pennsylvania, 1956.

E117 Stanton, Edgar Emmett, Jr. "Hegel and Thomas Wolfe." Ph.D. dissertation, Florida State University, 1960.

E118 Stanzel, Franz. "Das Amerikabild Thomas Wolfes, 1900-1938." Ph.D. dissertation, Graz, 1950.

E119 Strozier, Robert Ingram. "The Anatomy of Thomas Wolfe: A Study of the Question of Unity in the Gant-Webber Saga." Ph.D. dissertation, Florida State University, 1965.

E120 Suberman, Jack. "The Idealism of Thomas Wolfe." Master's thesis, University of Florida, 1947.

E121 Sullivan, J. B. "Changes in the Short Story from 1925 to 1935." Master's thesis, Texas Technological College, 1936.

E122 Sutliff, Harriet J. "Thomas Wolfe, American Legend." Master's thesis, Colorado College, 1942.

E123 Taylor, P. M. "Thomas Wolfe, American." Master's thesis, Boston University, 1942.

E124 Tekusch, Hiltgund H. "Thomas Wolfes Selbstporträt in seinen Briefen und Romanen." Ph.D. dissertation, Vienna, 1952.

E125 Treble, Cicely. "Thomas Wolfe: A Bibliography." Master's thesis, Carnegie Institute, 1950.

E126 Unger, Gerda. "Amerika und Europa im Urteil von Thomas Wolfes Romanen." Ph.D. dissertation, Vienna, 1952.

E127 Vause, Edward A. "Thomas Wolfe's Narrative Method." Master's thesis, University of North Carolina, 1949.

E128 Vickers, James Edward. "Theme and Form in *Of Time and the River*." Master's thesis, University of North Carolina, 1967.

E129 Voigt, Walter. "Die Bildersprache Thomas Wolfes mit besonderer Berücksichtigung der Metaphorik des Amerikanischen Englisch." Ph.D. dissertation, Tübingen, 1952.

E130 Weiss, Paul. "Thomas Wolfe, Far-Wanderer." Master's thesis, Columbia University, 1941.

E131 West, Alfred T. "The Development and Influence of the Folk-Interest in Contemporary Drama." Master's thesis, University of Alabama, 1933. Includes discussion of Wolfe's early plays.

E132 Williamson, Juanita V. "The Treatment of the Negro
in the Fiction of North Carolina, 1920-1940."
Master's thesis, Atlanta University, 1940.

E133 Wilson, Elizabeth G. "Thomas Wolfe: His Life and
Personality." Master's thesis, Cornell University, 1944.

E134 Witham, William T. "The Forge of Life: Problems
of Adolescence in American Novels, 1920-1958."
Ph.D. dissertation, University of Illinois, 1961.

E135 Woodruff, Lloyd B. "A Study of the Structure in the
Novels of Thomas Wolfe." Master's thesis,
University of Southern California, 1948.

E136 Yarmolinsky, Adam. "Thomas Wolfe and his America."
Bliss Prize Essay, Harvard University, 1939.

E137 Yoggerst, James Paul. "The Individualism of Thomas
Wolfe." Master's thesis, University of Illinois, 1950.

E138 Young, Phyllis D. "Manhattan Life in the Novel,
1920-1940." Master's thesis, Southern Methodist
University, 1948.

F. Articles About Wolfe

F1 Adams, Agatha B. "Thomas Wolfe at Chapel Hill,"
  Carolina Quarterly, II (December 1949), 21-29.

F2 ———. "Thomas Wolfe: The Friendliness of a Lonely
  Man," *Carolina Quarterly*, II (May 1950), 16-22.

F3 Adams, J. Donald. "A New Novel by Thomas Wolfe,"
  New York Times Book Review, June 25, 1939, p. 1.
  Review of *TWATR*.

F4 ———. "Thomas Wolfe's Last Book," *New York Times
  Book Review*, October 26, 1941, p. 1. Review of *THB*.

F5 ———. "Thomas Wolfe's Last Novel," *New York
  Times Book Review*, September 22, 1940, p. 1.
  Review of *YCGHA*.

F6 Adams, Phoebe. "The Truth About Thomas Wolfe,"
  Atlantic Monthly, CCVI (July 1960), 100.
  Review of Nowell.

F7 Adams, Walter S. (Review of *LHA*). *Asheville Times*,
  October 27, 1929.

F8 Albrecht, W. P. "Time as Unity in the Novels of Thomas Wolfe," *New Mexico Quarterly Review*, XIX (Autumn 1949), 320-329.

F9 ———. "The Title of *Look Homeward, Angel*," *Modern Language Quarterly*, XI (March 1950), 50-57.

F10 Aldington, Richard. (Review of *LHA*), *Sunday Referee* [London], July 6, 1930.

F11 Alker, Ernst. "Thomas Wolfe und die neue amerikanische Dichtung," *Wort und Wahrheit* [Vienna], III (November 1948), 852-857.

F12 Allen, Gay Wilson. "He Sought a World to Fit His Size," *Saturday Review*, XLIII (July 16, 1960), 17. Review of Nowell.

F13 ———. (Review of Austin), *New York Times Book Review*, June 23, 1968, p. 22.

F14 ———. (Review of Pamela Johnson), *American Literature*, XXI (1949), 253-254.

F15 Allen, Lee. "Wolfe in Retrospect," *American Mercury*, LXIV (March 1947), 381.

F16 Allsbrook, Raleigh. "The Novelist Thomas Wolfe Is Recalled by Local Man," *Charlotte News*, September 17, 1938.

F17 Alsterlund, B. "Thomas Wolfe," *Wilson Library Bulletin*, XIII (1938), 170-172.

F18 Ames, R. S. "Wolfe, Wolfe," *American Spectator*, III (January 1935), 5-6.

F19 Anastas'ev, N. A. "Faust ne umiraet: zametki o trorcestve Tomasa Vulfa," *Voprosy Literatury*, XI (August 1967), 87-105.

F20 Anderson, Mildred C. "Pious Dither about Form," *Saturday Review of Literature*, XIV (May 23, 1936), 9.

F21 Anderson, Patrick. "Ten Thousand Words a Day," *Times Literary Supplement* [London], April 21, 1961, p. 252. Review of Nowell.

F22 Andrews, G. R. "Thomas Wolfe's Mother Gives Glimpses of Famous Writer," *Uplift*, XXX (February 7, 1942), 6. Also in *Observer* [Charlotte], January 18, 1942.

F23 Angoff, Charles. "A Promise and a Legend," *North American Review*, CCXLVIII (Autumn 1939), 198-201. Review of *TWATR*.

F24 ———. "Thomas Wolfe and the Opulent Manner," *Southwest Review*, XLVIII (1963), 81-84.

F25 Anonymous. "About Tom Wolfe," *University of North Carolina Magazine*, LXVI (December 1936), 4.

F26 Anonymous. "Altamont, 50 Years Later," *Flair*, I (October 1950), 32-35. Illustrated.

F27 Anonymous. "Alumni Write Books," *University of North Carolina Alumni Review*, XVIII (November 1929), 45. On *LHA*.

F28 Anonymous. "As They Recall Thomas Wolfe," *Southern Packet*, IV (April 1948), 4, 9-10. Also in *Carolina Magazine*, LXXVII (May 1948), 28-33.

F29 Anonymous. "Asheville Is Altamont of Wolfe's Novels," *Life*, XIX (December 24, 1945), 60-62. Illustrated

F30 Anonymous. "Bitter Mystery," *Time*, XXXIII (June 26, 1939), 81. Review of *TWATR*.

F31 Anonymous. "Burning, Burning, Burning," *Time*, XXXVI (September 23, 1940), 78, 80. Review of *YCGHA*.

F32 Anonymous. "The Colossus of Asheville," *Times Literary Supplement* [London], September 26, 1958, 544. Review of *Letters*.

F33 Anonymous. "Death the Proud Brother: An Essay on Thomas Wolfe." *American Prefaces*, IV (October 1938), 7-9.

F34 Anonymous. "Edward Aswell Succeeds Perkins as Administrator of Wolfe Estate," *Publishers' Weekly*, CLII (August 9, 1947), 531.

F35 Anonymous. "Fine Play From Great Novel," *Life*, XLIII (December 16, 1957), 79-82.

F36 Anonymous. "First Night Flurry," *Newsweek*, L (December 9, 1957), 70-71. Review of Frings.

F37 Anonymous. "The Great Editor: M. E. Perkins," *Quick*, II (March 27, 1950), 34-36.

F38 Anonymous. "His Letters Tell Wolfe Life Story," *Times-Picayune* [New Orleans], October 14, 1956. Review of *Letters*.

F39 Anonymous. "Home-Grown Giant," *Time*, XCI (February 9, 1968), 94-95. Review of Turnbull.

F40 Anonymous. "Honorable Mention: The Letters of Thomas Wolfe," *Publishers' Weekly*, CLXXI (January 14, 1957), 20-21.

F41   Anonymous. "In Flooding Words," *Newsweek*, XLVIII (October 8, 1956), 92-94. Review of *Letters*.

F42   Anonymous. "In Memory of Thomas Wolfe," *Rock of Ages Magazine*, XVII, (February 1940), 9.

F43   Anonymous. "Is Genius Enough?" *Time*, LI (January 5, 1948), 78. Review of Muller.

F44   Anonymous. "Land of Smoke and Dreams," *Coronet*, XLVI (October 1959), 142-151. Illustrated.

F45   Anonymous. "The Last Look Around," *Time*, LVIII (July 2, 1951), 98, 100. Review of *A Western Journal*.

F46   Anonymous. "Laurels to an Editor," *Publishers' Weekly*, CXXVII (March 23, 1935), 1230-1231.

F47   Anonymous. "Legend of a Giant," *Time*, LXXVI (July 11, 1960), 102, 104. Review of Nowell.

F48   Anonymous. "Letters from Leviathan," *Time*, LXVIII (October 8, 1956), 113-114. Review of *Letters*.

F49   Anonymous. "Literary Estate," *New Yorker*, XXXII (February 9, 1957), 24-26.

F50   Anonymous. "*Look Homeward, Angel*: A New Play by Ketti Frings," *Playbill*, II (February 3, 1958), 11-32. This issue and others during the run of the play on Broadway contain the cast of characters and other information about the play.

F51   Anonymous. "Mabel Wolfe Wheaton, Novelist's Sister Dies," *Asheville Citizen*, September 30, 1958, pp. 1, 3.

F52 Anonymous. "The Measure of a Giant," *Newsweek*, LVI (July 11, 1960), 92, 94. Review of Nowell.

F53 Anonymous. "Memory of Thomas Wolfe Does Come Home Again," *Tar Heel* [University of North Carolina], November 1, 1940.

F54 Anonymous. "Mother and Son," *Time*, XLI (May 10, 1943), 100. Review of *LTHM*.

F55 Anonymous. "A New and Notable Wolfe Collection," *The Bookmark* [University of North Carolina Library], April 1952, pp. 1-2.

F56 Anonymous. "New Look Homeward," *New York Times Book Review*, August 6, 1950, p. 7.

F57 Anonymous. "New Play in Manhattan," *Time*, LXX (December 9, 1957), 72-74. Review of Frings.

F58 Anonymous. (Obituary of Aline Bernstein), *New York Times*, September 8, 1955, p. 31.

F59 Anonymous. "Papa Was the Character," *Carolina Comments*, January 1962, p. 2.

F60 Anonymous. (Review of *FDTM*), *Saturday Review*, XLVIII (October 23, 1965), 62.

F61 Anonymous. (Review of Frings), *Asheville Citizen*, November 7, 1957. See also issue of January 3, 1958.

F62 Anonymous. (Review of Kennedy), *Critic*, XXI (February-March 1963), 80.

F63 Anonymous. (Review of Kennedy), *Times Literary Supplement* [London], July 26, 1963, p. 550.

F64 Anonymous. (Review of *Letters*), *College English*, XIX (November 1957), 88.

F65 Anonymous. (Review of *Letters*), *New Yorker*, XXXII (October 20, 1956), 198.

F66 Anonymous. (Review of *Letters*), *Yale Review*, XLVI (Spring 1957), xviii.

F67 Anonymous. (Review of *LHA*), *Booklist*, XXVI (May 1930), 315.

F68 Anonymous. (Review of *LHA*), *Christian Register*, CX (January 9, 1930), 28.

F69 Anonymous. (Review of *LHA*), *Times Literary Supplement* [London], July 24, 1930.
Reprinted September 17, 1954.

F70 Anonymous. (Review of *LHA*), *Weekly* [Chapel Hill], October 18, 1929.

F71 Anonymous. (Review of *LHA*), *Tar Heel* [University of North Carolina], October 24, 1929.

F72 Anonymous. (Review of *Mannerhouse*), *New York Times*, December 19, 1948, p. 9.

F73 Anonymous. (Review of *Mannerhouse*), *Yale Daily News*, May 6, 1949.

F74 Anonymous. (Review of Nowell), *Booklist*, LVI (July 15, 1960), 681.

F75 Anonymous. (Review of Nowell), *English Journal*, XLIX (October 1960), 507-508.

F76 Anonymous. (Review of Nowell), *Nineteenth Century Fiction*, XV (December 1960), 280-281.

F77 Anonymous. (Review of Nowell), *New Yorker*, XXXVI (August 13, 1960), 105.

F78 Anonymous. (Review of Nowell), *New York Times*, July 8, 1960, p. 19.

F79 Anonymous. (Review of Nowell), *Times Literary Supplement* [London], April 21, 1961, p. 252.

F80 Anonymous. (Review of Nowell), *Times Weekly Review* [London], March 30, 1961, p. 13.

F81 Anonymous. (Review of *OTATR*), *Booklist*, XXXI (April 1935), 268.

F82 Anonymous. (Review of *OTATR*), *Literary Digest*, CXIX (March 16, 1935).

F83 Anonymous. (Review of Pollock), *United States Quarterly Book Review*, X (June 1954), 159.

F84 Anonymous. (Review of Raynolds), *Choice*, III (July 1966), 411.

F85 Anonymous. (Review of Reeves), *Books Abroad*, XXXI (Winter 1957), 45.

F86 Anonymous. (Review of Rubin), *New York Times Book Review*, May 15, 1955, p. 22.

F87 Anonymous. (Review of *Short Novels*), *Booklist*, LVII (May 15, 1961), 573.

F88 Anonymous. (Review of *Short Novels*), *Christian Science Monitor*, July 15, 1961, p. 11.

F89 Anonymous. (Review of *Short Novels*), *New York Herald Tribune Lively Arts*, May 28, 1961, p. 30.

F90 Anonymous. (Review of *Short Novels*), *San Francisco Sunday Chronicle*, May 14, 1961, p. 34.

F91 Anonymous. (Review of *Thomas Wolfe Reader*), *San Francisco Sunday Chronicle*, June 3, 1962, p. 34.

F92 Anonymous. (Review of *TWATR*), *Booklist*, XXXV (July 1, 1939), 365.

F93 Anonymous. (Review of Walser), *Times Literary Supplement* [London], May 26, 1961, p. 330.

F94 Anonymous. (Review of Walser), *Times Weekly Review* [London], May 11, 1961, p. 12.

F95 Anonymous. (Review of Watkins), *Asheville Citizen*, July 14, 1957.

F96 Anonymous. (Review of Watkins), *Booklist*, LIV (September 1, 1957), 14.

F97 Anonymous. (Review of *YCGHA*), *Booklist*, XXXVI (October 1, 1940), 37.

F98 Anonymous. (Review of *YCGHA*), *Newsweek*, XVI (September 23, 1940), 46.

F99 Anonymous. "Thomas Wolfe and Asheville," *Mainliner* [United Air Lines], VI (September 1963), 15-16.

F100 Anonymous. "Thomas Wolfe: Asheville's Famous Son," *Mountain Life and Work*, XXIV (April 1958), 25-26.

F101 Anonymous. "Thomas Wolfe: Der verdammte Ding," *Der Spiegel* [Hamburg], XI (1957), 42-46.

F102 Anonymous. "Thomas Wolfe: Novelist Dies,"
New York Herald Tribune, September 16, 1938.

F103 Anonymous. "Thomas Wolfe to Be Buried This
Afternoon," *Asheville Citizen*, September 18, 1938.

F104 Anonymous. "Thomas Wolfe Wins Applause of
Audiences," *The Mirror* [Colorado State College
of Education], August 2, 1935.

F105 Anonymous. "Thomas Wolfe's Mother Is Dead,"
Life, XIX (December 24, 1945), 59.

F106 Anonymous. "Thomas Wolfe's Simple Autobiographical
Sketch," *Herald-Sun* [Durham], September 18, 1938.

F107 Anonymous. "Tom Wolfe," *New Republic*, XCVI
(September 28, 1938), 197-198.

F108 Anonymous. "Unpredictable Imagination," *Time*,
XXXII (September 26, 1938), 66.

F109 Anonymous. "University of North Carolina Library
Gets John Skally Terry's Collection," *Daily News*
[Greensboro], August 1, 1954.

F110 Anonymous. "Whitmanesque Rhapsody," *Times Literary
Supplement* [London], February 1, 1947, p. 61.
Review of *TWATR*.

F111 Anonymous. "What Does Asheville Think of Thomas
Wolfe Now?" *Asheville Citizen*, July 22, 1957.

F112 Anonymous. "Wilde and Wolfe," *The Sign*, XXVII
(September 1947), 24-25.

F113 Anonymous. "Wolfe: die Versöhnung," *Der Spiegel* [Hamburg], XII (1958), 44-45.

F114 Anonymous. "Wolfe in the West," *Newsweek*, XXXVIII (July 2, 1951), 80, 82. Review of *A Western Journal*.

F115 Anonymous. "Wolfe in Waco," *Time*, LXXIII (April 27, 1959), 44-48.

F116 Anonymous. "Wolfe: so herzerschuetternd," *Der Spiegel* [Hamburg], XVI (1962), 106-107.

F117 Anonymous. "Wolfe Speaks in City Informally," *Daily Tribune* [Greeley, Col.], July 31-August 1, 1935, p. 5

F118 Anonymous. "Wolfe's Home to Become Museum," *Asheville Times*, May 2, 1956.

F119 Anonymous. "Wolfe's Mighty Masterpiece Molded into Brilliant Play by Ketti Frings," *Beaumont Enterprise* [Texas], April 17, 1960.

F120 Anonymous. "Wolfe's Student Days," *Weekly* [Chapel Hill], June 7, 1935.

F121 Anonymous. "Write Hard and at Home, Advises Author at C. U." *Rocky Mountain News*, August 8, 1935.

F122 Appel, Benjamin. "Elizabeth Nowell and Thomas Wolfe," *Carleton Miscellany*, VIII (Winter 1967), 70-77.

F123 Armstrong, Anne W. "As I Saw Thomas Wolfe," *Arizona Quarterly*, II (Spring 1946), 5-14.

F124 Aston, Frank. "Wolfe Novel Now Fine Play," *New York World Telegram*, November 29, 1957.

F125 Aswell, Edward C. "En Route to a Legend," *Saturday Review of Literature*, XXI (November 27, 1948), 7, 34-36.

F126 ———. "Letter to Editor," *Commentary*, XIII (April 1952), 395. This is in reply to Hans Meyerhoff's "Death of a Genius."

F127 ———. "Note on 'A Western Journey,'" *Virginia Quarterly Review*, XV (Summer 1939), 333-334.

F128 ———. "A Note on Thomas Wolfe," *Omnibook Magazine*, IV (January 1942), 129-132.

F129 ———. "Thomas Wolfe Did Not Kill Maxwell Perkins," *Saturday Review of Literature*, XXXIV (October 6, 1951), 16-17, 44-46.

F130 ———. "Thomas Wolfe: The Playwright Who Discovered He Wasn't," *Playbill*, II (February 3, 1958), 9, 32.

F131 ———. "Thomas Wolfe's Unpublished Works," *Carolina Magazine*, LXVIII (October 1938), 19-20.

F132 Atkinson, Brooks. "Theatre: A Wolfe Novel," *New York Times*, November 30, 1957.

F133 Aubery, Pierre. "L'Image de la France chez le romancier Thomas Wolfe," *Revue de Psychologie des Peuples*, XII (1957), 205-215.

F134 Avery, May J. "Tom Wolfe Paints Picture Relentless for Truthfulness With Homefolks Characters," *Observer* [Charlotte], March 30, 1930.

F135 Bagg, D. B. (Review of Wheaton), *Springfield Republican*, February 12, 1961, p. D4.

F136 Baker, Carlos. "Thomas Wolfe's Apprenticeship," *Delphian Quarterly*, XXIII (January 1940), 20-25.

F137 Balakian, Nona. (Review of Raynolds), *New York Times*, March 30, 1966, p. 41.

F138 Ball, Joseph. (Review of *FDTM*), *Best Sellers*, XVII (March 15, 1958), 431.

F139 Barber, P. W. "Thomas Wolfe Writes a Play," *Harper's Magazine*, CCXVI (May 1958), 71-76.

F140 Baro, Gene. (Review of Pollock), *New York Herald Tribune Book Review*, April 18, 1954, p. 3.

F141 ———. (Review of Walser), *New York Herald Tribune Book Review*, August 30, 1953, p.7.

F142 ———. (Review of Watkins), *New York Herald Tribune Book Review*, July 14, 1957, p. 1.

F143 ———. (Review of *A Western Journal*), *New York Herald Tribune Book Review*, July 29, 1951, p. 3.

F144 Barr, Stringfellow. "The Dandridges and the Gants," *Virginia Quarterly Review*, VI (Spring 1930), 310-313. Review of *LHA*.

F145 Barton, Robert. "Works of Wolfe, the Student, to Be Published in Book Form," *Asheville Citizen*, June 19, 1960.

F146 Basso, Hamilton. "Mountain View," *New Republic*, LXXXV (January 1, 1936), 232. Review of *FDTM*.

F147 ———. "A New Look Homeward," *New York Times Book Review*, January 22, 1961, p. 6. See also March 5, 1961, p. 42 and March 26, 1961, p. 41. Review of Wheaton.

132

F148 ———. (Review of *PTW*), *New Yorker*, XXII (September 14, 1946), 107.

F149 ———. "Thomas Wolfe, A Portrait," *New Republic*, LXXXVII (June 24, 1936), 199-202. Review of *SOAN*.

F150 ———. "Thomas Wolfe, A Summing Up," *New Republic*, CIII (September 23, 1940), 422-423. Review of *YCGHA*.

F151 Bates, Ernest S. "Thomas Wolfe," *English Journal*, XXVI (September 1937), 519-527.

F152 ———. "Thomas Wolfe," *Modern Quarterly*, XI (Fall 1938), 86-89.

F153 Bay, Andre. "Aux sources de Thomas Wolfe," *Information et Documents* [Paris], no. 34, November 1, 1956.

F154 Beebe, Maurice, and Field, Leslie A. "Criticism of Thomas Wolfe: A Selected Checklist," *Modern Fiction Studies*, XI (Autumn 1965), 315-328. A bibliography.

F155 Beja, Morris. "Why You Can't Go Home Again: Thomas Wolfe and 'The Escapes of Time and Memory,'" *Modern Fiction Studies*, XI (Autumn 1965), 297-314.

F156 Bell, Alladine. "T. Wolfe of 10 Montague Terrace," *Antioch Review*, XX (Fall 1960), 377-390.

F157 Benet, Stephen V. "Thomas Wolfe's Torrent of Recollection," *Saturday Review of Literature*, XXII (September 21, 1940), 5. Review of *YCGHA*.

F158 Bentinck-Smith, William. "The Legacy of Thomas Wolfe," *Harvard Alumni Bulletin*, L (November 22, 1947), 210-214.

F159 Berman, Barney. "Wolfe Without Art," *Saturday Review of Literature*, XIV (May 23, 1936), 9.

F160 Bhattacharya, Lokenath. "Thomas Wolfe: A Tragic Giant," *Span* (New Delhi), XII (October 1961), 36-39.

F161 Bianchini, Angela. "Tom Wolfe dopo venti anni," *Approdo*, V (1959), 67-70.

F162 Bigart, Homer. "Thomas Wolfe at 35 Is Tired of Being a Legend," *New York Herald Tribune*, November 3, 1935.

F163 Bigger, Frank. "Fred Wolfe, GE '22, Comes Home Again," *Georgia Tech Alumnus*, XL (December 1961), 16-17.

F164 Bishop, Donald E. "Fame Came from Essay on Labor," *Herald-Sun* [Durham, N. C.], April 20, 1941. See also *News and Observer* [Raleigh], October 20, 1941 for similar article.

F165 ———. "Group Out to Prove Wolfe No Monster," *Observer* [Charlotte], May 20, 1951.

F166 ———. "Terry Promises Wolfe Life within One Year," *Observer* [Charlotte], April 30, 1950.

F167 ———. "Thomas Wolfe," *Carolina Magazine*, LXXI (March 1942), 28-29, 35, 47-48.

F168 ———. "Thomas Wolfe Biographer Is Interrupted
by Death," *Asheville Citizen-Times,* May 10, 1953.

F169 ———. "Thomas Wolfe's Official Biography Is Being
Prepared," *Morning Herald* [Durham, N. C.],
May 25, 1947.

F170 ———. "Under No Censor," *Daily Tar Heel* [University
of North Carolina], October 5, 1939.

F171 ———. " 'Wolfe, American' Is Symphonic Poem,"
Observer [Charlotte, N. C.], October 15, 1950.

F172 Bishop, John P. "The Myth and Modern Literature,"
Saturday Review of Literature, XX (July 22, 1939),
3-4, 14.

F173 ———. "The Sorrows of Thomas Wolfe," *Kenyon
Review,* I (Winter 1939), 7-17.

F174 Blackmur, R. P. "Notes on the Novel," *Southern Review,*
I (Spring 1936), 898-899.

F175 Blanzet, M. J. (Review of *TWATR*), *Le Figaro Littéraire,*
II (October 18, 1947), 5.

F176 Blythe, LeGette. "Eliza Gant's Monologue," *Saturday
Review of Literature,* XXX (April 5, 1947), 21.
Review of Norwood.

F177 ———. "Papa Wolfe Takes Children to Fair," *Daily
News* [Greensboro, N. C.], October 11, 1964, pp. D1,
D11. Also in *Morning Herald* [Durham, N. C.],
same date.

F178 ———. "The Thomas Wolfe I Knew," *Saturday Review
of Literature,* XXVIII (August 25, 1945), 18-19.
This contains an excerpt of a letter from Wolfe to Blythe.

F179 ———. "Wolfe 'Legend' Irks Biographer," *Observer* [Charlotte], June 20, 1947.

F180 Bower, Warren. "Washington Square," *Saturday Review*, XLIX (June 4, 1966), 23-24.

F181 Boyle, Thomas E. "Thomas Wolfe: Theme Through Imagery," *Modern Fiction Studies*, XI (Autumn 1965), 259-268.

F182 Braham, Lionel. "Wolfean Baby Talk," *American Speech*, XXXI (December 1956), 302-303.

F183 Braswell, William. "Thomas Wolfe Lectures and Takes a Holiday," *College English*, I (October 1939), 11-22.

F184 Bräunig, Werner. "Auf der Strasse Leben: Thomas Wolfe," *Sinn und Form*, XIX (1967), 983-988.

F185 Breit, Harvey. "A Walk With Faulkner," *New York Times Book Review*, January 30, 1955, pp. 4, 12.

F186 Brenner, H. G. "Junges Amerika," *Berliner Tageblatt*, April 19, 1936. Review of *OTATR*.

F187 Brickell, Herschel. (Review of *FDTM*), *New York Post*, December 14, 1935, p. 15.

F188 ———. (Review of OTATR), *New York Post*, March 9, 1935, p. 7.

F189 Brighouse, Harold. (Review of Pamela Johnson), *Manchester Guardian*, September 26, 1947, p. 3.

F190 Brion, Marcel. "Thomas Wolfe," *Revue des Deux Mondes*, XVI (August 15, 1952), 731-740.

136

F191 Brown, E. K. "Thomas Wolfe: Realist and Symbolist,"
University of Toronto Quarterly, X (January 1941),
153-166.

F192 Brown, John Mason. "Blue Pencil to Parnassus:
The Letters of Maxwell E. Perkins," *Saturday Review of
Literature*, XXXIII (April 8, 1950), 7-8, 32.

F193 ———. (Review of Nowell), *Book of the Month Club
News*, July 1960, pp. 2-3.

F194 ———. "Thomas Wolfe as a Dramatist," *New York
Post*, September 21, 1938.

F195 Brown, Lauren. "The Noble Savage as Novelist,"
American Review, VII (May 1936), 221-224.
Review of *SOAN*.

F196 Buchanan, Kenneth C. "Thomas Wolfe," *Bluets*,
[Asheville] XX (1947), 10-12.

F197 Budd, Louis J. "The Grotesques of Anderson and Wolfe,"
Modern Fiction Studies, V (Winter 1959-1960),
304-310.

F198 Burger, Nash K. "Mother of a Genius," *New York
Times Book Review*, February 9, 1947, p. 37.
Review of Norwood.

F199 ———. "A Story to Tell: Agee, Wolfe, Faulkner,"
South Atlantic Quarterly, LXIII (1964), 32-43.

F200 Burgum, Edwin B. "Thomas Wolfe's Discovery of
America," *Virginia Quarterly Review*,
XXII (1946), 421-437.

F201 Burt, Struthers. "Catalyst for Genius: Maxwell Perkins," *Saturday Review of Literature*, XXXIV (June 9, 1951), 6-8, 36-39. See also June 23, 1951, issue, p. 24.

F202 ———. "Wolfe and Perkins," *Saturday Review of Literature*, XXXIV (August 11, 1951), 22-25.

F203 Butcher, Fanny. (Review of Nowell), *Sunday Tribune* [Chicago], July 10, 1960, p. 1.

F204 Butz, R. C. (Review of *Letters*), *San Francisco Chronicle*, October 21, 1956, p. 19.

F205 Calverton, V. F. "Cultural Barometer," *Current History*, XLIX (November 1938), 47.

F206 ———. (Review of *OTATR*), *Modern Monthly*, IX (June 1935), 249-250.

F207 Cameron, Kenneth W. (Review of Watkins), *South Atlantic Bulletin*, XXIII (March 1958), 4.

F208 Cameron, May. "An Interview with Thomas Wolfe," *New York Post*, March 14, 1936.

F209 Canaday, Julia. "Dixieland: Home of Tom Wolfe Always Seemed in Need of Paint," *Morning Herald* [Durham N. C.], August 29, 1948, p. 3.

F210 Canby, Henry S. (Review of *TWATR*), *Book of the Month Club News*, July 1939, p. 1.

F211 ———. "The River of Youth," *Saturday Review of Literature*, XI (March 9, 1935), 529-530. Review of *OTATR*.

F212 Cantwell, Robert. (Review of *OTATR*), *New Outlook*, CLXV (April 1935), 10, 58.

F213 Capek, Abe. "The Development of Thomas Wolfe in the Light of his Letters," *Zeitschrift für Anglistik und Amerikanistik*, X (1962), 162-178.

F214 Cargill, Oscar. "Gargantua Fills His Skin," *University of Kansas City Review*, XVI (Autumn 1949), 20-30.

F215 ———. (Review of *Letters*), *Saturday Review*, XXXIX (October 13, 1956), 13-14.

F216 ———. (Review of Nowell), *American Literature*, XXXIII (May 1961), 238-240.

F217 ———. (Review of Pfister), *American Literature*, XXVII (March 1955), 127-128.

F218 ———. (Review of Watkins), *American Literature*, XXX (March 1958), 132-133.

F219 Carland, Lucy. "A Tribute to Thomas Wolfe," *Bluets*, [Asheville] XII (1939), 12.

F220 Carlisle, Robert E. "Musical Analogs in Thomas Wolfe's *Look Homeward, Angel*," *Modern Fiction Studies*, XIV (Summer 1968), 215-223.

F221 Carpenter, Frederic I. "Frame of Reference," *Saturday Review of Literature*, XIII (January 25, 1936), 9.

F222 ———. "Thomas Wolfe: The Autobiography of an Idea," *University of Kansas City Review*, XII (Spring 1946), 179-187.

F223 Carraway, Gertrude. "Thomas Wolfe Looks Homeward," *State* [Raleigh, N. C.], October 30, 1937, pp. 12, 20.

F224 ———. "Thomas Wolfe, 37 Today," *Observer* [Charlotte], October 3, 1937.

F225 Cash, W. J. "His Sister Knew Thomas Wolfe Well,"
News [Charlotte], July 30, 1939.

F226 Cassill, R. V. "The Wolfe Revival," *Western Review*,
XVI (Summer 1952), 258, 337.

F227 Chamberlain, John. "A Prodigious 'Putter-Inner,' "
National Review, XII (July 30, 1960), 55-56.
Review of Nowell.

F228 ————. (Review of *FDTM*), *New York Times*,
November 15, 1935.

F229 ————. (Review of *LHA*), *Bookman*, LXX
(December 1929), 449-450.

F230 Chamberlain, John. (Review of *OTATR*), *Current
History*, XLII (April 1935), iii.

F231 Chapman, John. "*Look Homeward, Angel*: A Play of
Splendid and Stirring Beauty," *Daily News* [New York],
November 29, 1957. Review of Frings.

F232 Chapman, Mary Lewis B. "Thomas Wolfe," *Literary
Sketches* [Williamsburg, Va.], VI (December 1966), 1-4.

F233 Chittick, V. L. O. "Tom Wolfe's Farthest West,"
Southwest Review, XLVIII (1963), 93-110.

F234 Christadler, Martin. (Review of Voigt), *Jahrbuch für
Amerikastudien*, VI (1960), 340-342.

F235 Church, Margaret. "Thomas Wolfe: Dark Time,"
Publications of the Modern Language Association,
LXIV (September 1949), 629-638.

F236 Clements, Clyde C. "Symbolic Patterns in *You Can't Go Home Again," Modern Fiction Studies,* XI (Autumn 1965), 286-296.

F237 Clurman, Harold. (Review of Frings), *Nation,* CLXXXV (December 14, 1957), 463-464.

F238 Coates, Albert. "I Agree Tom Wolfe Had Another Dimension," *Weekly* [Chapel Hill], July 7, 1950.

F239 Codman, Florence. "The Name Is Sound and Smoke," *Nation,* CXL (March 27, 1935), 365-366. Review of *OTATR.*

F240 Cohn, Louis H. "Thomas Clayton Wolfe," *Publishers' Weekly,* CXX (August 15, 1931), 615.

F241 Coindreau, Maurice. "Thomas Wolfe ou l'Apprenti Sorcier," *Les Oeuvres Nouvelles* [New York], V (1945).

F242 Coleman, Robert. "*Look Homeward* Is Superb Drama," *Daily Mirror* [New York], November 29, 1957. Review of Frings.

F243 Collins, Thomas L. "Letters Tom Wolfe Sent Home," *New York Times Book Review,* May 2, 1943, p. 6. Review of *LTHM.*

F244 ———. "Thomas Wolfe," *Sewanee Review,* L (October 1942), 487-504.

F245 Colton, Gerald B. "Talking about Reading Thomas Wolfe," *Assistant Librarian* [London], XLVIII (August 1955), 135-138.

F246 Colum, Mary M. (Comparison of Wolfe, Proust and Joyce), *Scribner's Magazine*, C (December 1936), 102. See also p. 100.

F247 ———. "The Limits of Thomas Wolfe," *Forum*, CII (November 1939), 227-228.

F248 ———. (Review of *OTATR*), *Forum*, XCIII (April 1935), 218-219.

F249 Conklin, R. J. (Review of TWATR), *Springfield Republican*, July 2, 1939, p. E7.

F250 Corrington, John W. "An Objective Biographer Misses the Real Wolfe," *National Observer*, February 26, 1968, p. 21. Review of Turnbull.

F251 Coughlan, Robert. "Grand Vision, A Final Tragedy," *Life*, XLI (September 24, 1956), 168-184. Illustrated.

F252 ———. "Tom Wolfe's Surge to Greatness," *Life*, XLI (September 17, 1956), 168-184. Illustrated. See also October 8, 1956, issue, p. 22.

F253 Cowley, Malcolm. "The 40 Days of Thomas Wolfe," *New Republic*, LXXXII (March 20, 1935), 163-164. Review of *OTATR*.

F254 ———. "The Life and Death of Thomas Wolfe," *New Republic*, CXXXV (November 19, 1956), 17-21.

F255 ———. "Maxwell Perkins," *New Yorker*, XIX (April 8, 1944), 30-43. See also April 1, 1944, issue, p. 22-36.

F256 ———. "Miserly Millionaire of Words," *Reporter*, XVI (February 7, 1957), 38-40.

F257 ———. "Sherwood Anderson's Epiphanies,"
London Magazine, VII (July 1960), 61-66.

F258 ———. "Thomas Wolfe," *Atlantic Monthly*, CC
(November 1957), 202-212.

F259 ———. "Thomas Wolfe's Legacy," *New Republic*, XCIX
(July 19, 1939), 311-312.

F260 ———. "Twenty-five Years After—The Lost Generation
Today," *Saturday Review of Literature*, XXXIV (June 2,
1951), 6-7, 33-34.

F261 ———. "Unshaken Friend," *New Yorker*, XX (April 1,
1944), 32-36; (April 8, 1944), 30-34.

F262 ———. "Wolfe and the Lost People," *New Republic*,
CV (November 3, 1941), 592-594. Review of *THB*.

F263 Crawley, Oliver. "Thomas Wolfe Comes Back,"
The State [Raleigh], February 27, 1937, p. 9.

F264 Creedy, John. (Editorial on Wolfe), *Carolina Magazine*,
XLVIII (October 1938), 21.

F265 Cross, Neal, "If I Am Not Better," *Pacific Spectator*, IV
(1950), 488-496.

F266 Crossen, Forrest, "Future of Writers' Conference
Discussed," *Daily Camera* [Boulder, Col.], August 12,
1935. Wolfe was present and is quoted on several points.

F267 Culkin, J. M. (Review of Walser), *America*, XC
(January 30, 1954), 460.

F268 Culver, John W. "Thomas Wolfe," *Andean Quarterly*, VIII (Summer 1945), 61-66.

F269 Cummin, W. P. (Review of *Mannerhouse*), *North Carolina Historical Review*, XXVI (July 1949), 368-369.

F270 Cummings, Ridgely. "Wolfe and Perkins," *Saturday Review of Literature*, XXXII (August 11, 1951), 22.

F271 Curley, T. F. "Novelist of the Normal," *Commonweal*, LXV (November 23, 1956), 209-211. Review of *Letters*.

F272 Curtiss, Mina. "Wolfe among the monstres sacrés," *Nation*, CCVI (April 1, 1968), 446-448. Review of Turnbull.

F273 Daniels, Jonathan. "A Native at Large," *Nation*, CLI (October 12, 1940), 332.

F274 ———. "Thomas Wolfe," *Saturday Review of Literature*, XVIII (September 24, 1938), 8.

F275 ———. "Thomas Wolfe: October Recollections," *Southeastern Librarian*, XI (Fall 1961), 205-212.

F276 ———. "A Voice That Will Not Soon Be Silent," *Saturday Review of Literature*, XX (October 14, 1939), 7. Review of *FOAN*.

F277 ———. "Wolfe's First Is Novel of Revolt," *News and Observer* [Raleigh], October 20, 1929. Review of *LHA*.

F278 Danielson, R. E. (Review of *THB*), *Atlantic Monthly*, CLXVIII (December 1941), unpaged section.

F279 Davenport, Basil. "C'est Maitre François," *Saturday Review of Literature*, VI (December 21, 1929), 584. Review of *LHA*.

F280 Davis, H. J. (Review of *SOAN*), *Canadian Forum*, XVI (July 1936), 29.

F281 Davis, Robert G. "Coach into Pumpkin," *New York Times Book Review*, February 11, 1968, pp. 1, 34, 36. Review of Turnbull. See also p. 17.

F282 ———. "Of Time and Thomas Wolfe," *New York Times Book Review*, May 10, 1953, p. 4. Review of Walser.

F283 Day, A. Grove. (Review of Muller), *American Literature*, XX (1948), 71-72.

F284 Dean, G. Earl. "Thomas Wolfe Born Half Century Ago," *News and Observer* [Raleigh], October 1, 1950.

F285 ———. "Dad's Personality Helped Thomas Wolfe," *Daily News* [Greensboro, N. C.], July 30, 1950.

F286 ———. "Thomas Wolfe's Mother," *State* [Raleigh], October 26, 1935, p. 3.

F287 Delakas, Daniel. "L'expérience française de Thomas Wolfe," *Revue de Littérature Comparée*, XXIV (July-September 1950), 417-436.

F288 ———. "Thomas Wolfe and Anatole France," *Comparative Literature*, IX (Winter 1957), 33-50.

F289 Dever, Joe. (Review of Wheaton), *Commonweal*, LXXIV (April 7, 1961), 56-68.

F290 DeVoto, Bernard. "American Novels, 1939," *Atlantic Monthly*, CLXV (January 1940), 69-71. Includes *TWATR*.

F291 ———. "English '37," *Saturday Review of Literature*, XVI (August 21, 1937), 8, 14.

F292 ———. "Genius Is Not Enough," *Saturday Review of Literature*, XIII (April 25, 1936), 3-4, 14-15. Review of *SOAN*.

F293 Dewey, E. H. "The Storm and Stress Period," *Survey Graphic*, XXIV (May 1935), 255. Review of *OTATR*.

F294 Dick, Kay. (Review of Nowell), *Punch*, May 3, 1961, 699.

F295 Dickson, Frank A. "Look Homeward, Angel," *Independent* [Anderson, S. C.], July 9, 17, 24, 31; August 7, 14, 21, 28; September 4, 1948. A series of articles on Wolfe and his family.

F296 Dollard, W. A. S. (Review of *THB*), *New York Herald Tribune Books*, October 19, 1941, p. 6.

F297 Donahugh, Robert H. (Review of Kennedy), *Library Journal*, LXXXVII (December 1, 1962), 4438-4439.

F298 Downing, Susan. "Thomas Wolfe: Point of View," *Lit*, (Spring 1965), 50-55.

F299 Driver, Tom F. "As It Was," *Christian Century*, LXXV (April 16, 1958), 469. Review of Frings.

F300 Duncan, Norvin C. "Background of Thomas Wolfe, Author," *Observer* [Charlotte], April 7, 1935.

F301 Dykeman, Wilma, and Stokely, James. "Thomas Wolfe Comes Home," *New York Times Magazine*, December 15, 1957, pp. 18, 46, 48.

F302 Earnest, Ernest. "The American Ariel," *South Atlantic Quarterly*, LXV (Spring 1965), 192-200.

F303 East, Charles. "Thomas Wolfe Is Brought into Clearer Focus," *Morning Advocate* [Baton Rouge, La.], September 25, 1960, p. 2E. Review of Nowell.

F304 Eaton, Clement. "Student Days with Thomas Wolfe,"
      Georgia Review, XVII (Summer 1963), 146-155.

F305 Eaton, W. P. (Review of *Mannerhouse*), *New York
      Herald Tribune Weekly Book Review*,
      January 30, 1949, p. 20.

F306 Effelberger, Hans. (Review of *OTATR*), *Die Neuren
      Sprachen*, XLIV (1936), 158-159.

F307 Ehle, John M. "An Unfound Door," *American Adventure*,
      Series 1, no. 13, (1953).

F308 Ehrsam, Theodore G. "I Knew Thomas Wolfe,"
      Book Collector's Journal, I (June 1936), 1, 3. Also in
      Fact Digest, V (March 1938), 14-17.

F309 Eichelberger, Clayton L. "Wolfe's 'No Door' and the
      Brink of Discovery," *Georgia Review*, XXI (1967),
      319-327.

F310 Einseidel, Wolfgang von. (Review of *OTATR*),
      Europäische Revue, XII (October 1936), 841-844. See
      also pp. 760, 923.

F311 Elliott, Hubert. "The Death of Thomas Wolfe," *State*
      [Raleigh], September 24, 1938, pp. 12, 26.

F312 Ellis, Mary Helen. "A Voice from the Wasteland:
      Thomas Wolfe," *Living Church*, LXXX (May 12, 1957),
      10-13.

F313 Engels, Gunther. "Die Daseinsnot des modernen
      Menschen in der Amerikanischen Litteratur," *Begegnung*,
      V (January 1950), 59-61.

F314 Erdmann, Lothar. "Thomas Wolfe," *Das deutsche Wort*,
      XIV (May-June 1938), 151-152.

F315 Eschenberg, Harold. "Thomas Wolfe," *Der Bücherwurm*, XXIV (November 1938), 87.

F316 Estes, Rice. (Review of Holman), *Library Journal*, XCI (August 1966), 3729.

F317 Evans, Robert O. "Wolfe's Use of *Iliad* I. 49," *Modern Language Notes*, LXX (December 1955), 594-595.

F318 Fadiman, Clifton. "Of Nothing and the Wolfe," *American Spectator*, IV (October 1935), 4, 14.

F319 ———. "Party of One: My Un-Favorite Classics," *Holiday*, XXIII (February 1958), 13.

F320 ———. (Review of *OTATR*), *New Yorker*, XI (March 9, 1935), 68-70, 79-82.

F321 ———. (Review of *SOAN*), *Nation*, CXLII (May 27, 1936), 681-682.

F322 ———. (Review of *THB*), *New Yorker*, XVII (October 18, 1941), 93-94.

F323 ———. (Review of *TWATR*, *New Yorker*, XV (June 24, 1939), 82-84.

F324 ———. (Review of *YCGHA*), *New Yorker*, XVI (September 21, 1940), 79.

F325 Fagin, N. Bryllion. "In Search of an American Cherry Orchard." *Texas Quarterly*, I (Summer-Autumn 1958), 132-141. See 134-136 on *Mannerhouse*.

F326 Falk, Robert. "Thomas Wolfe and the Critics," *College English*, V (January 1944), 186-192.

F327 Faverty, F. E. (Review of Kennedy), *Chicago Sunday Tribune Books*, December 30, 1962, p. 4.

F328 ———. (Review of *TWR*), *Chicago Sunday Tribune Books*, June 24, 1962, p. 2.

F329 ———. (Review of Wheaton), *Chicago Sunday Tribune Books*, January 29, 1961, p. 2.

F330 Fay, Bernard. "L'école de l'infortune, ou, La nouvelle génération littéraire aux États-Unis," *Revue de Paris*, August 1, 1937, pp. 664-665. Includes Wolfe.

F331 Fecher, C. (Review of *Letters*), *Books On Trial*, XV (November 1956), 124.

F332 Ferguson, De Lancey. (Review of Nowell), *New Leader*, XXXIII (October 3, 1960), 27-28.

F333 Field, Leslie A. "Wolfe's Use of Folklore," *New York Folklore Quarterly*, XVI (Autumn 1960), 203-215.

F334 Fifield, Benjamin. "Joyce's Brother, Lawrence's Wife, Wolfe's Mother, Twain's Daughter," *Texas Quarterly*, X (1967), 69-87.

F335 Figueira, Gaston. "Poetas y prosistas americanos: II. Thomas Wolfe," *Revista Ibero-Americana*, XI (October 1946), 329-332. Partly translated in *Carolina Quarterly*, (March 1949), 40-41.

F336 Findeisson, Helmut. "Unser Porträt der Woche: Thomas Wolfe," *Börsenblatt für den Deutschen Buchhandel* [Leipzig], CXXII (1955), 622-623.

F337 Fisher, Vardis. "My Experiences with Thomas Wolfe," *Tomorrow*, X (April 1951), 24-30.

F338 ————. "Thomas Wolfe—Maxwell Perkins," *Tomorrow*, X (July 1951), 20-25.

F339 Fiskin, A. M. I. (Review of Norwood), *Chicago Sun Bookweek*, March 9, 1947, p. 11.

F340 Flaccus, Kimball. "Gotham Gambit," *Dartmouth Alumni Magazine*, XLIX (December 1956), 24-27.

F341 Fleckenstein, Adolf. (Review of *FDTM*), *Hochland*, XXXV (November 1937), 145-146.

F342 Fleming, Carl. "Thomas Wolfe: The Tortured Genius Hated by His Home Town," *Atlanta Journal and Constitution Magazine*, July 16, 1961, pp. 6-7, 32.

F343 Flora, Joseph. (Review of Fisher), *American Book Collector*, XIV (1964), 3.

F344 Forrey, Robert. "Whitman to Wolfe," *Mainstream*, XIII (October 1960), 19-27. Review of Nowell.

F345 Forsythe, Robert. "Reminiscences of Wolfe," *New Masses*, XXXVII (September 27, 1938), 14.

F346 Foster, R. E. "Fabulous Tom Wolfe," *University of Kansas City Review*, XXIII (June 1957), 260-264.

F347 Fowler, Bob. "Sales of First Book by Thomas Wolfe Passes 250,000 Mark," *Daily News* [Greensboro], May 8, 1954.

F348 Franke, Hans. "Unerwünschte Einfuhr," *Die neue Literatur*, XXXVIII (October 1937), 501-508.

F349 Frederick, J. T. (Review of *LTHM*), *Chicago Sun Book Week*, May 9, 1943, p. 4.

F350 Frenz, Horst. "Bemerkungen über Thomas Wolfe," *Die neueren Sprachen*, II, n.s., (1953), 371-377.

F351 ———. "A German Home for *Mannerhouse*," *Theatre Arts*, XL (August 1956), 62-63, 95.

F352 ———. "Thomas Wolfe als Dramatiker," *Die neueren Sprachen*, IV, n.s., (1956), 153-157.

F353 Frere, A. S. "My Friend Thomas Wolfe," *Books and Bookmen* [London], I (September 1958), 15.

F354 Friedman, M. J. (Review of Kennedy), *Books Abroad*, XXXVII (Winter 1964), 71-72.

F355 Friedrich, Delta (Review of *OTATR*), *Die christliche Welt*, L (December 19, 1936), 1117.

F356 Frings, Ketti. "O Lost! At Midnight," *Theatre Arts*, XLII (February 1958), 30-31, 91.

F357 Frise, Adolf. (Review of *LHA*), *Der Gral*, XXVIII (1933), 277.

F358 ———. (Review of *OTATR*), *Die Tat*, XXVII (November 1935), 639.

F359 Frohock, W. M. "Thomas Wolfe: Of Time and Neurosis," *Southwest Review*, XXXIII (Autumn 1948), 349-360.

F360 Fuchs, Konrad. "Thomas Wolfe, der süchende Realist," *Die neueren Sprachen*, XI, n.s., (1963), 110-117.

F361 Fuller, Edmund. "Rabelaisian, Eloquent U. S. Literary Giant," *Wall Street Journal*, February 6, 1968, p. 18. Review of Turnbull.

F362 ———. (Review of *Letters*), *Episcopal Church News* [Richmond], CXXII (October 1956), 3.

F363 ———. (Review of Raynolds), *Wall Street Journal*, January 7, 1966, p. 4.

F364 Gannett, Lewis. (Review of *FDTM*), *New York Herald Tribune*, November 15, 1935, p. 15.

F365 Gardner, Martin. (Review of Pamela Johnson and Muller), *Ethics*, LVIII (July 1948), 304.

F366 Gardner, Thomas. "The Form of *Look Homeward, Angel*," *Archiv für das Studium der neueren Sprachen und Literaturen*, CCII (November 1965), 189-193.

F367 Garrett, J. C. (Review of Muller), *Canadian Forum*, XXVII (February 1948), 260.

F368 Gehman, Richard. "Asheville, North Carolina," *Woman's Day*, XXI (June 1958), 46-47, 92-93. Largely on Wolfe.

F369 Geismar, Maxwell. "Faithfully Yours, Thomas Wolfe," *New York Times Book Review*, October 7, 1956, pp. 1, 34. Review of *Letters*.

F370 ———. "He Wrote His Life in an Open Book," *New York Times Book Review*, July 10, 1960, pp. 1, 29. Review of Nowell.

F371 ———. "Hillman and the Furies," *Yale Review*, (Summer 1946), 649-665.

F372 ———. "Man, Place and Time," *New York Times Book Review*, May 15, 1955, p. 22.

F373 ———. (Review of Pollock), *New York Times Book Review*, January 31, 1954, p. 3.

F374 ———. (Review of Watkins), *New York Times*, July 14, 1957, p. 6.

F375 Gerard, Albert. "Big Bad Wolfe," *Revue des Langues Vivantes* [Brussels], XXIII (February 1957), 86-89.

F376 Gerards, David. "Discussion of Chickamauga," *Civil War Times*, I (November 1959), 6.

F377 Gessner, R. "Gargantua of the Mews," *Saturday Review*, XXXVII (February 20, 1954), 21. Review of Pollock.

F378 Giaccari, Ada. "Struttura e stile nell' opera di Thomas Wolfe," *Studi Americani* [Rome], IX (1964), 287-352.

F379 Giaconi, Claudio. "Gogol y Thomas Wolfe," *Cuadernos Americanos*, XXI (1962), 214-228.

F380 Gibbs, Wolcott. "At Home with the Gants," *New Yorker*, XXXIII (December 7, 1957), 93-95. Review of Frings.

F381 Giese, Helmut. "Thomas Wolfe," *Das deutsche Wort*, XIII (1937), 242.

F382 Gilman, Richard. "The Worship of Thomas Wolfe," *New Republic*, CLVIII (February 24, 1968), 31-32, 34. Review of Turnbull.

F383 Gilpin, Pete. "Tom Wolfe Is Still Vibrant Personality," *Asheville Citizen-Times*, September 21, 1958.

F384 Glicksberg, Charles I. "The Letters of Thomas Wolfe," *Prairie Schooner*, XXXI (Summer 1957), 102, 157-161.

F385 ———. "Thomas Wolfe," *Canadian Forum*, XV (January 1936), 24-25. Review of *FDTM*.

F386 Golden, Harry. "Thomas Wolfe," *Carolina Israelite*, XIV (September-October, 1956), 3.

F387 Gordon, Caroline. "Rooted in Adolescence," *New York Times Book Review*, March 7, 1948, pp. 10, 12. Review of Pamela Johnson and Muller.

F388 Gould, Gerald. (Review of *LHA*), *Observer* [London], August 17, 1930.

F389 Gourlay, Bruce. "Wolfe Story Told in Splendor," *Asheville Citizen-Times*, October 5, 1961.

F390 Grace, George W. (Review of *Mannerhouse*), *Theatre Arts*, XXXIII (March 1949), 8.

F391 Green, C. B. (Review of Holman), *Georgia Review*, XV (1961), 364-365.

F392 ———. (Review of Walser), *American Literature*, XXXIII (1962), 544.

F393 ———. (Review of Watkins), *Georgia Review*, XIII (1959), 105.

F394 Green, Lewis W. "Asheville's Attitude Toward Wolfe Changes," *Daily News* [Greensboro], August 2, 1964.

F395 ———. "Relentless Time Is Thinning the Ranks of Those Whose Paths Touched Wolfe's," *Asheville Citizen-Times*, August 2, 1964.

F396 Green, Paul. "Appreciation," *Carolina Magazine,*
LXVIII (October 1938), 7.

F397 Greenblatt, William. "Thomas Wolfe: An Appreciation,"
City College Monthly, May 1939, 5-8, 24-25.

F398 Gregory, Horace. (Review of *SLD*), *New York Herald
Tribune Weekly Book Review,* January 13, 1946, p. 4.

F399 Griffin, Lloyd W. (Review of *TWR*), *Library Journal,*
LXXXVII (May 1, 1962), 1792.

F400 Gronke, E. (Review of Pfister), *Zeitschrift für Anglistik
und Amerikanistik,* III (1955), 115-117.

F401 Gunther, Albrecht E. "Amerika in der Krise," *Deutsches
Volkstum* [Potsdam], (July 1933), 584-587.
Includes critical notes on Wolfe and *LHA.*

F402 Gurganus, Ransom. "Thomas Wolfe, Undergraduate,"
Washington Square Critic, I (May 1935), 1-2.

F403 Hadecke, W. "Nekrolog auf Thomas Wolfe,"
Sinn und Form, VII (August 2, 1956).

F404 Hale, Nancy. "Can Writers Ignore Critics?" *Saturday
Review,* LI (March 23, 1968), 22-24, 60-61.

F405 Halperin, Irving. "Faith as Dilemma in Thomas Wolfe,"
Prairie Schooner, XXVII (1953), 213-217.

F406 ———. "Hunger for Life: Thomas Wolfe, A Young
Faust," *American-German Review,* XXX (August-
September 1964), 12-14, 31.

F407 ———. "Jews in the Novels of Thomas Wolfe,"
Jewish Day-Journal, March 16, 1958.

F408 ———. "Man Alive," *Delphian Quarterly*, XLI (Winter 1958), 1-3, 31.

F409 ———. "Torrential Production: Thomas Wolfe's Writing Practices," *Arizona Quarterly*, XIV (Spring 1958), 29-34.

F410 ———. "Wolfe's *Of Time and the River*," *Explicator*, XVIII (November 1959), 1, 3.

F411 Hamblen, Abigail Ann. "Ruth Suckow and Thomas Wolfe: A Study in Similarity," *Forum* [Houston, Texas], III (Winter 1961), ix, 27-31.

F412 Hamilton, A. (Review of *FDTM*), *Books and Bookmen*, VII (December 1965), 52.

F413 Hamner, Earl. "Thomas Wolfe: Biography in Sound," *Carolina Quarterly*, IX (Fall 1956), 5-19.

F414 Handlin, Oscar. (Review of Turnbull), *Atlantic Monthly*, CCXXI (March 1968), 130.

F415 Hansen, Harry. "Ah, Life! Life!" *World* [New York], October 26, 1929. Review of *LHA*.

F416 Harris, Arthur S. "The House on Spruce Street," *Antioch Review*, XVI (Winter 1956-1957), 506-511.

F417 ———. "Thomas Wolfe's One Great Book," *World in Books*, I (September 1946), 5.

F418 Hart, Henry. (Review of *YCGHA*), *New Masses*, XXXVII (October 22, 1940), 25-26.

F419 Hartley, Lois. "Theme in Thomas Wolfe's 'The Lost Boy' and 'God's Lonely Man,'" *Georgia Review*, XV (1961), 230-235.

F420 Hartung, Rudolph. "Der amerikanische Schriftsteller Thomas Wolfe in seinen Briefen," *Die Zeit* [Hamburg], XVII, no. 6 (1962), 13.

F421 Haugen, Einar. "Thomas Wolfe's siste bok," *Samtiden* [Oslo], LV (1946), 641-645.

F422 Hawthorne, Mark D. "Thomas Wolfe's Use of the Poetic Fragment," *Modern Fiction Studies*, XI (Autumn 1965), 234-244.

F423 Hayes, Richard. "The Shock of Recognition," *Commonweal*, LXVIII (April 4, 1958), 16-18. Review of Frings.

F424 Heiderstadt, Dorothy. "Studying under Thomas Wolfe," *Mark Twain Quarterly*, VIII (Winter 1950), 7-8.

F425 Heiseler, Bernt von. "Neue Amerikaner," *Deutsche Zeitschrift*, XLIX (August-September 1936), 465-466.

F426 Hellman, Geoffrey T. (Review of *LHA*), *New Republic*, LXI (December 18, 1929), 122.

F427 Helmcke, Hans. "Die 'Thomas Wolfe renaissance' in den Vereinigten Staaten," *Jahrbuch für Amerikastudien*, IX (1964), 181-195.

F428 Henderson, Archibald. "The Puzzle Thomas Wolfe Left for Posterity," *News and Observer* [Raleigh], March 30, 1941.

F429 ———. "Thomas Wolfe, Playmaker," *Carolina Play-book*, XVI (March-June 1943), 27-33.

F430 Hennecke, Hans. "Thomas Wolfe," *Europäische Revue*, XIV (January 1938), 74.

F431 Hesse, Hermann. (Review of *LHA*), *Die neue Rundschau*,
XLVI (December 1935), 670.

F432 Hewes, Henry. "The Lonely American,"
Saturday Review, XLII (May 6, 1959), 30.

F433 ———. "Thomas Wolfe's 'Angel,'" *Saturday Review*,
XL (November 23, 1957), 27-28. Review of Frings.
See also December 14, 1957, issue, p. 22.

F434 Hicklen, J. B. "Two Giants of Letters," *State*
[Raleigh], April 1, 1939.

F435 Hicks, Granville. "Our Novelists' Shifting Reputations,"
English Journal, XL (January 1951), 1-4.

F436 ———. "The Volcanic Mr. Wolfe," *Saturday Review*,
LI (February 3, 1968), 23-24, 66. Review of Turnbull.

F437 Higham, Claire. "Thomas Wolfe," *Rosary College Eagle*,
XXVII (1953), 19-22.

F438 Hilfer, Anthony C. "Wolfe's Altamont: The Mimesis
of Being," *Georgia Review*, XVIII (Winter 1964),
451-456.

F439 Hill, John S. "Eugene Gant and the Ghost of Ben,"
Modern Fiction Studies, XI (Autumn 1965), 245-249.

F440 Hillyer, Robert. "Prose Poems from Thomas Wolfe,"
New York Times Book Review, September 30, 1945, p. 7.
Review of *SLD*.

F441 Hindus, Milton. "American Writer," *Commentary*, XXII
(December 1956), 585-588.

F442 ———. (Review of *Letters*), *Chicago Sunday Tribune*, October 14, 1956, p. 2.

F443 Hoagland, Clayton. (Review of *FDTM*), *New York Sun*, November 14, 1935.

F444 Hodges, Ed. "Wolfe Led Busy 'Solitary' Life," *Morning Herald* [Durham, N. C.], May 22, 1955.

F445 Hoelscher, Ruth. "Einige Worte über Thomas Wolfe," *Wochenpost*, XLVI (January 1951), 7.

F446 Hoentzsch, Alfred. "Thomas Wolfe: ein Versuch," *Eckart* [Wittenberg], XXIV (1954-1955), 132-139.

F447 Hoepfl, H. "Thomas Wolfe," *Hanoverscher Kurier*, 1939, p. 305.

F448 Hoffman, Frederick J. (Review of Rubin), *American Literature*, XXVII (1956), 602-604.

F449 Hoffman, Paul. (Review of *FDTM*), *Atlantic Monthly*, CLVII (April 1936), 9.

F450 ———. (Review of *OTATR*), *Atlantic Monthly*, CLVI (August 1935), 6.

F451 Hogan, William. (Review of Nowell), *San Francisco Chronicle*, July 10, 1960, p. 26.

F452 ———. (Review of Wheaton), *San Francisco Chronicle*, January 24, 1961, p. 27.

F453 Holman, C. Hugh. "Hungry Wolfe," *Christian Century*, LXXVIII (April 26, 1961), 540. Review of Wheaton.

F454 ———. "Loneliness at the Core," *New Republic*, CXXXIII (October 10, 1955), 16-17.

F455 ———. "Portrait of an American Romantic," *Virginia Quarterly Review*, XLIX (Spring 1968), 329-332. Review of Turnbull.

F456 ———. "Thomas Wolfe: A Bibliographical Study," *Texas Studies in Literature and Language*, I (Autumn 1959), 427-445.

F457 ———. "Thomas Wolfe and the Stigma of Autobiography," *Virginia Quarterly Review*, XL (1964), 614-625.

F458 ———. "Thomas Wolfe as Artist," *Virginia Quarterly Review*, XXXIX (Winter 1963), 132-135. Review of Kennedy.

F459 ———. "Thomas Wolfe's Berlin," *Saturday Review*, L (March 11, 1967), 66, 69, 90.

F460 ———. "Wolfe and His Public Persona," *Virginia Quarterly Review*, XXXVI (Autumn 1960), 646-649.

F461 Hornberger, Theodore. (Review of Pollock), *College English*, XV (May 1954), 485-486.

F462 Hough, Robert L. (Review of Nowell), *Prairie Schooner*, XXV (1961-1962), 284-285.

F463 Hoult, Norah. (Review of *TWATR*), *Foylibra* [London], no. 236 (1947), 7.

F464 Howard, William. "Praise for Thomas Wolfe," *New Republic*, LXXXII (May 1, 1935), 343.

F465 Howe, Irving. "Thomas Wolfe's Genius and Anguish in His Letters," *New York Herald Tribune Book Review*, October 7, 1956, pp. 1, 8. Review of *Letters*.

F466 Howell, Mildred. "Thomas Wolfe and His Home," *Coraddi* [Greensboro], XLIII (October 1938), 3-6.

F467 Hubbard, Louise. "Boardinghouse Home of Wolfe Achieves Immortality in North Carolina," *Daily Advocate* [Baton Rouge], April 27, 1958.

F468 Huehnerfeld, P. "Thomas Wolfes Briefe an die Mutter: Einwände gegen ein Vorwort von Ina Seidel," *Die Zeit*, V, no. 25 (1950), 5.

F469 Huff, William H. "Thomas Clayton Wolfe," *Wilson Library Bulletin*, XXV (September 1950), 72-74.

F470 Hughes, Aline. "Thomas Wolfe," *State* [Raleigh], December 29, 1934, p. 24.

F471 Hutsell, James K. "Thomas Wolfe and 'Altamont,'" *Southern Packet*, IV (April 1948), 1-8.

F472 ———. "The Wolfe Legend Continues to Grow," *Asheville Citizen-Times*, October 19, 1947.

F473 Ivey, Pete. "Tommy Wolfe's School Days," *State* [Raleigh], May 25, 1935, pp. 9, 22.

F474 Izaguirre, Rodolfo. "Thomas Wolfe, al huida hacia el frenesi," *Sardia* [Caracas], VI (1961), 32-41.

F475 Jack, Peter M. "Remembering Thomas Wolfe," *New York Times Book Review*, October 2, 1938, pp. 2, 28.

F476 ———. (Review of *FDTM*), *New York Times Book Review*, November 24, 1935, p. 6.

F477 ———. (Review of *OTATR*), *New York Times Book Review*, March 10, 1935, p. 1.

F478 ———. (Review of *SOAN*), *New York Times Book Review*, May 3, 1936, p. 2.

F479 Jackson, Katherine G. (Review of Raynolds), *Harper's Magazine*, CCXXXII (April 1966), 123.

F480 ———. (Review of Turnbull), *Harper's Magazine*, CCXXXVI (March 1968), 149-150.

F481 ———. (Review of Wheaton), *Harper's Magazine*, CCXXII (February 1961), 106.

F482 Jaffard, Paul. "L'oeuvre de Thomas Wolfe," *Critique*, VII (August-September 1951), 686-693.

F483 Jaloux, Edmond. "Thomas Wolfe: La Toile et le Roc," *Psyche*, IV (February 1, 1947), 202-210. Review of *TWATR*.

F484 James, Olive B. (Review of *TWATR*), *Delphian Quarterly*, XXII (July 1939), 53-54.

F485 Jeffares, A. N. (Review of Nowell), *Time and Tide*, XXX (March 30, 1951), 528.

F486 Jellife, Belinda. "More on Tom Wolfe," *American Mercury*, LXV (July 1947), 125-126.

F487 Johnson, Elmer D. "On Translating Thomas Wolfe," *American Speech*, XXXII (May 1957), 95-101.

F488 ———. "Thomas Wolfe Abroad," *Louisiana Library Association Bulletin*, XVIII (1955), 9-11.

F489 ———. "Thomas Wolfe as a Literary Critic," *Radford Review*, XX (Summer 1966), 107-117.

F490 Johnson, Pamela H. "Thomas Wolfe, A Critical Study," *Windmill*, II (1947), 40-48.

F491 ———. "Thomas Wolfe and the Kicking Season," *Encounter*, XII (April 1959), 77-80. Review of *Letters*.

F492 Johnson, Stewart. "Mrs. Julia Wolfe," *New Yorker*, XXXIV (April 12, 1958), 39-44.

F493 Johnson, William P. "Some of Thomas Wolfe's Quaker Connections," *The North Carolinian*, I (December 1955), 100-102.

F494 Jones, Howard M. (Review of *THB*), *Saturday Review of Literature*, XXIV (October 25, 1941), 7-8.

F495 ———. (Review of *TWATR*), *Boston Transcript*, July 1, 1939, p. 1.

F496 ———. "Social Notes on the South," *Virginia Quarterly Review*, XI (July 1935), 452-457. Includes criticism of *OTATR*.

F497 ———. "Thomas Wolfe's Short Stories," *Saturday Review of Literature*, XIII (November 30, 1935), 13. Review of *FDTM*.

F498 Jones, Weimar. (Review of *OTATR*), *Asheville Citizen-Times*, April 21, 1935.

F499 Kantor, Seymour. (Review of *OTATR*), *Washington Square Critic*, I (May 1935), 15-16.

F500 Karsten, Otto. (Review of *LHA* and *OTATR*),
Die Literatur, XXXVIII (February-March 1936),
308-311. See also *Das deutsche Wort*, XII
(April 1936), 454.

F501 ———. (Review of *FDTM*), *Die Literatur*, XXXIX
(May 1937), 503.

F502 Katz, Joseph. "Balzac and Thomas Wolfe: A Study of
Self-Destructive Overproductivity," *Psychoanalysis*,
V (Summer 1957), 3-19.

F503 Kauffman, Bernice. "Bibliography of Periodical Articles
on Thomas Wolfe," *Bulletin of Bibliography*, XVII
(May-August 1942), 162-165, 172-190.

F504 Kazin, Alfred. "Chile Takin' Notes," *New Republic*,
CVIII (May 3, 1943), 607-609.

F505 ———. "Rhetorik und Verzweiflung," *Der Monat*,
I (October 1941), 55-63, 78-80.

F506 ———. (Review of Turnbull), *Washington Post Book
World*, January 28, 1968, pp. 1, 3.

F507 ———. (Review of *TWATR*), *New York Herald
Tribune Books*, June 25, 1939, p. 1.

F508 ———. "Thomas Wolfe," *Die amerikanische
Rundschau*, II, no. 5 (1946).

F509 ———. "The Writer's Friend," *New Yorker*, XXVII
(February 17, 1951), 88-92.

F510 Kearns, Frank. "Tom Wolfe on the Drama,"
Carolina Quarterly, XI (Spring 1960), 5-10.
Contains Wolfe's autobiographical statement.

F511 Keever, T. W. "The Legend of a Lost Man,"
Bluets, [Asheville] XVIII (January 1945), 43-48.

F512 Keister, Don A. "From Fitzgerald to Thomas Wolfe,"
Cleveland Plain Dealer, February 4, 1968.
Review of Turnbull.

F513 Kelly, W. W. (Review of Holman), *South Atlantic
Quarterly*, LXVI (Spring 1967), 275.

F514 Kennedy, Richard S. "Thomas Wolfe and the American
Experience," *Modern Fiction Studies*, XI (Autumn
1965), 219-233.

F515 ———. "Thomas Wolfe at Harvard," *Harvard Library
Bulletin*, IV (Spring-Autumn 1950), 172-190,
304-319.

F516 ———. "Thomas Wolfe's Don Quixote," *College
English*, XXIII (December 1961), 185-191.

F517 ———. "Wolfe's *Look Homeward, Angel* as a Novel
of Development," *South Atlantic Quarterly*, LXIII
(Spring 1964), 218-226.

F518 Kennedy, William F. "Are Our Novelists Hostile to the
American Economic System?" *Dalhousie Review*,
XXXV (Spring 1955), 32-44. Largely on Fitzgerald
and Wolfe.

F519 ———. "Economic Ideas in Contemporary Literature:
The Novels of Thomas Wolfe," *Southern Economic
Journal*, XX (July 1953), 35-50.

F520 Kerr, David. "Wolfe Gives Second Lecture in His Life,"
Silver and Gold [University of Colorado],
August 8, 1935.

F521 Kerr, Walter. "*Look Homeward, Angel,*" *New York
Herald Tribune*, November 29, 1957. Review of Frings.

F522 Kilgore, Carl J. "Thomas Wolfe: A Flash of Genius,"
Aurora, [Emory, Va.] VI (Spring 1949), 8-10, 22-34.

F523 Kinne, Wisner P. "Enter Tom Wolfe," *Harvard Alumni
Bulletin*, LVII (October 23, 1954), 101-102, 122-123.

F524 Klau, Werner. "Ein Dichter Amerikas," *Deutsche
Zukunft*, V (January 10, 1937).

F525 Klausler, Alfred P. "Hungry Wolfe," *Christian Century*,
LXXVIII (April 26, 1961), 540-542.
Review of Nowell.

F526 Knesebeck, Paridam von den. "Thomas Wolfe: die
Legende seines Lebens," *Deutsche Beiträge*, III
(1949), 220-234.

F527 Koch, Frederick H. "Thomas Wolfe, Playmaker,"
Carolina Play-book, VIII (June 1935), 65-69.
See also September 1938 and March-June 1943 issues.

F528 ———. "A Young Man of Promise," *Theatre Arts*,
XXIII (February 1939), 150.

F529 Kohler, Dayton. "All Fury Spent: A Note on Thomas
Wolfe," *Southern Literary Messenger*, II (October
1940), 560-563. Review of *YCGHA*.

F530 ———. "Thomas Wolfe: Prodigal and Lost,"
College English, I (October 1939), 1-10. Also in English
Journal, XXVIII (October 1939), 609-618.

F531 Koischwitz, Otto. (Review of YCGHA), Die Literatur,
XLIII (February 1941), 240.

F532 Korn, Karl. "Thomas Wolfe," Die Tat, XXIX
(May 1937), 128-129.

F533 Kreymborg, Alfred. "Thomas Wolfe, Poet," Saturday
Review of Literature, XXVIII (November 3, 1945),
32. Review of SLD.

F534 Krim, Seymour. "Wolfe, the Critics, and the People,"
Commonweal, LVIII (September 4, 1953),
540-542.

F535 Kronenberger, Louis. "Thomas Wolfe—
Autobiographer," Nation, CXLIX (July 15, 1939),
75-76. Review of TWATR.

F536 Kussy, Bella. "The Vitalist Trend and Thomas Wolfe,"
Sewanee Review, L (July-September 1942), 306-323.

F537 Lalou, M. R. (Review of TWATR), Les Nouvelles
Littéraires, January 8, 1948, p. 3.

F538 Lane, Lauriest. (Review of Kennedy), Dalhousie
Review, LXIII (Autumn 1963), 424-425.

F539 Lanzinger, Klaus. "Die Reise im Zug als Vorwürf und
Sinnbild bei Thomas Wolfe," Die Neueren Sprachen,
VII (1962), 293-307.

F540 Lask, Thomas. "Giant in the Land," New York Times,
February 13, 1968, p. 45. Review of Turnbull.

F541 Lathrop, Virginia T. "Hendersonville Monument Identified as Thomas Wolfe's 'Angel,'" *Asheville Citizen-Times*, November 20, 1949.

F542 ———. "Wolfe's Golden October," *Morning Herald* [Durham, N. C], October 21, 1951.

F543 Latimer, Margery. "The American Family," *New York Herald Tribune Books*, November 3, 1929, p. 20. Review of *LHA*.

F544 Leary, Lewis. "Romans à cléf," *Saturday Review*, XL (October 5, 1957), 13. Review of Watkins.

F545 Le Breton, W. (Review of Nowell), *Études Anglaises*, XV (1962), 100-101.

F546 Ledig-Rowohlt, Heinrich M. "Thomas Wolfe in Berlin," *Der Monat, I* (October 1948), 69-77. See also a translation and adaptation of this article in *American Scholar*, XXII (Spring 1953), 185-201; also a similar article with the same title, *Berlin im Spiegel* (Berlin and the U. S. A. Special Issue), 1962, 86-89.

F547 Lessing, Doris. "Thomas Wolfe, Myth-Maker," *Manchester Guardian*, October 9, 1958, p. 11. Review of *Letters*.

F548 Lichtinhagen, Leo. "Thomas Wolfe's *Herrenhaus*," *Zeitschrift für Kultur und Politik* [Frankfurt], II (February 1954).

F549 Lieber, Maxim. "Letter to the Editor," *Times Literary Supplement* [London], June 16, 1961, p. 373.

F550 Little, Thomas. "The Thomas Wolfe Collection of William B. Wisdom," *Harvard Library Bulletin*, I (Autumn 1947), 280-287.

F551 Littlejohn, Daniel. (Review of Turnbull), *Reporter*, XXXVII (May 30, 1968), 41-43.

F552 Lucignani, Luciano. "Lettera da Roma sull' annata teatrale," *Communita*, no. 72 (August-September 1959), 78-89. Includes comments on Wolfe play.

F553 Ludwig, Heinz. "Ein Beitrag zum Verständnis von Thomas Wolfe's 'Death the Proud Brother,' " *Die Neueren Sprachen*, IV, n.s. (1966), 173-182.

F554 Lynch, W. J. (Review of Turnbull), *America*, CXVIII (March 9, 1968), 326.

F555 Lynn, Kenneth S. "Cry Wolfe!" *Nation*, CXCI (July 23, 1960), 56. Review of Nowell.

F556 McAfee, Helen. (Review of *OTATR*), *Yale Review*, XXIV (Summer 1935), vi-vii.

F557 Macaulay, Thurston. "Thomas Wolfe: A Writer's Problems," *Publishers' Weekly*, CXXXIV (December 24, 1938), 2150-2152.

F558 McClain, John. "Wolfe's Novel Made into Huge Success," *Journal-American* [New York], November 29, 1957. Review of Frings.

F559 McCole, Camille. "Thomas Wolfe Embraces Life," *Catholic World*, CXLIII (April 1936), 42-48.

F560 McCoy, George W. "Asheville and Thomas Wolfe," *North Carolina Historical Review*, XXX (April 1953), 200-217.

F561 ———. "Asheville Man Is New Author," *Asheville Citizen*, July 26, 1929.

F562 ———. (Review of Walser), *North Carolina Historical Review*, XXXVIII (1961), 414-415.

F563 McCoy, Lola Love. (Review of *LHA*), *Asheville Citizen-Times*, October 20, 1929.

F564 McDonald, Donald. "Thomas Wolfe's 'Bloody Barn' to Become Memorial to Him." *Daily News* [Greensboro], August 22, 1948.

F565 McDowell, David. "The Renaissance of Thomas Wolfe," *Sewanee Review*, LVI (Summer 1948), 536-544.

F566 McElderry, B. R., Jr. "The Autobiographical Problem in Thomas Wolfe's Earlier Novels," *Arizona Quarterly*, IV (Winter 1948), 315-324.

F567 ———. "The Durable Humor of *Look Homeward, Angel*," *Arizona Quarterly*, XI (Summer 1955), 123-128.

F568 ———. (Review of Purdue Speech), *Personalist*, XLVI (Winter 1965), 120-121.

F569 ———. (Review of Kennedy), *Personalist*, XLIV (Fall 1963), 410-411.

F570 ———. "Thomas Wolfe, Dramatist," *Modern Drama*, VI (May 1963), 1-11.

F571 ————. "Wolfe and Emerson on 'Flow,' " *Modern Fiction Studies*, II (1956) 77-78.

F572 McGovern, Hugh. "A Note on Thomas Wolfe," *New Mexico Quarterly*, XVII (Summer 1947), 198-200.

F573 ————. (Review of Muller), *New Mexico Quarterly*, XVIII (Spring 1948), 109-110.

F574 MacLachlan, J. M. "Folk Concepts in the Novels of Thomas Wolfe," *Southern Folklore Quarterly*, IX (December 1945), 175-186.

F575 Macmillan, Mary J. "Thomas Wolfe Returns," *Carolina Magazine*, LXVIII (October 1938), 6-7.

F576 McNeil, Ben Dixon. "Reporter Reminisces on Wolfe's Visit Here," *News and Observer* [Raleigh], November 9, 1950.

F577 Maddocks, Melvin. "Can Thomas Wolfe Go Home Again?" *Christian Science Monitor*, February 8, 1968, p. 11. Review of Turnbull.

F578 ————. "Wolfe Biography: Abundance or Excess?" *Christian Science Monitor*, July 7, 1960, p. 7. Review of Nowell.

F579 Madry, Robert W. "Wolfe's Greatest Ambition Unfulfilled at His Death," *Journal* [Winston-Salem, N. C.], September 25, 1938. Similar article in *Herald-Sun* [Durham, N. C.], and *Daily News* [Greensboro], same date.

F580 Magnus, Peter "Thomas Wolfe," *Syn og Segn* [Oslo], LIII (March 1947), 138-144.

F581 Maloff, Saul. "Man Mountain," *Newsweek*, LXXI
(February 5, 1968), 78-80. Review of Turnbull.

F582 Maloney, Martin. "A Study of Semantic States:
Thomas Wolfe and the Faustian Sickness,"
General Semantics Bulletin, nos. 16-17, 1955, pp. 15-25.

F583 Mandel, Siegfried. (Review of *A Western Journal*),
Saturday Review, XXXIV (August 18, 1951),
31-32.

F584 Mannes, Marya. "Look Backward, Playwright,"
Reporter, XVII (December 26, 1957), 33-34.
Review of Frings.

F585 Mansfield, Gardner. "Gin and Tom Wolfe," *New York
Times Book Review*, March 26, 1961, p. 41.

F586 Mariella, Sister. (Review of *THB*), *Commonweal*,
XXXV (November 14, 1941), 97.

F587 Martin, F. D. "The Artist, Autobiography, and
Thomas Wolfe," *Bucknell Review*, V (1955), 15-28.

F588 Mary William, Sister. (Review of Turnbull), *Best Sellers*,
XXVII (February 15, 1968), 437.

F589 Meade, Julian R. "Thomas Wolfe on the Use of Fact
in Fiction," *New York Herald Tribune Books*,
April 14, 1935, p. 8.

F590 Meade, Robert D. "You Can't Escape Autobiography:
New Letters of Thomas Wolfe," *Atlantic Monthly*,
CLXXXVI (November 1950), 80-83.

F591 Mebane, John. "Laughter and Tears," *University of
North Carolina Magazine*, LIX (February 2, 1930), 4.
Review of *LHA*.

F592 Meder, Thomas. "Notes on Thomas Wolfe and the
American Spirit," *Carolina Magazine*, LXVIII
(October 1938), 22-24.

F593 Menck, Clara. "Unermesslich und grausam wie Gott,"
Wort und Wahrheit, V (1950), 256-266.

F594 Meyerhoff, Hans. "Death of a Genius: The Last Days
of Thomas Wolfe," *Commentary*, XIII (January 1952),
44-51. German translation in *Der Monat*, V (1953),
581-589.

F595 Middlebrook, L. Ruth. "Further Memories of Tom
Wolfe," *American Mercury*, LXIV (April 1947),
413-420.

F596 ———. "Reminiscences of Tom Wolfe," *American
Mercury*, LXIII (November 1946), 544-549.

F597 Miles, George. (Review of Muller), *Commonweal*,
XLIX (December 12, 1947), 231.

F598 Miller, Draughn. "Asheville Proud of Him Now,"
Observer [Charlotte], October 12, 1952.

F599 Miller, Edward M. "Gulping the Great West: Here's
How Three Men Rambled Through 11 Western National
Parks in a Two-Week Vacation," *The Oregonian*
[Portland], July 31, 1938, pp. 1, 9.

F600 ———. "Gulping the West. . . . But You Can't Eat
Scenery," *The Oregonian* [Portland], August 7, 1938,
p. 6. These two articles report on the trip Wolfe
made just prior to his death.

F601 Miller, H. "Mother and Son," *Nation*, CLVI (June 5, 1943), 811. Review of *LTHM*.

F602 Miller, Nolan. "Joyce and Wolfe," *Antioch Review*, XVI (December 1956), 511-517. Review of *Letters*.

F603 Mims, Edwin. "A Semi-Centennial Survey of North Carolina's Intellectual Progress," *North Carolina Historical Review*, XXIV (April 1947), 235-257. See 253-257 for Mims' view of Wolfe.

F604 Mitgang, Herbert. (Review of Nowell), *New York Times*, July 8, 1960, p. 19.

F605 Mjöberg, Jöran. "Thomas Wolfe och Amerika," *Ord och Bild* [Stockholm], LXIII (1954), 163-170.

F606 Molzahn, Ilse. "Dem Andenken Thomas Wolfes," *Deutsches Zukunft*, VI (September 25, 1938), 9.

F607 Moring, Richard. "Thomas Wolfe," *Die neue Rundschau*, XLIX (March 1938), 310.

F608 Mosher, John. (Review of *YCGHA*), *New Yorker*, XVI (September 21, 1940), 78-79.

F609 Mott, Sara Louise. "Strait-Jacket on a Whale," *The Search* [Columbia, S. C.], I (April 1962), 44-49.

F610 Moynahan, Julian. "Hick Napoleons," *Spectator*, CCVI (April 21, 1961), 568-569.

F611 Muller, Herbert J. "Life of Thomas Wolfe 'Gets Him Right,'" *New York Herald Tribune Book Review*, July 10, 1960, p. 3. Review of Nowell.

F612 Murphy, Eugene. (Review of Reeves), *Books Abroad*, XXXI (Winter 1957), 45.

F613 Nagelschmidt, Joe. "Ungentlemanly, with a Temper," *Weekly* [Chapel Hill], July 7, 1960. Review of Nowell.

F614 Napier, Elizabeth. "Wolfe Data to Be Presented to U.N.C.," *Observer* [Charlotte], April 23, 1950.

F615 Natanson, M. A. "Privileged Moment: A Study in the Rhetoric of Thomas Wolfe," *Quarterly Journal of Speech*, XLIII (April 1957), 143-150.

F616 Naves, Glen. "Brother of Noted Author Recalls Life with Wolfe," *Journal* [Spartanburg, S. C.], November 2, 1955.

F617 Nichols, Mark. (Review of Frings), *Coronet*, XLIII (March 1958), 20.

F618 Norman, Charles. "Tom Wolfe's Books Record Agony," *Herald-Sun* [Durham, N. C.], September 16, 1938.

F619 Norman, James. "The Gargantuan Gusto of Thomas Wolfe," *Scholastic*, XXVII (November 2, 1935), 5, 12.

F620 North, Sterling. (Review of *SLD*), *Book Week*, September 23, 1945, p. 2.

F621 Norwid, Helena. "Thomas Wolfe na tle nurtow literakich w Ameryce niedzywojennej," *Kwartalnik Neofilologiczny* [Warsaw], XII (1965), 255-270.

F622 ———. "Ucieczka od samego siebie: Thomas Wolfe," *Kwartalnik Neofilologiczny* [Warsaw], XIV (1967), 395-413.

F623 Norwood, Hayden. "Julia Wolfe: Web of Memory," *Virginia Quarterly Review*, XX (April 1944), 236-250.

F624 Nowell, Elizabeth. "The Death of Tom Wolfe," *Esquire*, LIV (April 1960), 144-147.

F625 Nuhn, Ferner. (Review of *FDTM*), *New York Herald Tribune Books*, November 17, 1935, p. 7.

F626 Obendick, Edward. (Review of Voigt), *Anglia*, LXXX (1960), 359-360.

F627 Odets, Clifford. "When Thomas Wolfe Went Home Again," *Mountain Life and Work*, XXIV (April 1958), 26-28.

F628 ———. "When Wolfe Came Home," *New York Times*, September 14, 1958, pp. x, 3.

F629 O'Faolain, Sean. (Review of *OTATR*), *Spectator*, CLV (August 23, 1935), 300.

F630 O'Meara, Frank. "Thomas Wolfe," *Bluets*, [Asheville] XV (1942), 20.

F631 Orkeny, Istvan. "Néhány szó Thomas Wolfe-ról." *Nagyvilág* [Budapest], IV (1958), 491-492.

F632 Ownbey, E. H. "The Marble Man's Wife," *Bluets*, [Asheville] XIX (1947), 21.

F633 Paeschke, Hans. "Thomas Wolfe," *Deutsche Zukunft*, IV (January 20, 1936), 20.

F634 Parris, John. "October Was Tom Wolfe's Month," *Asheville Citizen*, October 5, 1941.

F635 Patterson, Isobel M. "Turns with a Bookworm," *New York Herald Tribune* Books, February 24, 1935, p. 18. Review of *OTATR*.

F636 Penley, Grover. "Thomas Wolfe: An Interview with His Sister," *Bluets*, [Asheville] XIII (1940), 9-10.

F637 Perkins, Maxwell. "Reply to Wolfe's Last Letter," *Harvard Library Bulletin*, I (August 1947), 279.

F638 ———. "Scribner's and Thomas Wolfe," *Carolina Magazine*, LXVIII (October 1938), 15-17.

F639 ———. "Thomas Wolfe," *Scribner's Magazine*, CV (May 1939), 5.

F640 ———. "Thomas Wolfe," *Harvard Library Bulletin*, I (Autumn 1947) 269-277. Parts of this in *Vogue* (February 1, 1948), pp. 177, 260-261.

F641 Peterson, Houston. "From Movable Type to Thomas Wolfe," *Saturday Review*, XLIII (April 23, 1960), 46-48. See also p. 12.

F642 Phillips, Gene. "Milton and Wolfe," *Saturday Review of Literature*, XL (December 21, 1957) 26.

F643 Phillipson, J. S. (Review of Wheaton), *Catholic Library World*, XXXIII (November 1961), 183-184.

F644 ———. "Thomas Wolfe: The Appeal to Youth," *Catholic Library World*, XXXII (November 1960), 101-102.

F645 Phinney, A. W. (Review of *Short Novels*), *Christian Science Monitor*, June 15, 1961, p. 11.

F646 Pickrel, Paul. "A Novelist's Life," *Harper's Monthly*, CCXXI (August 1960), 97-98.

F647 Polk, William. "Thomas Wolfe," *Carolina Magazine*, LXVIII (October 1938), 4-5.

F648 Powell, Desmond. "Of Thomas Wolfe," *Arizona Quarterly*, I (Spring 1945), 28-36.

F649 ———. "Wolfe's Farewells," *Accent*, I (Winter 1941), 114-118.

F650 Prescott, Orville. (Review of *Letters*), *New York Times*, October 5, 1956, p. 23.

F651 Preston, George R., Jr. "Thomas Wolfe, American Literary Genius," *News and Observer* [Raleigh, N. C.], May 10, 1953.

F652 Pritchett, V. S. "The Talking Dinosaur," *New Statesman and Nation*, LXI (March 31, 1961), 516. Review of Nowell.

F653 ———. "Self-Portrait of a Mastodon," *New Statesman and Nation*, LVI (September 27, 1958), 423-424. Review of *Letters*.

F654 Pruette, Lorine. (Review of *LTHM*), *New York Herald Tribune Weekly Book Review*, May 2, 1943, p. 4.

F655 ———. (Review of Norwood), *New York Herald Tribune Books*, February 16, 1947, p. 6.

F656 Pugh, C. E. "Of Thomas Wolfe," *Mark Twain Quarterly*, VII (Summer-Fall 1945), 13-14.

F657 Pusey, William W. "The German Vogue of Thomas Wolfe," *Germanic Review*, XXIII (April 1948), 131-148.

F658 Quennell, Peter. (Review of *OTATR*), *New Statesman and Nation*, X (August 24, 1935), 253.

F659 Radecki, Sigismund von. (Review of *LHA*), *Der Querschnitt*, XIII (October 1933), 503.

F660 Raimbault, R. N. "Un romancier fleuve," *Nouvelles Littéraires Artistiques et Scientifiques* [Paris], XXX, no. 1234 (1951), 1.

F661 Ramsay, Warren. (Review of Delakas), *Comparative Literature*, VI (Spring 1954), 174-176.

F662 Rascoe, Burton. (Review of *LHA*), *Arts and Decorations*, LIX (February, 1930), 106.

F663 ———. "Of Time and Thomas Wolfe," *Newsweek*, XIII (June 26, 1939), 36. Review of *OTATR*.

F664 ———. "Thomas Wolfe Sings and Shouts in His Gargantuan New Novel," *New York Herald Tribune Books*, March 10, 1935, p. 1.

F665 ———. "Wolfe, Farrell, and Hemingway," *American Mercury*, LI (December 1940), 493-494.

F666 Rauch, Karl. "Das realistisch-romantische Epos
Amerikas," *Kölnische Zeitung*, April 26, 1936.
Review of *OTATR*.

F667 Raynolds, Robert. (Review of *LHA*), *Scribner's
Magazine*, LXXXVI (December 1929), unpaged.

F668 Reaver, J. Russell, and Strozier, Robert I. "Thomas Wolfe
and Death," *Georgia Review*, XVI (Fall 1962),
330-350.

F669 Redman, Ben Ray. "Biography of Thomas Wolfe Shows
Man as He Really Was," *Herald-American Stars*
[Syracuse], July 10, 1960, p. 13.

F670 Reed, Douglas. "Wolfe Biography Monumental Effort
to 'Get Tom Right,' " *Asheville Citizen-Times*,
June 19, 1960. Review of Nowell.

F671 ———. "Thomas Wolfe Exhibit Set at Library Monday,"
Asheville Citizen-Times, September 30, 1956, p. 6.

F672 Reeves, George M., Jr. "Mr. Eliot and Thomas Wolfe,"
South Atlantic Bulletin, XXXII (November 1967),
7-8.

F673 ———. "A Note on the Life and Letters of Thomas
Wolfe," *South Atlantic Quarterly*, LVII (Spring
1958), 216-221.

F674 Reeves, Walter Paschal, Jr. "The Humor of Thomas
Wolfe," *Southern Folklore Quarterly*, XXIV
(June 1960), 109-120.

F675 ———. (Review of Kennedy), *South Atlantic Quarterly*,
LXII (Summer 1963), 435-436.

F676 ———. (Review of *Short Novels*), *South Atlantic Quarterly*, LXI (Winter 1962), 115.

F677 ———. (Review of Wolfe's *Purdue Speech*), *South Atlantic Quarterly*, LXIV (Summer 1965), 428.

F678 ———. "Thomas Wolfe: Notes on Three Characters," *Modern Fiction Studies*, XI (Autumn 1965), 275-285.

F679 ———. "Thomas Wolfe on Publishers: Reaction to Rejection," *South Atlantic Quarterly*, LXIV (Summer 1965), 385-389.

F680 ———. "Thomas Wolfe and His Scottish Heritage," *Southern Folklore Quarterly*, XXVIII (1964), 134-141.

F681 ———. "Thomas Wolfe's Old Catawba," *Names*, XI (December 1963), 254-256.

F682 ———. "Wolfe's *Of Time and the River*," *Explicator*, XXVI (1967), item 18.

F683 Reynolds, Horace. (Review of *Letters*), *Christian Science Monitor*, October 4, 1956, p. 7.

F684 Ribalow, Harold H. "Jews in Thomas Wolfe's World," *Congress Weekly*, XIV (January 31, 1947), 13-15.

F685 ———. "Of Jews and Thomas Wolfe," *Congress Weekly*, XIV (January 24, 1947), 15-25. Similar article with same title in *Chicago Jewish Forum*, XIII (1954), 89-99.

F686 Rice, Jerry. "A Slice of Life," *Literary Sketches* [Williamsburg, Va.], VI (December 1966), 4, 9.

F687 Rivers, Rudy. "Last of the Tom Wolfe Family," *News and Observer* [Raleigh], July 28, 1963.

F688 Robbins, Frances L. (Review of *LHA*), *Outlook and Independent*, CLIII, (December 25, 1929), 669.

F689 Roberts, J. M., Jr. "Former *Morning Herald* Staff Member Gives Views on Thomas Wolfe's Mother," *Morning Herald* [Durham, N. C.], January 26, 1947, pp. i, 6.

F690 ———. (Review of *A Western Journal*), *Atlanta Journal*, July 1, 1951.

F691 ———. "Thomas Wolfe," *Life*, October 8, 1956, p. 22.

F692 Robertson, Michael. "Giant from Asheville," *Cosmopolitan*, CXLV (August 1958), 46-51.

F693 Robinson, Henry M. "Thomas Wolfe as a Writer and Man," *Saturday Review of Literature*, XXXI (February 7, 1948), 8. Review of Muller.

F694 Roch, Herbert. "Die Amerikanische Wirklichkeit im Roman," *Die Hilfe*, XLII (October 17, 1936), 47-48.

F695 Rogers, W. G. "Thomas Wolfe," *Advertiser* [Lafayette, La.], July 3, 1960, p. 3. Review of Nowell.

F696 ———. "Thomas Wolfe: Giant Who Stirred Literature," *Blade* [Toledo, O.] February 4, 1968. Review of Turnbull. These two articles by Rogers are samples of syndicated reviews of Wolfe's books which have appeared in newspapers all over the United States.

F697 Rose, Frank. "Thomas Wolfe," *Tempo*, Spring, 1938, p. 20-22.

F698 Rousseaux, André. "Thomas Wolfe est-il méconnu?" *Figaro Littéraire*, no. 553 (1956), 2.

F699 Rubin, Larry Jerome. "Thomas Wolfe and the Lost Paradise," *Modern Fiction Studies*, XI (Autumn 1965), 250-258.

F700 Rubin, Louis D., Jr. "The Historical Image of Modern Southern Writing," *Journal of Southern History*, XXII (1956), 147-166.

F701 ———. (Review of Holman), *American Literature*, XXXVIII (1966-1967), 574-575.

F702 ———. (Review of Kennedy), *Journal of Southern History*, XXIX (1963), 420-422.

F703 ———. (Review of Kennedy), *The New Leader*, XXXV (January 7, 1963), 24-26.

F704 ———. (Review of *Letters*), *American Literature*, XXIX (March 1957), 106-107.

F705 ———. "The Self Recaptured," *Kenyon Review*, XXV (Summer 1963), 393-415.

F706 ———. "The South and the Faraway Country," *Virginia Quarterly Review*, XXXVIII (1962), 444-459.

F707 ———. "Thomas Wolfe in Time and Place," *Hopkins Review*, VI (Winter 1953), 117-132.

F708 Rugoff, Milton. (Review of Muller and Pamela Johnson), *New York Herald Tribune Books*, April 4, 1948, p. 1.

F709 ———. (Review of *YCGHA*), *New York Herald Tribune Books*, September 22, 1940, p. 5.

F710 Russell, Francis. (Review of Pollock),
      Christian Science Monitor, April 29, 1954, p. 11.

F711 Russell, H. K. (Review of Holman), *South Atlantic
      Quarterly*, LX (Winter 1961), 115.

F712 Russell, Phillips. "The Meaning of Thomas Wolfe,"
      Carolina Magazine, LXVIII (October 1938), 3.

F713 Sain, Bob. "A Letter to Thomas Wolfe," *News*
      [Charlotte], July 7, 1951. Review of *A Western Journal*.

F714 Sancton, Thomas. "Time and the River," *Item* [New
      Orleans], October 26, 1950.

F715 Saunders, J. Marion. "Tom Wolfe Returns," *University
      of North Carolina Alumni Review*, XXV (January
      1937), 3.

F716 ———. "Alumniana: Thomas Wolfe," *University of
      North Carolina Alumni Review*, XLVII (Fall
      1958), 43, 49.

F717 Schickert, Werner. "Thomas Wolfe," *Die Literatur*,
      XLI (June 1939), 577-578.

F718 Schneider, Duane. (Review of Austin), *Library Journal*,
      XCIII (May 15, 1968), 1999.

F719 ———. (Review of Turnbull), *Library Journal*, XCIII
      (February 1, 1968), 544.

F720 Schoenberner, Franz. "Wolfe's Genius Seen Afresh,"
      New York Times Book Review, August 4, 1946, pp. 1, 25.
      Originally in *Das Silberboot* [Vienna], II (1946),
      217-219.

F721 Schorer, Mark. "The Flaw Is the 'I' " *New York Times Book Review*, July 1, 1951, p. 4. Review of *A Western Journal*.

F722 ———. "Technique as Discovery," *Hudson Review*, I (Spring 1948), 67-68.

F723 Schramm, Wilbur L. "Careers at Crossroads," *Virginia Quarterly Review*, XV (October 1939), 627-632.

F724 Schroeder, James. (Review of Walser), *College English*, XXIII (December 1961), 242.

F725 Scott, Evelyn. "Colossal Fragment," *Scribner's Magazine*, XCVII (June 1935), 2, 4. Review of *OTATR*.

F726 Shaw, Albert. "The Carolina Playmakers," *Review of Reviews*, LX (September 1919), 302-303. Includes notes and pictures on Wolfe's play, "The Return of Buck Gavin."

F727 Shaw, Thomas J., Jr. "Rare Wine Mixed with Stiff Corn," *The Archive* [Duke University], XLII (March 1930), 23-24. Review of *LHA*.

F728 Simmons, Fritz "Thomas Wolfe's Novel Reveals Marked Advance in His Writing," *Daily News* [Greensboro, N. C.], June 25, 1939. Review of *TWATR*.

F729 Simpson, Claude M., Jr. "A Note on Wolfe," *Fantasy*, VI (1939), 17-21.

F730 ———. "Of Wolfe and the Critics," *Southwest Review*, XXXVIII (Summer 1953), 264-265. Review of Walser.

F731 ———. (Review of Holman), *Southwest Review*, XLV (Autumn 1960), 363.

F732 ———. (Review of Kennedy), *Southwest Review,* XLVIII (Autumn 1963), 412.

F733 ———. (Review of Nowell), *Southwest Review,* XLV (Autumn 1960), 362.

F734 ———. (Review of *YCGHA*), *Southwest Review,* XXV (1940), 132-135.

F735 ———. "Thomas Wolfe: A Chapter in his Biography," *Southwest Review,* XXV (1940), 308-321.

F736 Skipp, Francis E. "The Editing of *Look Homeward, Angel,*" *Bibliographical Society of America Papers,* LVII (1963), 1-13.

F737 ———. "Thomas Wolfe, Maxwell Perkins, and Politics," *Modern Fiction Studies,* XIII (Winter 1967-1968), 503-511.

F738 Slay, Joseph M. "Wolfe and Perkins," *Saturday Review of Literature,* XXXIV (September 1, 1951), 27.

F739 Sloane, William M. "Literary Prospecting," *Saturday Review of Literature,* XIX (December 3, 1938), 4.

F740 Slocum, John. (Review of *OTATR*), *North American Review,* CCXL (June, 1935), 175-177.

F741 Slotnick, Emanuel. (Review of *LTHM*), *Springfield Republican,* May 2, 1943, p. E7.

F742 Sloyan, G. S. "American Novelists Through Fifty Years," *America,* LXXXV (June 16, 1941), 291-293.

F743 ———. (Review of *Letters*), *America,* XCVI (November 3, 1956), 132-133.

F744 Smathers, Anita. "Tom Wolfe's 'Other Brother,' "
Daily News [Greensboro, N. C.], January 17,
1965, p. 82.

F745 Smith, Chard P. "Perkins and the Elect," *Antioch
Review*, XXII (Spring 1962), 85-102.

F746 Smith, Harrison. "Midwife to Literature," *Saturday
Review of Literature*, XXX (July 12, 1947), 15-16.

F747 Snelling, Paula. "Thomas Wolfe: The Story of a Marvel,"
Pseudopodia [Atlanta], I (Spring 1936), 1, 8-12.

F748 Snyder, C. L. (Review of Kennedy), *New York Times
Book Review*, April 7, 1963, p. 45.

F749 ———. (Review of *LTHM*), *Yale Review*, XXXIII
(Winter 1944), 373.

F750 Solomon, L. B. (Review of *YCGHA*), *Nation*, CLI
(September 28, 1940), 278.

F751 Solon, S. L. "The Ordeal of Thomas Wolfe," *Modern
Quarterly*, XI (Winter 1939), 45-53.

F752 Spearman, Walter. "Thomas Wolfe's View of Himself,"
Weekly [Chapel Hill], June 23, 1968, p. 4. Review
of revised *LTHM*.

F753 ———. "Tom Wolfe Is Revealed as Teacher,"
Daily News [Greensboro, N. C.], January 31, 1954.
Review of Pollock.

F754 Spencer, Theodore. (Review of *TWATR*), *Atlantic
Monthly*, CLXIV (August 1939), unpaged section.

F755 Spiller, Robert E. (Review of Kennedy), *Times Literary
Supplement* [London], July 26, 1963, p. 550.

F756 ———. (Review of *Short Novels*), *Sewanee Review*, LXXI (Autumn 1963), 568-569.

F757 ———. "The Unfinished Artist," *Saturday Review*, XLVI (January 12, 1963), 69, 74. Review of Kennedy.

F758 Stafford, Jean. "Wolfe Hunting," *New York Review of Books*, May 9, 1968, pp. 17-20. Review of Turnbull and revised *LTHM*.

F759 Stahl, Hermann. "Übertreibung zur Wahrheit hin zu Thomas Wolfes Romanwerk," *Welt und Wort*, IX (1954), 231-232.

F760 Stahr, Alden. "Thomas Wolfe at Chapel Hill," *Carolina Magazine* LXI (April 10, 1932), 1, 8.

F761 Stallings, Laurence. (Review of "A Portrait of Bascom Hawke"), *New York Sun*, March 31, 1932.

F762 Starkey, M. L. (Review of *OTATR*), *Boston Transcript*, March 9, 1935, p. 1.

F763 ———. "Thomas Wolfe from North Carolina," *Boston Transcript*, September 26, 1931, Book Section, pp. 1-2.

F764 Stearns, Monroe M. "The Metaphysics of Thomas Wolfe," *College English*, VI (January 1945), 193-199.

F765 Stedman, John. (Review of Nowell), *Canadian Forum*, XLI (November 1969), 186.

F766 Stefano, Luciana de. "La soledad y el mundo perdido in Thomas Wolfe," *Revista Nacional de Cultura* [Caracas], XXV (1963), clviii-clix, 59-80.

F767 Stevens, George. "Always Looking Homeward," *Saturday Review of Literature*, XX (June 24, 1939), 5-6. Review of *TWATR*.

F768 Stevens, N. (Review of Muller), *Arizona Quarterly*, IV (Summer 1948), 188-189.

F769 Stevens, Virginia. "L'America di Thomas Wolfe," *Contemporaneo*, VII, no. 55 (1963), 8-39.

F770 ———. "Thomas Wolfe's America," *Mainstream*, XI (January 1958), 1-24.

F771 Stokely, James, "Perkins and Wolfe," *Saturday Review of Literature*, XXXIV (July 7, 1951), 22.

F772 Stone, Edward. "The Paving Stones of Paris: Psychometry From Poe to Proust," *American Quarterly*, V (1953), 121-131.

F773 ———. "A Rose for Thomas Wolfe," *Ohio University Review*, V (1963), 17-24.

F774 Stone, Geoffrey, "In Praise of Fury," *Commonweal*, XXII (May 10, 1935), 36-37. Review of *OTATR*.

F775 ———. "Thomas Wolfe: Romantic Atavism," *The Examiner*, I (Fall 1938), 385-393.

F776 Stoney, George. "Eugene Returns to Pulpit Hill," *Carolina Magazine*, LXVIII (October 1938), 11-14.

F777 Straumann, Heinrich. "Thomas Wolfe und das Drama," *Neue Zürcher Zeitung*, October 14, 1962, p. 4.

F778 Styron, William. "The Shade of Thomas Wolfe,"
      Harper's Magazine, CCXXXVI (April 1968), 96-104.
      Review of Turnbull. See also the June 1968 issue
      for letters to the editor concerning this review.

F779 Sugarman, Joseph. "Thomas Wolfe Hungers On,"
      Carolina Magazine, LXIV (April 1935), 22-24.
      Review of *OTATR*.

F780 Sugrue, Thomas. "Thomas Wolfe Looks Homeward,"
      Saturday Review of Literature, XXVI (May 29, 1943), 17.
      Review of *LTHM*.

F781 Sutton, Horace. "Look Homeward, Asheville,"
      Saturday Review, XXXVII (November 6, 1954), 45-48.

F782 Swinnerton, Frank. (Review of *LHA*), *London Evening
      News*, August 8, 1930.

F783 Sylvester, Harry. (Review of *TWATR*), *Commonweal*,
      XXX (July 31, 1939), 321.

F784 ———. (Review of *YCGHA*), *Commonweal*, XXXIII
      (October 25, 1940), 29.

F785 Talmey, Allene. "Wolfe and the Angel," *Vogue*, CXXXI
      (March 1, 1958), 142-143, 180-181, 183.

F786 Taucher, Franz. "Gulliver entdeckt Amerika: Thomas
      Wolfe und die Welt," *Die Heimat und die Welt*
      [Vienna], 1947, pp. 90-100.

F787 Taylor, Walter F. "Thomas Wolfe and the Middle-Class
      Tradition," *South Atlantic Quarterly*, LII (October
      1953), 543-554.

F788 Tebbel, John. "The Long Dream of Thomas Wolfe," *American Mercury*, LIII (December 1941), 752-754.

F789 Tedd, Eugene. "Hours of Hell and Anguish," *Prairie Schooner*, XXIX (Summer 1955), 95-108.

F790 Terry, John Skally. "En Route to a Legend," *Saturday Review of Literature*, XXXI (November 27, 1948), 7-9.

F791 ———. (Review of Delakas), *American Literature*, XXIV (March 1952), 114-116.

F792 Tettau, Franz. "Thomas Wolfes letztes Kapitel," *Berlin Neuen Zeitung*, December 30, 1950. Review of *YCGHA*.

F793 Theunissen, Gert H. (Review of *OTATR*), *Der Bücherwurm*, XXI (1936) 194-195.

F794 Thoer, Gunther. "Die klassiker Amerikas sind zeitgenossen zu Büchern von Thomas Wolfe und William Faulkner," *Die Yacht* [Berlin], IX, no. 11 (1954), 6.

F795 Thompson, Betty. "Thomas Wolfe: Two Decades of Criticism," *South Atlantic Quarterly*, XLIX (July 1950), 378-392.

F796 Thompson, Lawrence. "Tom Wolfe, Amerikas Skildrare," *Bonniers Litterara Magazine*, VIII (September 1939), 541-546.

F797 Thompson, Leslie M. "The Promise of America in Whitman and Thomas Wolfe," *Walt Whitman Review*, XII (June 1966), 27-34.

F798 Thompson, Ralph. (Review of *Letters*), *Book of the Month Club News*, October, 1956, p. 8.

F799 Thorp, Willard. (Review of Wheaton), *New York Herald Tribune Lively Arts*, May 28, 1961, p. 29.

F800 Tinker, Edward L. (Review of *FOAN*), *New York Times Book Review*, November 19, 1939, p. 33.

F801 Todd, Joseph W. "Thomas Wolfe: Inexhaustible," *Scholastic*, XXXVIII (May 12, 1941), 23.

F802 Tornai, József. (Review of *LHA*), *Élet és Irodalom* [Budapest], December 1963, p. 6.

F803 Townsend, Marion. (Review of *Mannerhouse*), *Observer* [Charlotte], December 5, 1948.

F804 Trilling, Lionel. "Contemporary Literature in Its Relation to Ideas," *American Quarterly*, I (1949), 195-208.

F805 Tschumi, R. (Review of Pfister), *English Studies*, XXXVII (October 1956), 233-235.

F806 Turnbull, Andrew. "Perkins' Three Generals," *New York Times Book Review*, July 16, 1967, pp. 2, 25-27.

F807 ———. "Thomas Wolfe Arrives," *Atlantic Monthly*, CCXX (December 1967), 60-66.

F808 Ungvári, Tamás. (Review of *LHA*), *Magyar Nemzet* [Budapest], March 31, 1963, p. 9.

F809 Vance, E. G. "Modern Men of Letters," *Saturday Review of Literature*, XXXII (January 22, 1949), 30.

F810 Vanderbilt, Sanderson. "Interview with Thomas Wolfe," *New York Herald Tribune*, February 18, 1935.

F811 Van Doren, Carl. (Review of *LHA*), *Wings* [Literary Guild], February, 1930, p. 3.

F812 ———. (Review of *SOAN*), *New York Herald Tribune Books*, May 17, 1936, p. 5.

F813 Van Gelder, Robert. "Thomas Wolfe as Friends Remember Him," *New York Times Book Review*, September 29, 1940.

F814. Vilmos, Zolnay. (Review of *LHA*), *A Könyvtáros* [Budapest], May, 1963, p. 301.

F815 Vining, Lou Myrtis. "I Cover a Writers' Conference," *Writer's Digest*, XV (September 1935), 30-32.
On the conference at Boulder, Col., which Wolfe attended in 1935.

F816 ———. "Thomas Wolfe: In Memoriam," *Writer's Digest*, XIX (July 1939), 47-50.

F817 Vogel, Albert W. "The Education of Eugene Gant," *New Mexico Quarterly*, XXXVI (1966), 278-292.

F818 Volkening, Henry T. "Thomas Wolfe: Penance No More," *Virginia Quarterly Review*, XV (Spring 1939), 196-215.

F819 Wade, John Donald. "Prodigal, An Essay on Thomas Wolfe," *Southern Review*, I (July 1935), 192-198.

F820 Wagner, Heinrich. (Review of *OTATR*), *Das Deutsche Wort*, XII (1936), 879-880.

F821 Wainwright, Alexander D. (Review of E. D. Johnson), *Bibliographical Society of America Papers*, LV (1961), 258-263.

F822 Walbridge, Earle F. (Review of Daniels), *Library Journal* LXXXVI (May 15, 1961), 1887.

F823 ———. (Review of *Letters*), *Library Journal*, LXXXI (October 1, 1956), 2555.

F824 ———. (Review of Nowell), *Library Journal*, LXXXV (June 1, 1960), 2159.

F825 ———. (Review of *Short Novels*), *Library Journal*, LXXXVI (April 1, 1961), 1482.

F826 ———. (Review of Watkins), *Library Journal*, LXXXII (March 15, 1957), 747.

F827 ———. (Review of Wheaton), *Library Journal*, LXXXVI (January 1, 1961), 92.

F828 Walker, Gerald. "Tom Wolfe's Search for a Father," *Cosmopolitan*, CXLIX (August 1960), 35.

F829 Wallace, Margaret. "A Novel of Provincial American Life," *New York Times Book Review*, October 27, 1929, p. 7. Review of *LHA*.

F830 Walpole, Hugh. "A Londoner in New York," *New York Herald Tribune Books*, March 16, 1930, p. 9.

F831 Walser, Richard. "An Early Wolfe Essay—and the Downfall of a Hero," *Modern Fiction Studies*, XI (Autumn 1965), 269-274.

F832 ———. (Review of Kennedy), *Modern Philology*, LXI (1964), 323-324.

F833 ———. (Review of Watkins), *South Atlantic Quarterly*, LVII (Spring 1958), 271-272.

F834 ———. (Review of Wheaton), *American Literature*, XXXIII (November 1961), 391-392.

F835 ———. "Some Notes on Wolfe's Reputation Abroad," *Carolina Quarterly*, I (March 1949), 37-41.

F836 ———. "The Terrible Book," *State* [Raleigh], October 11, 1952, pp. 3, 25.

F837 Walter, Felix. "Thomas Wolfe," *Canadian Forum*, XI (October 1930), 25-26.

F838 Warren, Robert Penn. "A Note on the Hamlet of Thomas Wolfe," *American Review*, V (May 1935), 191-208. Review of *OTATR*.

F839 Watkins, Floyd C. "De Dry Bones in de Valley," *Southern Folklore Quarterly*, XX (June 1956), 136-140.

F840 ———. (Review of Kennedy), *American Literature*, XXXV (May 1963), 254-255.

F841 ———. (Review of Reeves), *American Literature*, XXVII (1956), 604-606.

F842 ———. (Review of Walser), *South Atlantic Quarterly*, LX (1961), 514-515.

F843 ———. "Rhetoric in Southern Writing: Wolfe," *Georgia Review*, XII (Spring 1958), 79-82.

F844 ———. "Thomas Wolfe," *Mississippi Quarterly*, XX (1967), 90-96.

F845 ———. "Thomas Wolfe and the Nashville Agrarians," *Georgia Review*, VII (Winter 1953), 410-423.

F846 ———. "Thomas Wolfe and the Southern Mountaineer," *South Atlantic Quarterly*, L (1951), 58-71.

F847 ———. "Thomas Wolfe's High Sinfulness of Poetry," *Modern Fiction Studies*, II (December 1956), 197-206.

F848 Watts, Georgia. "An Afternoon with Thomas Wolfe," *Writer's Digest*, XXXIX (February 1959), 30-34.

F849 Watts, Richard. "A Moving and Beautiful New Drama," *New York Post*, November 29, 1957. Review of Frings.

F850 Weigle, Edith. (Review of *FDTM*), *Chicago Daily Tribune*, December 14, 1935, p. 16.

F851 Wellman, Manly Wade. "Tom Wolfe's Own Football Hero," *Morning Herald* [Durham, N. C.], November 13, 1960.

F852 Weltman, Lutz. (Review of *LHA*), *Die Literatur*, XXV (May 1933), 478-479.

F853 Wenzell, Ron. "The Tom Wolfe Legend Burns Bright," *The State* [Columbia, S. C.], January 1, 1963, p. B1.

F854 West, Jessamin. "Tom Wolfe's My Name," *New Mexico Quarterly Review*, XIV (Summer 1944), 153-165.

F855 Westecker, Wilhelm. " 'Altamont,' Thomas Wolfes Jugendrama in Zurich aufgeführt," *Christ und Welt* [Stuttgart], XV, no. 43 (1962), 2.

F856 White, Elwyn Brooks. "Literary Estate," *New Yorker*, XXXII (February 9, 1957), 24-26.

F857 White, Katherine S. "Wolfe Call," *New York Times Book Review*, February 5, 1961, p. 44.

F858 Whitson, Max. "Thomas Wolfe's Cabin," *State* [Raleigh, N. C.], January 12, 1946, p. 5.

F859 Wilder, Roy, Jr. "Here Are Mother's Memories of Thomas Wolfe," *News and Observer* [Raleigh], October 29, 1950. Review of Norwood.

F860 Williams, Cecil B. (Review of Walser), *Midcontinent American Studies Journal*, III (Fall 1962), 60-61.

F861 ———. "Thomas Wolfe Fifteen Years After," *South Atlantic Quarterly*, LIV (October 1955), 523-547.

F862 Wilson, Elizabeth. (Review of *OTATR*), *Bluets*, [Asheville] VII (1935), 31-32.

F863 Winkler, Eugene G. "Thomas Wolfe," *Hochland*, XXXIII (1936), 554-555.

F864 Wisdom, William B. "Book on Wolfe," *Times-Picayune* [New Orleans], January 25, 1963, pp. 1, 14. Review of Kennedy.

F865 Wittig, Hans. "Thomas Wolfe: Philosoph, Kulturkritiker, Pädagoge," *Sammlung*, XIII (1958), 169-177, 242-255.

F866 Wolfe, Fred W. "My Brother Tom," *Time*, XCI (February 23, 1968), 6.

F867 ———. "Letter to the Editor," *New York Times Book Review*, March 31, 1968, p. 20; March 26, 1961, p. 41; March 6, 1961, p. 41; July 31, 1960, p. 18.

F868 ———. "Wolfe and Perkins," *Saturday Review of Literature*, XXXIV (August 11, 1951) 23-24. See also November 20, 1965, issue, p. 33.

F869 Wolfe, Julia E. "Letter from His Mother," *Carolina Play-Book*, XVI (March-June 1943), 13-14.

F870 ———. "Look Homeward, Angel," *Saturday Review of Literature*, XXIX (January 6, 1946), 13-14, 31-32. Interview transcribed by Ruth Davis.

F871 Woodburn, John. (Review of *Mannerhouse*), *New Republic*, CXX (January 17, 1949), 24.

F872 Wright, Cuthbert. (Review of *LTHM*), *Commonweal*, XXXVIII (May 21, 1943), 127.

F873 Wylie, Nancy C. "Mother of Thomas Wolfe Reaches 85th Milestone with Keen Mind," *News and Observer* [Raleigh], February 18, 1945.

F874 ———. "Of Tom Wolfe—And Going Home Again," *Daily News* [Greensboro, N. C.], November 8, 1962, p. D 1, 7.

F875 Young, Perry D. "Asheville Dramatizes the Tom Wolfe Story," *New York Times*, September 23, 1962, Travel Section, p. 13.

F876 ———. "Plaque Memorializes Life, Works of Wolfe," *Daily News* [Greensboro, N. C.], October 3, 1964.

G. Parts of Books About Wolfe

G1 Aaron, Daniel. *Writers on the Left* (1961), 309, 392, 431.

G2 Adamic, Louis. *My America* (1938), 54.

G3 Adams, Eugene T. *The American Idea* (1942), 138, 171-172.

G4 Adams, J. Donald. *The Shape of Books to Come* (1944), 10, 72, 79, 84-102, 131, 141, 142, 163.

G5 ———. *Speaking of Books and Life* (1965), 8, 11, 21, 29, 35, 60, 62, 68, 103, 243, 249, 269.

G6 ———. *The Writer's Responsibility* (1946), 99-103.

G7 Albrecht, W. P. "Time as Unity in Thomas Wolfe," Walser, 239-248.

G8 Aldridge, J. W. *After the Lost Generation* (1951), 19, 53, 198.

G9 ———. *In Search of Heresy* (1956), 11, 66, 86, 117, 119, 180.

G10 ———. *Time to Murder and Create: The Contemporary Novel in Crisis* (1966), 11, 16, 32, 151, 184.

G11 Allen, Walter. *Tradition and Dream: The English and American Novel from the Twenties to Our Time* (1964), 98-102, 131, 258, 295.

G12 Altick, Richard D. *The Art of Literary Research* (1963), 28, 80, 155.

G13 Anderson, Sherwood. Horace Gregory, ed., *The Portable Sherwood Anderson*, (1949), 30, 611, 616-617, 623-624.

G14 ———. *Letters* (1953), 314, 368-372, 386, 393-394, 401, 411-412, 435.

G15 Angoff, Allan, ed. *American Writing Today* (1957), 83, 165, 167, 183, 209, 374-376.

G16 Angoff, Charles. "Thomas Wolfe and the Opulent Manner," *The Tone of the Twenties and Other Essays* (1966), 84-92. See also 11, 71.

G17 Anonymous. "Lebensbericht Thomas Wolfes," *Uns Bleibt die Erde* (Munich, 1952), 153-158.

G18 Anonymous. (Review of *Look Homeward, Angel*), Allen Angoff, ed., *American Writing Today* (1957) 374-376.

G19 Aswell, Edward C. "An Introduction to Thomas Wolfe, *The Adventures of Young Gant* (1948), vii-xii. Also in Walser, 103-108; and Jerome Beatty, Jr., ed., *The Saturday Review Gallery* (1959), 353-357; originally in *Saturday Review*, November 27, 1948, with title "En Route to a Legend."

G20 ———. "A Note on Thomas Wolfe," in *THB* (1941), 351-386. Also *THB* (Perennial Library, 1964),

143-181; *The Lost Boy* (Perennial Library, 1965), 209-247; and in German translation, *Hinter jenen Bergen* (1956), 251-280. Excerpts in Holman, 45-48; and in Field, 149-151.

G21 ———. "Note on 'A Western Journey,' " *A Western Journal,* v-vi.

G22 ———. "Thomas Wolfe Did Not Kill Maxwell Perkins," *Saturday Review Reader No. 2* (1953), 68-100.

G23 ———. "Thomas Wolfe: The Playwright Who Discovered He Wasn't," Frings, vii-ix.

G24 Baiwir, Albert. *Abregé de l'Histoire du Roman Américain* (1946), 16, 89-90.

G25 ———. *Le Declin de l'Individualism chez les Romanciers Américains Contemporains* (1948), 353-354.

G26 Basso, Hamilton. "Thomas Wolfe," Malcolm Cowley, ed., *After the Genteel Tradition* (1936), 202-212. See also 213, 224, 225, 233, 248, 262.

G27 Bay, André. "Thomas Wolfe," *De la Mort au Matin* (1948), 7-14.

G28 Beach, Joseph W. "Thomas Wolfe: The Search for a Father," *American Fiction, 1920-1940* (1942), 173-215. The German translation appears in his *Amerikanische Prosadichtung, 1920-1940,* 161-202, and an excerpt in Holman, 96-100.

G29 Beatty, Jerome, ed. *The Saturday Review Gallery* (1959), 226, 231-233, 353-357, 389, 393, 403, 435.

G30 Beatty, Richmond C., ed. *The Literature of the South* (1952), 622-625, 994.

G31 Beebe, Maurice, and Field, Leslie A. "Criticism of Thomas Wolfe: A Selected Checklist," in Field, 273-293.

G32 Bement, Douglas. *The Fabric of Fiction* (1949), 16, 72, 128, 147.

G33 Benet, Stephen V. "A Torrent of Recollection," in Walser, 154-157.

G34 Benet, William R., ed. *The Reader's Encyclopedia* (1948), 419, 649, 791, 1221.

G35 Benn, Gottfried. "Thomas Wolfe," *Ausdruckswelt: Essays und Aphorismen* (1949), 96-98.

G36 Bernard, Harry. *Le Roman Régionaliste aux États-Unis, 1913-1940* (1949), 39, 80-81, 351, 354, 355.

G37 Bernstein, Irving. *The Lean Years, 1920-1933* (1960), 312-313.

G38 Bigelow, Gordon E. *Frontier Eden: The Literary Career of Marjorie Kinnan Rawlings* (1966), 1, 12, 18, 24, 34-35, 71.

G39 Bishop, Donald E. "Thomas Wolfe as a Student," in Walser, 8-17.

G40 Bishop, John Peale. "The Myth and Modern Literature," *Collected Essays* (1948), 127-128.

G41 ———. "The Sorrows of Thomas Wolfe," *Collected Essays* (1948), 129-137. Also in J. C. Ransom, ed., *The Kenyon Critics* (1951), 3-12. J. W. Aldridge, ed., *Literature in America* (1958), 391-399; A. W. Litz, ed., *Modern American Fiction* (1963), 256-264; and excerpt in Holman, 92-95.

G42 Blackmur, R. P. "Notes on the Novel," *Expense of Greatness* (1940), 176-198.

G43 Blair, Walter, ed. *The Literature of the United States* (1946), 863-867, 1085.

G44 Blankenship, Russell. *American Literature as an Expression of the National Mind* (1949), 749-751.

G45 Bloecker, Gunter. "Thomas Wolfe," *Die neuen Wirklichkeiten* (1957), 206-214.

G46 Bloom, Edward A. "Critical Commentary on 'Only the Dead Know Brooklyn,' " *The Order of Fiction* (1964), 143-146. Also in Field, 269-272.

G47 Blotner, Joseph. *The Modern American Political Novel, 1900-1960* (1966), 204, 360.

G48 Bluestone, George. *Novels into Film* (1957), 56-57, 211, 216.

G49 Blythe, LeGette. "Foreword," *Thomas Wolfe and His Family* (1961), 9-10.

G50 Bob, Julius. *Über den Tag hinaus: Kritische Betrachtungen* (1960), 246-248.

G51 Bode, Carl, ed. *The Young Rebel in American Literature* (1959), 53, 61, 73, 121.

G52 Bond, Marjorie N. "This Side Olympus," *Adventures in Reading, 8th Series* (1936), 18-20. On *OTATR.*

G53 Botkin, B. A. ed. *A Treasury of Southern Folklore* (1949), 306, 309, 413, 550.

G54 Bowden, Edwin. *The Dungeon of the Heart: Human Isolation and the American Novel* (1961), 66-72, 89, 102. 152, 155.

G55 Boynton, Percy H. "Thomas Wolfe," *America in Contemporary Fiction* (1940), 204-224.

G56 Bradbury, John M. *Renaissance in the South: A Critical History of the Literature* (1963), 5, 8, 11, 14-16, 19, 36, 88, 92-94, 106, 122, 124, 168, 197.

G57 Braswell, William. "Introduction," *Harper's Modern Classics TWATR* (1958), ix-xix.

G58 ———. "Introduction," *Thomas Wolfe's Purdue Speech* (1964), 9-17, 21-23.

G59 ———. "Thomas Wolfe Lectures and Takes a Holiday," *Thomas Wolfe's Purdue Speech* (1964), 117-129; also in Walser, 64-76; and M. M. Bryant, ed., *Essays Old and New* (1940), 399-407.

G60 Breit, Harvey, ed. *The Writer Observed* (1956), 31, 179-180, 282.

G61 Brewster, Dorothy, and Burrell, John. *Modern World Fiction* (1960), 65-66.

G62 Bridgers, Emily. "Thomas Wolfe," *The South in Fiction* (1948), 42-44.

G63 Brodin, Pierre. "Thomas Wolfe," *Les Écrivains Américains de l'Entre Deux Guerres* (1946).

G64 Brooks, Van Wyck. *An Autobiography* (1965), 32, 33, 376-377, 476, 570-571, 574, 582.

G65 ———. *The Confident Years* (1952), 337-342.

G66 ———. *Days of the Phoenix* (1957), 124-125.

G67 ———. *From the Shadow of the Mountain* (1961), 26, 120-121, 124, 132.

G68 ———. *The Opinions of Oliver Allston* (1941), 120, 173, 260, 275, 278.

G69 ———. *Our Literary Heritage* (1956), 138, 216, 337.

G70 ———. *The Writer in America* (1953), 64-65, 82.

G71 Brown, E. K. "Thomas Wolfe: Realist and Symbolist," in Walser, 206-221.

G72 Brown, John. *Panorama de Littérature Contemporaine aux États-Unis* (1954), 16, 23, 24-25, 53, 91, 170, 196, 210-213, 219, 301.

G73 Brown, John Mason. "Thomas Wolfe as a Dramatist," *Broadway in Review* (1940), 282-286. See also his *Dramatis Personae*, 398-401.

G74 ———. "Thomas Wolfe as a Dramatist," George Oppenheimer, ed., *The Passionate Playgoer* (1958), 55-58.

G75 ———. *Still Seeing Things* (1950), 39-40; 43-45; 285.

G76 Burgum, Edwin Berry. "Thomas Wolfe's Discovery of America," *The Novel and the World's Dilemma* (1947), 302-321. Also Walser, 179-184; and Holman, 115-119.

G76a Burke, William J., ed. *American Authors and Books* (1962), 118, 447, 540, 785, 819, 830.

G77 Burlingame, R. "Loyalties," *Of Making Many Books.* (1946), 169-190. See also 40-42, 324-326.

G78 Burt, Struthers. "Catalyst for Genius: Maxwell Perkins," *The Saturday Review Reader, No. 2* (1953), 70-85.

G79 Burtis, Mary E. *Recent American Literature* (1961), 338-341.

G80 Butcher, Margaret J. *The Negro in American Culture* (1956), 169-170.

G81 Cameron, May "An Interview with Thomas Wolfe," *Press Time* (1936), 247-252.

G82 Canby, Henry S. "Literary Gymnastics," *American Memoir* (1947), 330-338 .

G83 ———. "River of Youth," *Seven Years' Harvest* (1936), 163-170. See also 124-125. Also in Walser, 133-139.

G84 Cardwell, Guy A., ed. *Readings from the Americas* (1947), 978-982.

G85 Cargill, Oscar. "Gargantua Fills His Skin," Field, 3-15.

G86 ———. *Intellectual America* (1941), 167, 170, 349.

G87 Carpenter, Frederic I. "Thomas Wolfe," *American Literature and the Dream* (1955), 155-166. See also 10, 12, 17, 47, 194, 195.

G88 Cash, Wilbur J. *The Mind of the South* (1941), 376-379.

G89 *Cassell's Encyclopedia of World Literature* (1953), v.2. 2076-2077.

G90 Cerf, Bennett, ed. *Reading for Pleasure* (1957), 745-746.

G91 Chamberlain, John. "Look Homeward, Angel," Louis D. Rubin, Jr., and John Rees Moore, eds., *The Idea of an American Novel* (1961), 344-346.

G92 Chase, Richard. "Introduction," Dell edition of *YCGHA* (1960), 9-21.

G93 ———. "Introduction," Dell edition of *TWATR* (1960), 7-19.

G94 Church, Margaret. "Dark Time," *Time and Reality: Studies in Contemporary Fiction* (1963), 207-226. See also 184, 205-206, 227-228, 274-275. Also in Walser, 249-262; and Field, 85-103.

G95 Clements, Clyde C., Jr. "Symbolic Patterns in *You Can't Go Home Again*," Field, 229-240.

G96 Clough, Wilson O. *The Necessary Earth: Nature and Solitude in American Literature*, (1964), 178-180, 183.

G97 Coan, Otis W. *America in Fiction* (1956), 61-62.

G98 Coindreau, M. E. "Thomas Wolfe," *Aperçus de Littérature Américaine* (1946), 198-208.

G99 Collins, Thomas L. "Wolfe's Genius vs. Its Critics," Walser, 161-176.

G100 Commager, Henry Steele. *The American Mind*, 267-268, 275-276. Also Holman, 139-140.

G101 Congdon, Don, ed. *The Thirties: A Time to Remember*, (1962), 502-503.

G102 Connolly, C. "Thomas Wolfe," *Previous Convictions* (1963), 308-312.

G103 Cook, Albert. *The Meaning of Fiction* (1960), 272, 274.

G104 Cowie, Alexander. *American Writers Today* (1956), 50-52.

G105 ———. *The Rise of the American Novel* (1948), 175, 245, 743, 752, 754.

G106 Cowley, Malcolm. *After the Genteel Tradition* (1937), 213, 224, 225, 233, 248, 262.

G107 ———. *The Exiles Return* (1951), 9, 291-292.

G108 ———, ed. *The Faulkner-Cowley File: Letters and Memories, 1944-1962* (1966), 14, 112, 152, 159, 173.

G109 ———. "The Forty Days of Thomas Wolfe," Henry Dan Piper, ed., *Think Back On Us: A Contemporary Chronicle of the 1930's* (1967), 261-274. See also xiv, 90, 276, 353.

G110 ———. "Life and Death of Thomas Wolfe," *New Republic: Faces of Five Decades* (1946), 379-382.

G111 ———. *The Literary Situation* (1954), 41, 118, 129, 184, 191, 227.

G112 ———. "Thomas Wolfe," Holman, 167-174.

G113 ———. "Thomas Wolfe: The Professional Deformation," H. L. Beaver, ed., *American Critical Essays: 20th Century* (1959), 89-105.

G114 ———. "Thomas Wolfe's Legacy," Henry Dan Piper, ed., *Think Back on Us: A Contemporary Chronicle of the 1930's* (1967), 342-347.

G115 ——— ed. *Writers at Work: The Paris Review Interviews* (1958), 15, 94, 234, 289, 293.

G116 Crichton, Kyle. *Total Recoil* (1960), 13-14, 20-22, 29-30, 33-34, 73-75, 132-133, 135-136, 182-184, 304-308.

G117 Cunliffe, Marcus. *Literature of the United States* (1961), 14, 289-291, 306, 343, 363.

G118 Daniels, Jonathan. "Poet of the Boom," *Tar Heels* (1941), 218-235. Also in Walser, 77-90.

G119 ———. *The Time Between the Wars* (1966), 171, 177.

G120 Davenport, Basil. "C'est Maitre François." Holman, 54-56; also in Henry S. Canby, *Designed for Reading* (1935), 329-332; and A. P. Hudson, ed., *Nelson's College Caravan*, (1940), 157-159.

G121 Davenport, Marcia. *Too Strong for Fantasy: A Personal Record* (1967), 21, 138, 210-211, 213, 223-226, 298-299.

G122 Davidson, Donald. "Farewell — and Hail," *The Spyglass* (1963), 40-44.

G123 ———. *Southern Writers in the Modern World* (1958), 65-66.

G124 DeVoto, Bernard. "Genius Is Not Enough," *Forays and Rebuttals* (1936), 324-333. Also Walser, 140-148; Field, 131-138; and Holman, 86-91.

G125 ———. *The World of Fiction* (1950), 85, 161, 260-264. Excerpt in Holman, 72-74.

G126 Dickinson, Asa Don. *The World's Best Books* (1953), 381-382.

G127 Dodd, Martha. *Through Embassy Eyes* (1939), 89-95.

G128 Dow, Robert. "And Gladly Teche. . . ," Pollock, 104-107.

G129 Doyle, A. Gerald. "Drunk with Words," Pollock, 87-89.

G130 Dusenbury, Winifred L. *The Theme of Loneliness in Modern American Drama* (1960), 3, 38, 39, 130, 180.

G131 Dykeman, Wilma. "The Chateau and the Boarding House," *The French Broad* (1955), 210-227.

G132 Earnest, Ernest. *A Foreword to Literature* (1945), 122, 146, 149-150.

G133 Edmunds, Pocahontas W. "Thomas Wolfe, Mountaineer in Literature," *Tar Heels Track the Century* (1966).

G134 Eisinger, Chester E. *Fiction of the Forties* (1963), 4, 49, 330.

G135 Ellman, Richard. *James Joyce* (1959), 593, 806.

G136 Enzensberger, Hans M. "Thomas Wolfe," *Finn Veien, Engel!* (1963), 449-453.

G137 Eppelsheimer, Hans W., ed. *Handbuch der Weltliteratur* (1960), 673-674.

G138 Eyssen, Jürgen. "Thomas Wolfe," *Der Roman Fuehrer* (1960), v. 11, 355-365.

G139 Fadiman, Clifton, ed. *The American Treasury, 1455-1955* (1955), xxv, 478, 545.

G140 ———. "My Unfavorite Classics," *Enter Conversing* (1962), 161-162. See also 171, 173.

G141 ———— "Of Nothing and the Wolfe," Burling Lowrey,
ed., *Twentieth Century Parody* (1960), 75-80.
Also Robert P. Falk, ed., *American Literature in Parody*
(1955), 266-270; and Robert P. Falk, ed., *Antic Muse*
(1961), 245-249.

G142 ————. (Review of *TWATR*), in Walser, 149-153.

G143 ————. "The Wolfe at the Door," *Party of One*
(1955), 455-460, See also 278. Also in Holman, 37-39.

G144 Faverty, Frederic E. *Your Literary Heritage*
(1959), 209-211, 251.

G145 Fechter, Paul. "Mannerhouse," *Das Europäische Drama*
(1958), 480-482.

G146 Fiedler, Leslie A. *Love and Death in the American
Novel* (1960), 441-443.

G147 ————. *Waiting for the End* (1964), 38-39, 46,
79-81, 101, 148, 175.

G148 Field, Leslie A. "*The Hills Beyond*: A Folk Novel of
America," *Thomas Wolfe: Three Decades of Criticism*
(1968), 241-252.

G149 Finkelstein, Sidney. *Existentialism and Alienation in
American Literature* (1965), 186, 212.

G150 Fisher, John. *The Stupidity Problem and Other
Harassments* (1964), 95, 135, 136.

G151 Fisher, Vardis. "My Experiences with Thomas Wolfe,"
in Pollock, 127-145.

G152 Fitzgerald, F. Scott. *Letters. . .* , Andrew Turnbull, ed. (1963), 97-98, 100-101, 224, 227, 244, 251, 259, 262-264, 270, 276, 278-279, 284, 288, 291, 344, 365, 443, 496, 508, 552, 592.

G153 Foerster, Norman. *Literary Scholarship: Its Aims and Methods* (1941), 197-198, 200.

G154 Freeman, William. *Dictionary of Fictional Characters* (1963), 166, 221, 229, 438.

G155 French, Warren. *The Social Novel at the End of an Era* (1966), 16, 44, 140.

G156 Frenz, Horst. "Thomas Wolfe als Dramatiker," *Willkomen in Altamont*, 175-179. Also in Franz Lennartz, ed., *Auslandische Dichter und Schriftsteller unsere Zeit* (1955), 729-732.

G157 Friederich, Werner P. *Outline of Comparative Literature* (1954), 276, 282, 382, 423.

G158 Friedman, Melvin. *Stream of Consciousness: A Study in Literary Method* (1955), 77, 255.

G159 Frohock, W. M. *Strangers to This Ground: Cultural Diversity in Contemporary American Writing* (1961), 5, 6, 8, 18, 40, 143, 144.

G160 ———. "Thomas Wolfe: Of Time and Neurosis," *Novel of Violence in America* (1950), 47-66. Also in H. M. Ruitenbeek, ed., *The Literary Imagination* (1965), 211-231; and Holman, 69-71, 136-138; and Walser, 222-238.

G161 Gassner, John. *Theatre at the Crossroads* (1961), 294-296.

G162 Geismar, Maxwell. *American Moderns* (1958),
7, 17, 20, 24, 55, 73, 109, 119-144, 148, 153, 155, 164,
175, 217.

G163 ———. "A Cycle of Fiction," R. E. Spiller, ed.,
A Literary History of the United States (1948), v.2,
1309-1311. Also Holman, 133-135.

G164 ———. *The Last of the Provincials* (1947),
129, 193, 226, 283, 342, 356, 365.

G165 ———. *Rebels and Ancestors* (1953), 33, 49,
169, 170, 345.

G166 ———. "Thomas Wolfe: The Unfound Door,"
Writers in Crisis (1942) 185-236. Excerpt in Walser,
109-119.

G167 Geist, Stanley. "Thomas Wolfe," *Dizionario Letterario
Bompiani degli Autori* (Milan, 1957), v.3., 916-917.

G168 Gelfant, Blanche. *The American City Novel* (1952),
95-132. Excerpt in Holman, 153-156.

G169 Gerstenberger, Donna, and Hendrick, George, eds.
*The American Novel, 1789-1959: A Checklist of Twentieth
Century Criticism* (1961), 263-268.

G170 Goldhurst, William. *F. Scott Fitzgerald and His
Contemporaries* (1963), 31, 36, 107.

G171 Gordon, Caroline. *How to Read a Novel* (1957),
21-22, 194, 215.

G172 Gossett, Louise Y. "The Climate of Violence: Wolfe,
Caldwell, Faulkner," *Violence in Recent Southern Fiction*
(1965) 3-47. See also 52, 115, 199-200.

G173 Gray, James. "Forever Panting and Forever Young," *On Second Thought* (1946), 98-110.

G174 ———. "Thomas Wolfe," *Hälbgotter auf der Litterarischen Bühne* (1950), 131-144.

G175 Grebstein, Sheldon N. *Sinclair Lewis* (1962), 121, 125, 168n.

G176 *Der Grosse Herder* (Freiburg, 1956), v.3, pp. 1271-1272.

G177 Gurjot, Charles. *Les Romanciers Américains d'Aujourd'hui* (Paris, 1948), 100-101.

G178 Gurko, Leo. *Heroes, Highbrows, and the Popular Novel* (1953), 57-58, 78, 81, 193-198, 249, 252, 282, 305.

G179 ———. "The Laying of the Wind-Grieved Ghosts," *The Angry Decade* (1947), 148-170. See also 28-32.

G180 Gwynn, Frederick L., ed. *Faulkner in the University* (1959), 15, 142-144, 206, 233-234, 281.

G181 Haines, Helen E. *What's in a Novel* (1942), 17, 25, 58, 66.

G182 Hale, Nancy. *The Realities of Fiction: A Book about Writing* (1962), 22, 48, 51-56, 60-65, 240.

G183 Halperin, Irving. "Wolfe's *Of Time and the River*," Field, 217-219.

G184 Hart, James D., ed. *America's Literature*, (1941), 790-791, 911.

G185 ———. *Oxford Companion to American Literature* (1965), 493-494, 616, 940-941.

G186 Hartley, Lois. "Theme in Thomas Wolfe's 'The Lost Boy' and 'God's Lonely Man,' " Field, 261-267.

G187 Hassan, Ihab. *Radical Innocence: Studies in the Contemporary Novel* (1961), 52, 54, 55.

G188 Hatcher, Harlan. *Creating the Modern American Novel* (1939), 287-289.

G189 Haueis, Albert. "Nachwort," *Die Leute von Alt-Catawba*, 82-86.

G190 Heiney, Donald W. *Essentials of Contemporary Literature* (1954), 48, 119, 128-133, 134.

G191 ———. *Recent American Literature* (1958), 165-173, 580.

G192 Helmstadter, Frances. *Picture Book of American Authors* (1962), 47-49.

G193 Henderson, Archibald. *Pioneering a People's Theatre* (1945), viii, 3, 21, 22, 26, 29-30, 33, 75, 87.

G194 Herron, Ima H. *The Small Town in American Literature* (1939), 423-425.

G195 Herzberg, Max J., ed. *The Reader's Encyclopedia of American Literature* (1962), 54, 616, 656, 698, 726, 872, 1008, 1201-1202, 1247-1248, 1264.

G196 Hicks, Granville, ed. *The Living Novel, A Symposium* (1957), 25, 29, 33, 36, 128-129, 134-141, 167, 171.

G197 ———. *Part of the Truth* (1965), 84-85.

G198 Highet, Gilbert. *The Anatomy of Satire* (1962), 146-147.

G199 ———. *People, Places, and Books* (1953), 59, 204, 208.

G200 ———. *The Powers of Poetry* (1960), 105, 110, 161.

G201 Highsaw, Robert B., ed. *The Deep South in Transformation* (1964), 149-150, 152, 155, 157, 163, 167.

G202 Hoffman, Frederick J. *The Modern Novel in America, 1900-1950* (1951), 164-170, 178, 190. See also the 1956 edition, 180-187.

G203 Hogan, Robert, *The Independence of Elmer Rice* (1956), 142-143.

G204 Holman, C. Hugh. " 'The Dark, Ruined Helen of His Blood': Thomas Wolfe and the South," Louis D. Rubin and Robert D. Jacobs, eds., *South: Modern Southern Literature in Its Cultural Setting* (1961), 177-197. Also in Field, 17-36.

G205 ———. "Europe as Catalyst for Thomas Wolfe," *Essays in American and English Literature Presented to Bruce Robert McElderry, Jr.,* (1967), 122-127.

G206 ———. "Introduction," *The Letters of Thomas Wolfe to His Mother, Newly Edited. . .* by C. Hugh Holman and Sue Fields Ross (1968), ix-xiv.

G207 ———. "Introduction," *Of Time and the River: Young Faustus and Telemachus* (1965), xi-xvii.

G208 ———. "Introduction," *The Short Novels of Thomas Wolfe* (1961), vii-xx. See also 3, 75, 157, 235, 281.

G209 ———. "Introduction," *TWR*, 2-10.

G210 ———. "Introduction," Holman, 1-3.

G211 ———. "The Loneliness at the Core," Holman, 57-59.
Also in Louis D. Rubin, Jr. and John Rees Moore,
eds., *The Idea of An American Novel* (1961), 348-351.

G212 ———. "Thomas Wolfe," W. V. O'Connor, ed.,
Seven Modern American Novelists (1964), 189-225.
Also in Spanish, *Tres Escritores Norteamericanos*
(Madrid, 1961), 97-140. Excerpts in Holman, 175-178.

G213 ———. "Thomas Wolfe and the Stigma of
Autobiography," Jessie Rehder, ed., *Chapel Hill Carousel*
(1967), 121-133. See also xii, xiv.

G214 Holthusen, Hans E. "Nachwort," *Tod, der stolze Bruder*
(1953), 61-62.

G215 Hopper, Stanley R. *Spiritual Problems in Contemporary
Literature* (1952), 156-161.

G216 Horan, James D. *The Desperate Years: A Pictorial
History of the Thirties* (1962), 191, 192, 252.

G217 Horton, Rod W. *Backgrounds of American Literary
Thought* (1952), 241, 322, 358, 386.

G218 Howard, Leon. *Literature and the American Tradition*
(1960), 298-299, 305, 306.

G219 Howard, Robert W. *This is the South* (1959).
242, 250, 259.

G220 Hubbell, Jay B. *South and Southwest: Literary Essays
and Reminiscences* (1965), 87, 335, 344, 346, 351.

G221 ———. *Southern Life in Fiction* (1960), 11, 29, 86.

G222 Hutsell, James K. "Thomas Wolfe," *North Carolina Authors: A Selective Handbook* (1952), 131-132.

G223 Hyman, Stanley. *Armed Vision: A Study in the Methods of Modern Literary Criticism* (1948), 97, 125, 255, 372.

G224 Ilyich, Vera. [Introduction], *Pogledaj dom Svoj, Andjele* (1954), 5-33.

G225 Jessup, Josephine. *The Faith of our Feminists* (1965), 87, 92-95, 118.

G226 Johnson, Edgar. "Thomas Wolfe and the American Dream," *A Treasury of Satire* (1945), 741-745. See also 35, 77, 695. Also in Holman, 112-114.

G227 Johnson, Elmer D. "Introduction," *Of Time and Thomas Wolfe* (1959), v-ix.

G228 Johnson, Merle, ed. *American First Editions* (1942), 549-550.

G229 Johnson, Pamela. "Hungry Gulliver," Holman, 130-132.

G230 ———. "The Style," Holman, 64-68.

G231 ———. "Thomas Wolfe and the Kicking Season," Holman, 60-62.

G232 Jones, Joseph, et al, eds. *American Literary Manuscripts* (1960), 416-417.

G233 Jovanovich, William. *Now Barabbas* (1964), 79, 102, 206.

G234 Kazin, Alfred. *On Native Grounds* (1956), 90, 289, 305, 352, 361-377, 389. See also the 1942 edition, 118, 257,

370, 393, 419, 455, 466-484, 497. This has been translated into German as *Amerika—Selbsterkenntnis und Befreiung* (Munich, 1951).

G235 ———. "Thomas Wolfe's Significance as a Writer," Harry A. Warfel and E. W. Manwaring, eds., *Of the People* (1942), 546-551.

G236 ———. "The Writer's Friend," *The Innermost Leaf* (1955), 185-190.

G237 Kennedy, Richard S. "Thomas Wolfe," *The Dictionary of American Biography*, XXII, Supplement 2, (1958), 730-733.

G238 ———. "Wolfe's Harvard Years," Walser, 18-32.

G239 ———. "Wolfe's *Look Homeward, Angel* as a Novel of Development," Field, 195-203.

G240 Kennedy, William F. "Economic Ideas in Contemporary Literature — The Novels of Thomas Wolfe," Holman, 149-152.

G241 Kiell, Norman, ed. *The Adolescent Through Fiction: A Psychological Approach* (1959), 60-62, 115-120, 306, 338.

G242 Killinger, John. *The Failure of Theology in Modern Literature* (1963), 53-54, 105-106, 126, 167, 169-170.

G243 Kinne, Wisner P. "Enter Tom Wolfe," *George Pierce Baker and the American Theatre* (1954), 228-239.

G244 Klimke, Wolfgang. "Vorwort," *Verbannung und Entdeckung.* (1959), 3-7.

G245 Koch, Frederick, ed. *Carolina Folk-Plays* (1941), 115, 127-131.

G246 Kofsky, Bernard. "Overloaded Black Briefcase," Pollock, 90-92.

G247 Kohler, D. M. "Thomas Wolfe, Prodigal and Lost," Bryant, ed., *Essays Old and New* (1940), 391-398.

G248 Krauss, Russell. "Replacing Thomas Wolfe," Pollock, 146-152.

G249 Kronenberger, Louis. *The Republic of Letters* (1955), 257-260.

G250 Kunitz, Stanley, ed. *Twentieth Century Authors* (1942), 1541-1543.

G251 Kussy, Bella. "The Vitalist Trend and Thomas Wolfe," Holman, 306-324.

G252 *Laffont-Bompiani Dictionnaire Biographique des Auteurs* (Paris, 1956), II, 713.

G253 *Laffont-Bompiani Dictionnaire des Oeuvres de Tous Les Temps et Tous les Pays* (Paris, 1954), IV, 530, 572.

G254 Land, Myrick, *The Fine Art of Literary Mayhem: A Lively Account of Famous Writers and Their Feuds* (1963), 208-209.

G255 Lanzinger, Klaus. "Thomas Wolfe," *Die Epik in amerikanischen Roman* (1965), 141-162. See also 29, 33, 35, 36-37, 95, 111, 123, 140, 172-173.

G256 Laughton, Charles, ed. *The Fabulous Country: An Anthology* (1962), 2, 10, 23-24, 48-49, 67, 71, 119-120, 231, 242. Wolfe quoted on 10-12, 24, 49-51, 85-89, 120-121.

G257 Leary, Lewis. *Articles on American Literature, 1900-1950* (1954), 325-327.

G258 ───── ed. *Contemporary Literary Scholarship: A Critical Review* (1958), 215, 217, 277.

G259 ───── ed. *The Teacher and American Literature* (1965), 23, 41, 152.

G260 Ledig-Rowohlt, H. M. "Erinnerungen," *Uns Bleibt die Erde* (1951), 127-152.

G261 ───── "Thomas Wolfe in Berlin," *American Scholar Reader* (1960), 275-290.

G262 Lefler, Hugh T. *History of North Carolina* (1954), v.2, 824-825.

G263 Lerner, Max. *America as a Civilization* (1957), 102, 196-197, 280, 574, 577, 706, 791.

G264 LeRoy, Gaylord C. *Perplexed Prophets* (1953), 8-9.

G265 Levin, Harry. *Refractions: Essays in Comparative Literature* (1966), 78, 278-279.

G266 Lewis, Sinclair. *The Man from Main Street: A Sinclair Lewis Reader*, Harry Maule, ed. (1953), 17, 132, 158, 182, 188, 196, 211. This includes Lewis's 1931 Nobel Prize speech in which he praised Wolfe.

G267 Lewisohn, Ludwig. *The Story of American Literature* (1939), 594-595.

G268 *Lexikon der Weltliteratur* (Wien-Stuttgart, 1950), 886-887.

G269 Loggins, Vernon. "Dominant primordial," *I Hear America* (1937), 113-141.

G270 Lombardo, Agostino. *La Ricerca del Vero: Saggi Sulla Tradizione Letteraria Americana* (1961), 58, 339, 357.

G271 Longley, Marjorie, ed. *America's Taste, 1851-1959, From the Pages of the New York Times.* (1960), 216, 294, 321.

G272 Longstreet, Stephen. *The Last Man Comes Home: American Travel Journals* (1942), vii-viii, 87, 213, 358-359.

G273 Luccock, Halford E. *American Mirror* (1941), 39-60, 105-108.

G274 Ludwig, Richard M., *et al*, eds. *Literary History of the United States* (1959), 62, 131, 150, 167, 170, 213-215, 314, 784-786.

G275 Luedeke, Henry. *Geschichte der Amerikanischen Litteratur* (1952), 13, 413-415, 511-512.

G276 Lyons, John O. *The College Novel in America* (1962), 15, 77-85, 87-88, 141-144, 184, 186-187.

G277 McCole, Camille. "Thomas Wolfe Embraces Life," *Lucifer at Large* (1937), 231-254.

G278 McCormick, John. *Catastrophe and Imagination* (1957), 46-48, 53-54, 57, 75, 125-126, 161, 192-197, 201, 211, 248-254, 261-266, 276, 280.

G279 McElderry, Bruce R., Jr. "The Durable Humor of *Look Homeward, Angel*," Field, 189-194.

G280 McKinney, John C., and Thompson, Edgar T., eds. *The South in Continuity and Change* (1965), 384, 386, 395, 399-402.

G281 McLuhan, H. M. "Wolfe Has All the Passion. . . ," Fields, 81.

G282 Madison, Charles A. *Book Publishing in America* (1966), 206, 210, 211-215, 217.

G283 Magalaner, Marvin. *Joyce* (1956), 109, 184, 259, 261.

G284 Magill, Frank N., ed. *Cyclopedia of Literary Characters* (1963), 625-626, 796-797, 1232-1233, 1275-1276.

G285 ———. *Cyclopedia of World Authors* (1958), 1166-1169.

G286 Mailer, Norman. *Advertisements for Myself* (1959), 27, 70, 233, 474.

G287 Malcolmson, David. "Prodigal's Return," *Ten Heroes* (1941), 126-130.

G288 Maloney, Martin. "A Study of Semantic States: Thomas Wolfe and the Faustian Sickness," Field, 153-176.

G289 Mandel, James Lewis. "Thomas Wolfe, a Reminiscence," Pollock, 93-103.

G290 Manzini, Gianna "Thomas Wolfe," *Album di Ritratti* (Milan, 1963).

G291 Mayfield, Sara. *The Constant Circle: H. L. Mencken and His Friends* (1968), 183-185, 208, 237-238.

G292 Mencken, H. L. *Letters* . . . Selected and Annotated by Guy J. Forgue (1961) 312, 427, 437.

G293 Mendilow, A. A. *Time and the Novel* (1965), 55, 105, 137-138.

G294 Meriwether, James B., and Michael Millgate, eds. *Lion in the Garden: Interviews with William Faulkner* (1968), 53, 58, 81, 90, 107, 121-122, 179, 225, 268.

G295 Meyerhoff, Hans. "Death of a Genius," Rudolf Flesch, ed., *Best Articles of 1952*, 327-341.

G296 ———. *Time in Literature* (1955), 16, 26, 41, 44, 81.

G297 Millett, Fred B. *Contemporary American Authors* (1940), 34, 655-658.

G298 Millgate, Michael. *The Achievement of William Faulkner* (1965), 285-286.

G299 ———. *American Social Fiction: James to Cozzens*, (1964), 179, 198-199, 203.

G300 Minchero Vilasaro, Angel, ed. *Diccionario Universal de Escritores: Estados Unidos* (1957), 331-332.

G301 Morgan, H. Wayne. "Thomas Wolfe: The Web of Memory," *Writers in Transition* (1963), 127-151. See also 161-163, 169-170.

G302 Morris, Wright. "The Function of Appetite: Thomas Wolfe," *The Territory Ahead* (1958), 147-155. See also 13-14, 24, 26-27, 29-32, 129, 157, 170, 174-176. Portions of this are also in Granville Hicks, ed., *The Living Novel* (1957), 128-141; and A. W. Litz, ed., *Modern American Fiction* (1963), 349-354.

G303 Morrison, Joseph L. *W. J. Cash: Southern Prophet,
A Biography and Reader* (1967), 44, 54, 73, 92, 150-155,
157, 223, 249-250, 256, 288.

G304 Morsberger, Robert E. *James Thurber* (1964), 57, 199.

G305 Moser, Thomas C. "Thomas Wolfe, *Look Homeward,
Angel,*" Wallace Stegner, ed., *The American Novel
from James Fenimore Cooper to William Faulkner* (1965),
206-218. See also vii, x, xii, 113.

G306 Muller, Herbert J. "Thomas Wolfe," *Modern Fiction*
(1937), 404-418. Also in Holman, 120-129.

G307 Nadeau, Maurice. "Preface," *Aux Sources du Fleuve*
(1956), 7-14.

G308 Natanson, Maurice. "The Privileged Moment: A Study in
the Rhetoric of Thomas Wolfe," *Literature, Philosophy
and the Social Sciences* (1962), 131-140. Also in Holman,
78-84.

G309 Nelson, John H., and Cargill, Oscar, eds. *Contemporary
Trends: American Literature Since 1900* (1949), 1228-1229.

G310 Newquist, Roy, ed. *Counterpoint: Interviews with
People in Literary and Theatrical Worlds* (1965),
98, 255, 256, 261, 377, 409, 490.

G311 Nolte, William H. *H. L. Mencken: Literary Critic*
(1966), 111, 150, 192, 241.

G312 Nowell, Elizabeth. "Introduction," *Letters,* (1956)
xiii-xviii.

G313 Nyren, Dorothy, ed. *A Library of Literary Criticism:
Modern American Literature* (1960), 545-550.

G314 Odum, Howard W. *The Way of the South* (1947), 145-146.

G315 Ollen, Gunnar. "Inlednung," *Huset i den Gamla Stilen* 3-7.

G316 Oppenheimer, George, ed. "Thomas Wolfe Goes to Harvard," *Passionate Playgoer* (1958), 53-54. See also 1, 55-67.

G317 Országh, László. *Az Amerikai Irodalom Története* (Budapest, 1967), 330-333.

G318 Orvis, Mary B. *The Art of Writing Fiction* (1948), 234-235.

G319 Österling, Anders "Introduction," *Se Hemåt, Ängel!* (1932), v-vii.

G320 Perkins, Maxwell E. *Editor to Author* (1950), 99-102, 104, 110, 115-116, 119-125, 133, 140, 224-229. Letters from Perkins to Wolfe.

G321 ———— "Introduction," Scribner Library Edition and Modern Standard Authors Edition of *LHA*, vii-xiv.

G322 ———— "Scribner's and Thomas Wolfe," Walser, 57-63.

G323 ———— "Thomas Wolfe," Holman, 42-44; also Field, 139-147.

G324 Perosa, Sergio. *The Art of F. Scott Fitzgerald* (1965), 50, 129, 138, 142, 186, 217.

G325 Peyre, Henri. *Observations on Life, Literature and Learning in America* (1961), 91-92.

G326 Pivano, Fernando. *La Balena Bianca e Altri Miti* (1961), 385-388.

G327 Pollock, Thomas C. "Introductory Note," *The Correspondence of Thomas Wolfe and Homer Andrew Watt*, ix-xi.

G328 Powell, Lawrence C. *Books in My Baggage* (1960), 61-62, 66, 77, 183, 193.

G329 Price, Lawrence M. *The Reception of U. S. Literature in Germany* (1966), 123, 144, 150-152, 153, 154, 155-157, 172, 180, 225-226.

G330 Priestley, J. B. "Introduction," Heinemann edition of *TWATR*, ix-xii.

G331 ———. *Literature and Western Man* (1960), 433, 438-440. Also in Holman, 179-180.

G332 ———. *Rain upon Godshill* (1939), 108-110.

G333 Pritchett, V. S. *New York Proclaimed* (1965), 4, 5, 75.

G334 Quinn, Arthur H. *The Literature of the American People* (1951), 924-925, 1096.

G335 Rahv, Philip. *Image and Idea* (1957), 14, 22, 164.

G336 ———, ed. *Literature in America* (1957), 360, 363, 367-368, 369.

G337 Raimbault, R. N. "Introduction," *Au Fil du Temps* (1951), 7-10.

G338 Reaver, J. Russell, and Strozier, Robert I. "Thomas Wolfe and Death," Field, 37-58.

G339 Reeves, Walter Paschal, Jr. "Esther Jack as Muse," Field, 221-227.

G340 Rehder, Jessie C. *The Young Writer at Work* (1962),
27, 39, 40, 60, 69-72, 73, 156, 161, 250, 251.

G341 Reifenberg, Benno. *Lichte Schatten*
(1953), 313-317.

G342 Reynolds, Quentin. *By Quentin Reynolds* (1963),
143-144.

G343 Rice, Elmer. *Minority Report: An Autobiography* (1963),
266, 328, 348, 443-444.

G344 Richards, Robert, ed. *Concise Dictionary of American
Literature* (1955), 248-249.

G345 Rockwell, F. A. *Modern Fiction Techniques* (1962),
9, 28, 172, 204.

G346 Rosati, Salvatore. *Storia della Letteratura Americana*
(1961), 245, 293.

G347 Rothman, Nathan L. "Thomas Wolfe and James Joyce,"
Allan Tate, ed., *A Southern Vanguard* (1947), 52-77.
See also 33, 113, 117, 119-120. Also in Walser, 263-289.

G348 Rubin, Louis D., Jr. *The Curious Death of the Novel:
Essays in American Literature* (1967), 3-4, 97-98, 135,
139, 180, 185, 187, 193, 205, 271, 277-279, 284.

G349 ——— ed. *The Lasting South: Fourteen Southerners
Look at Their Home* (1957), 27, 42, 145-146, 161,
168, 171, 173-175, 179-180.

G350 ———. *The Teller in the Tale* (1967), 112, 117,
122-126, 129, 130-131, 150, 172n, 212.

G351 ———. "Thomas Wolfe in Time and Place," *Southern Renascence* (1953), 290, 305.

G352 ———. "Thomas Wolfe: Time and the South," *Faraway Country: Writers of the Modern South* (1963), 72-104; see also 8-9, 15-18, 133, 187, 194, 213-216, 233, 236, 239, 243, 244. Also in Field, 59-83.

G353 ———. "The Time of Thomas Wolfe," Holman, 157-163.

G354 Rubin, Louis D., Jr., and Jacobs, Robert, eds. *South: Modern Southern Literature in Its Cultural Setting* (1961), 12-13, 23-25, 31, 33-36, 38, 40-41, 43-46, 48, 52, 69, 75, 177-197, 264, 324, 350, 387, 430-431.

G355 Rubin, Louis D., Jr., and Moore, John Rees, eds. *The Idea of an American Novel* (1961), 143, 173, 267, 344-351, 382.

G356 *Saturday Review Treasury* (1957), 276, 331, 532.

G357 Scherman, David E. *Literary America* (1952), 158-161.

G358 Scheville, James. *Sherwood Anderson: His Life and Work* (1951), 324-327.

G359 Schirmer, Walter F. *Kurze Geschichte der englischen Literatur* . . . (1945), 303-304.

G360 Schoenberner, Franz. "Introduction," Letterio Calapai, *Twenty-five Original Wood Engravings Inspired by Thomas Wolfe's Look Homeward, Angel*.

G361 ———. "My Discovery of Thomas Wolfe," *The Inside Story of An Outsider* (1949). Also in Walser, 290-297.

G362 Schoenfelder, Karl-Heinz. "Nachtwort," *Der Ver-lorene Knabe*, 249-259.

G363 Scholes, Robert. *Approaches to the Novel* (1961), 262-263.

G364 ———. *The Nature of Narrative* (1966), 151, 155-156.

G365 Schorer, Mark. *Sinclair Lewis, An American Life* (1961), 4, 123, 538, 545, 548, 558-559, 574, 661.

G366 ———. "Technique as Discovery," William O'Connor, ed., *Forms of Modern Fiction* (1948), 9-29. Excerpts in James E. Miller, ed., *Myth and Method: Modern Theories of Fiction* (1960), 101-107.

G367 Seidel, Ina. "Geleitwort," *Briefe an die Mutter* (1949), 7-14.

G368 Sellers, Charles G., ed. *The Southerner as American* (1960), 186-187, 194, 198.

G369 Shipley, Joseph T., ed. *Encyclopedia of Literature* (1946), v.2, 988, 1186.

G370 Shirer, William L. *Berlin Diary* (1941), 66-67.

G371 Simon, Rita James, ed. *As We Saw the Thirties: Essays on Social and Political Movements of a Decade* (1967), 96-97, 101.

G372 Simonini, Rinaldo, ed. *Southern Writers: Appraisals in Our Time* (1964), vii, 49, 52, 59, 70, 105, 108, 111, 114, 116, 119, 120, 143, 163, 164, 190.

G373 Singleton, Marvin K. *H. L. Mencken and the American Mercury Adventure* (1962), 75, 212, 224.

G374 Slack, Robert C. "Thomas Wolfe: The Second Cycle," Arthur T. Broes, ed., *Lectures on Modern Novelists* (1963), 41-53. Also in Field, 105-120.

G375 Slochower, Harry. "Cosmic Exile," *No Voice Is Wholly Lost* (1945), 93-103.

G376 Sloyan, G. S. "Thomas Wolfe," H. C. Gardiner, ed., *Fifty Years of the American Novel* (1952), 197-215.

G377 Smith, Bernard, ed. *The Democratic Spirit* (1941), 346-347.

G378 Smith, G. C. *American Literature* (1960), 226-227, 254, 257.

G379 Smith, Page. *As a City Upon a Hill: The Town in American History* (1966), 234, 270-271, 273, 275-278, 280-282.

G380 Smith, Thelma M. *Transatlantic Migration: The Contemporary American Novel in France* (1955), 34-50.

G381 Snell, George. "The Education of Thomas Wolfe," *Shapers of American Fiction* (1947), 173-187.

G382 Spearman, Walter. "Thomas Wolfe, Major Novelist," *North Carolina Writers* (1949), 18-20.

G383 Sper, Felix. *From Native Roots: A Panorama of Our Regional Drama* (1948), 118-119.

G384 Spiller, Robert. *American Perspectives* (1961), 49, 57, 84.

G385 ———. *The Cycle of American Literature* (1955), 263-270. Excerpts in Holman, 164-166.

G386 ———. *A Time of Harvest*: *American Literature 1910-1960* (1962), 8, 40, 87-92, 94.

G387 Spiller, Robert E., et al, eds. *Literary History of the United States* (1963), 717, 1263-1264, 1309-1311, 1312, 1381, 1390, 1396-1397, 1480-1481.

G388 Springer, Anne M. *The American Novel in Germany* (1960), 7, 30, 75, 85, 88-95, 98.

G389 Starr, Nathan C. *The Dynamics of Literature* (1945), 33-34, 36-37, 60, 90-91.

G390 Starrett, Agnes Lynch. "Notes," *A Western Journal*, vii-ix.

G391 Stearns, Monroe M. "The Metaphysics of Thomas Wolfe," Walser, 195-205.

G392 Steen, Jos van der "De Icarus van Asheville," *Amerikanse Romanciers van Heden* (1954), 113-133.

G393 Stegner, Wallace. "An Analysis of 'The Lost Boy,'" *The Writer's Art* (1950), 178-183. Also in Field, 255-260.

G394 Steinbeck, John. *Travels with Charley* (1963), 200, 205.

G395 Steyick, Philip, ed. *The Theory of the Novel* (1967), 134, 136, 271, 278.

G396 Storm, Ole. [Foreword], Danish edition of *Mannerhouse* (1952), 5-9.

G397 Stovall, Floyd. *American Idealism* (1943), 154-158, 163-164.

G398 Straumann, Heinrich. *American Literature in the Twentieth Century* (1951), 67, 73, 79, 90, 94, 111-114, 116.

G399 Stuckey, William J. *The Pulitzer Prize Novels: A Critical Backward Look* (1966), 24, 104.

G400 Studena, Zora. "Thomas Wolfe a jeho tvorba," *Pavucina a Bralo*, 751-764.

G401 Summer, Richard. *Craft of the Short Story* (1948), 75, 88, 92, 113, 138.

G402 *Svensk Uppslagsbok* (1955), v.31, 686-687.

G403 Swados, Harvey. *A Radical's America* (1962), 194, 203.

G404 Swinnerton, Frank. *Figures in the Foreground: Literary Reminiscences* (1964), 113, 157.

G405 Talmey, A. "Wolfe and the Angel," *Vogue: World in Vogue* (1963), 368-369.

G406 Tanner, Louise. *All the Things We Were* (1968), 312-314.

G407 Tate, Allan. *Collected Essays* (1959), 514, 555.

G408 Taylor, Walter F. *The Story of American Letters* (1956), 397, 464-471.

G409 ———. "Thomas Wolfe and the Middle-Class Tradition," Holman, 141-148.

G410 Terry, John Skally. "Enroute to a Legend," Jerome Beatty, Jr., ed., *The Saturday Review Gallery* (1959), 357-361.

G411 ———. "Introduction," *LTHM*, vii-xxii.

G412 ———. "Wolfe and Perkins," Walser, 51-56.

G413 Theunissen, Gert H. "Thomas Wolfe," *Argernis und Zuversicht.* (1947).

G414 Thompson, Betty. "Thomas Wolfe: Two Decades of Criticism," W. B. Hamilton, ed., *Fifty Years of the South Atlantic Quarterly* (1952), 375-388. Also in Walser, 298-313.

G415 Thorp, Willard, *American Writing in the Twentieth Century* (1960), 173-177, 234.

G416 Tindall, George B. *The Emergence of the New South, 1913-1945* (1967), 104, 110, 304-305, 317, 650-653, 668.

G417 Tindall, W. Y. *James Joyce* (1950), 3, 11, 16-17.

G418 Trilling, Lionel. "The meaning of a literary idea," *The Liberal Imagination* (1950), 294-303. Also in 1957 edition, 285-290.

G419 ———, "Thomas Wolfe," Margaret Denny, ed., *The American Writer and the European Tradition* (1950), 144-149. See also 76, 170.

G420 ———, "Wolfe," Herbert Gold, ed. *Stories of Modern America* (1961), 487-491.

G421 Turnbull, Andrew. *Scott Fitzgerald* (1962), 118, 196-197, 219, 242, 309-310.

G422 Ulanov, Barry. *The Two Worlds of American Art: The Private and the Popular* (1965), 275-277, 459, 470.

G423 U.S. Library of Congress. *Guide to the Study of the United States of America* (1960), 152, 153, 198, 202.

G424 Untermeyer, Louis, ed. *The Britannica Library of Great American Writing* (1960), v. 2, 1613-1615.

G425 ———. "Foreword," *SLD*, v-vi.

G426 ———. "Thomas Wolfe," *Makers of the Modern World* (1955), 726-735.

G427 Uzzell, Thomas, *Techniques of the Novel* (1959), 239-240, 301.

G428 Van Doren, Carl, and Van Doren, Mark. *American and British Literature since 1890* (1940), 101-102, 365.

G429 Van Doren, Carl. "Thomas Wolfe," *The American Novel* (1940), 343-348.

G430 ———. *Three Worlds* (1936), 251, 267-269.

G431 Van Gelder. "Thomas Wolfe as Friends Remember Him," *Writers and Writing* (1946), 114-119. See also 80, 173-174.

G432 Van Nostrand, Albert. *The Denatured Novel* (1960), 61-62, 134.

G433 Vandiver, Frank E., ed. *The Idea of the South: Pursuit of a Single Theme* (1964), 30, 32, 34.

G434 Vauchier-Zananiri, Nelly. "Les romans-fleuves de Thomas Wolfe," *Voix d'Amérique* (1945), 85-92.

G435 Volkening, Henry T. "Penance No More," Walser, 33-50. Also Pollock, 108-126.

G436 Wade, John Donald. "Prodigal," *Selected Essays and Other Writings* (1966), 169-175. See also 8.

G437 Wagenknecht, E. C. "Gargantua as Novelist," *Cavalcade of the American Novel* (1952), 409-415.

G438 Waldmeir, Joseph J., ed. *Recent American Fiction: Some Critical Views* (1963), 86, 182, 184.

G439 Walker, Warren S. *Twentieth Century Short Story Explication* (1961), 361-363. See also *First Supplement* (1963), 127; and *Second Supplement* (1965), 171.

G440 Walser, Richard "A First Play by a Noted Novelist," *North Carolina Drama* (1956), 94-95.

G441 ———. *North Carolina in the Short Story* (1948), 143-144.

G442 ———. *North Carolina Parade: Stories of History and People* (1966), 190-193.

G443 ———. *Picture Book of Tar Heel Authors* (1957), 23.

G444 ———. "Preface," Brodin, 7-9.

G445 ———. "Preface," Walser, vii-xi.

G446 ———. "Thomas Wolfe: An Introduction and Interpretation," Field, 181-186.

G447 ———. "The Transformation of Thomas Wolfe," Warren French, ed., *The Thirties: Fiction, Poetry, Drama* (1967), 39-45.

G448 Warren, Robert Penn. "The Hamlet of Thomas Wolfe," *Selected Essays* (1958), 170-183. Translated into German, *Ausgewählte Essays* (1961), 208-223. Also M. D.

Zabel, ed., *Literary Opinion in America* (1937), 359-372; Walser, 120-132; and Field, 205-216.

G449 Wasserstrom, William. *Heiress of All the Ages* (1959), 100-101.

G450 Watkins, Floyd C. "Rhetoric in Southern Writing: Wolfe," Holman, 75-77. Also Field, 177-180.

G451 ———. "Thomas Wolfe: A Good Idea for a Story," *Writer to Writer* (1966), 7-15.

G452 ———. "Thomas Wolfe's Characters: Portraits," Holman, 49-51.

G453 Watt, William W. *An American Rhetoric* (1964), 44, 250-252, 278.

G454 Weales, Gerald. *American Drama Since World War II* (1963), 84, 154, 163.

G455 West, Paul. *The Modern Novel* (1963), 238, 245-254, 261, 265, 281-283, 298, 313-314, 336, 385.

G456 West, Ray B. *The Short Story in America, 1900-1950* (1952), 11, 24-25.

G457 Wheelock, John Hall. "Introduction," *FOAN*, v-vi.

G458 White, Roy Lewis, ed. *The Achievement of Sherwood Anderson* (1966), 4, 16, 17, 121, 224.

G459 *Who's Who in America, 1932-1933*, 2498. Also in editions of 1934-35, 1936-37, 1938-39.

G460 Widdemer, Margaret. *Do You Want to Write* (1937), 94-96.

G461 Wilson, Rufus R. *New York in Literature* (1947),
100, 172.

G462 —— ed. *Panorama of American Literature* (1947),
337-340.

G463 *Winkler-Prins Encyclopaedie* (Amsterdam 1954), v.4,
530, 572.

G464 Winterich, John T. *A Primer of Book-Collecting* (1946),
37, 131, 135, 136.

G465 Wolfe, Don M. *The Image of Man in America* (1957),
6, 359-360, 436, 457.

G466 Wolfe, Mrs. Julia Elizabeth "Reminiscences," *LTHM*,
xxii-xxv. Translated into German, *Uns Bleibt die
Erde*, 119-127.

G467 Wolfe, William Oliver. [Letter to Tom Wolfe, his son,
dated April 17, 1918], Hans Helmcke, *Die Familie in
Romanwerk von Thomas Wolfe* (1967), 300-301.

G468 Woodress, James, ed. *American Literary Scholarship:
An Annual, 1963* (1965), 132-134, 139-141,
214-215, 221, 222.

G469 ——. *American Literary Scholarship: An Annual,
1964* (1966), 148-149.

G470 ——. *American Literary Scholarship: An Annual,
1965* (1967), 162-163, 168, 170-172, 181, 200.

G471 ——. *Dissertations in American Literature, 1891-1961*
(1962), 46-47, 103.

G472 Woodward, C. Vann. *The Burden of Southern History*
(1960), 25, 29, 35.

H. Poetry and Fiction Concerning Wolfe

H1 Askew, Rual. "The Harp of Death for Thomas Wolfe,"
Southwest Review XXXIII (Autumn 1948), 348.
A poem.

H2 Ballou, Adin. "Catawba's Son," *New York Times*, October
19, 1956. A poem on the editorial page.

H3 Bernstein, Mrs. Aline. *An Actor's Daughter*. New York:
Alfred A. Knopf, 1941, 228 p.

H4 ———. "Eugene," *Three Blue Suits*. New York: Equinox
Cooperative Press, 1933, pp. 47-74. Also excerpt in
Bennett Cerf, ed., *Reading for Pleasure* (1957), 142-150.

H5 ———. *The Journey Down*. New York: Alfred A. Knopf,
1938, 305p.

H6 ———. *Miss Condon*. New York: Alfred A. Knopf,
1947, 244p.
Mrs. Bernstein's fiction, like Wolfe's, is largely
autobiographical. "Eugene" is a description of Wolfe,
while *The Journey Down* gives the woman's version of the
romance between George Webber and Esther Jack in
TWATR. *An Actor's Daughter* is based on Mrs. Bernstein's
youth, and describes some scenes similar to those told to
Webber by Mrs. Jack in Wolfe's novels.

H7 Bradbury, Ray. "Forever and the Earth," *Planet Stories*, Spring, 1950, pp. 26-33. Also in *Big Book of Science Fiction*, Conklin and Graff, eds. (1950).

H8 Brown, Rosellen. "On the Ghost of Thomas Wolfe," *New York Times*, April 11, 1957. A poem on the editorial page.

H9 Calverton, V. F. "To T. W.," *Modern Quarterly*, (Fall 1938), 89. A poem.

H10 Ehle, John Marsden. "An Unfound Door," *American Adventure* (1953). A play about Wolfe.

H11 Engell, Else. "Thomas Wolfe, 1900-1938," *Wilson Library Bulletin*, XIII (January 1939), 315. A poem.

H12 Fifield, William. "Tom Wolfe Slept Here," *Story*, XXII (March-April 1943), 9-16. A short story.

H13 Flaccus, Kimball. "Letter to Thomas Wolfe," *Scholastic*, XXXIV (May 13, 1939), 26E-27E. A poem. This also appears in the author's *The White Stranger* (1944), 110-115; and in *The Breadloaf Anthology* (1939).

H14 Hay, Sara H. "Once More, Ye Laurels . . . ," *Saturday Review*, XVIII (September 24, 1938), 8. A poem. Also in her *This, My Letter* (1939), with the title, "In Memoriam."

H15 Hodgin, David R. *The Ballad of Tall Tom Wolfe*. Asheville: Stephens Press, 1949, 8p. A poem in leaflet form.

H16 Mathews, Kathleen. "To Thomas Wolfe—Who Loved Maxwell Perkins," *North Carolina English Teacher*, IX (April 1952), 11. A poem.

H17 Schoeffle, Evelyn. "Requiem," *University of North Carolina Magazine*, LXVIII (1938), 21. A poem.

H18 Seif, Morton. "Sweet Tom," *Carolina Magazine*, May, 1948, p. 31. A poem.

H19 Tabler, Virginia H. "For Thomas Wolfe," *One and Twenty: Duke Narrative and Verse, 1924-1945* (1945), 185. A poem.

H20 Vance, Eleanor G. "Thomas Wolfe," *Saturday Review*, XXXII (January 22, 1949), 30. A poem. Also in her *Store in Your Heart* (1950).

H21 West, J. F. "At the Grave of Thomas Wolfe," *Carolina Magazine*, May 1948, p. 32. A poem.

H22 Wouk, Herman. *Youngblood Hawke.* Garden City, N. Y.: Doubleday, 1962, 783p.
This novel of a young writer's adventures was widely reviewed as a portrait of Wolfe. For example, the review in the *Saturday Review* (May 19, 1962, p. 36), said: ". . . despite the usual disclaimers, *Youngblood Hawke* is clearly a fictional account of Thomas Wolfe's tumultous life and career."

I. Miscellaneous

ART WORKS

I1 Two hundred sets of original wood engravings by Letterio
Calapai, inspired by *LHA*, were published in 1947 with
an introduction by Franz Schoenberner. There are twenty-five
different engravings, in two colors, with accompanying
text from *LHA* in calligraphy, enclosed in a gray cloth
portfolio, 52 by 38 cm.

I2 Nat Werner has made a head of Thomas Wolfe in clay
and cast twelve bronze replicas from it. They are $6\frac{3}{4}$ inches
high, mounted on hard wood bases $3\frac{1}{2}$ inches high.

MANUSCRIPT COLLECTIONS

I3 Harvard University Library has the best collection of
Wolfe manuscripts and source materials. Some description
of the contents of this collection can be seen in Kennedy,
439-441, and in Helmcke, 333-335. Much of this
collection came from William B. Wisdom, New Orleans
collector and friend of Wolfe.

I4 The University of North Carolina also has an excellent
Wolfe collection, including much manuscript material
relating to the Wolfe family and Wolfe's days in Chapel
Hill. The Wolfe Collection of John Skally Terry,
Wolfe's friend who was preparing a biography
of Wolfe before his untimely death in 1953,
is at Chapel Hill.

I6 The Pack Memorial Library, Asheville, N. C., has a
collection of Wolfeana, including books, letters,
legal documents, photographs, and newspaper clippings.

MUSIC SCORES

I7 Alexander Semmler composed a "Sinfonietta" based on the
life of Wolfe. It was played by the Columbia Concert
Orchestra over the Columbia Broadcasting System,
April 3, 1942.

I8 Howard Whittaker composed a song cycle, with text from
OTATR and scores for voice and piano (Cleveland,
Ohio, 1957).

I9 William Schuman composed a "Prelude for Women's
Voices," a vocal score with words taken from SLD.

I10 At least three songs with the title "Look Homeward, Angel"
and one with the title "You Can't Go Home Again"
have been copyrighted. There is no apparent connection
with Wolfe or his works except the titles.

I11 Don Gillis composed a music score entitled "Thomas Wolfe
—American." It was performed by the Cincinnati
Symphony Orchestra, October 27, 1950.

See also E 24.

RADIO PROGRAMS

I12 Norman Corwin directed a program of Wolfeana,
with readings from his works and a brief sketch of his life,
over the Columbia Broadcasting System,
October 5, 1941.

I13 A radio version of *OTATR* was presented over the
"Voice of America" broadcast, April 17, 1947.

I14 Wolfe was the subject of the radio program, "We, the
People," in October, 1950.

I15 John Marsden Ehle's drama about Wolfe, "An Unfound
Door," was presented in N.B.C.'s American
Adventures Series, November 13, 1953.

I16 Graham Hutton presented a program on "Thomas Wolfe,"
British Broadcasting Company, London, November 28,
1948.

I17 Martin Maloney presented a program with quotations
from Wolfe over WMAQ, Evanston, Ill., April 9, 1955.

I18 W. Neid presented a program entitled "Thomas
Wolfe: Der Homer der modernen Amerikanischen
Literatur," over the South German Radio, Munich,
August 29, 1955.

119 N.B.C.'s "Biography in Sound" featured Wolfe, November 1, 1955.

120 N.B.C. presented recordings of interviews with Mrs. Mabel Wolfe Wheaton concerning Thomas Wolfe, on "Radio Monitor," October 3, 1957, and January 10, 1958.

121 *LHA* was discussed on C.B.S., "Invitation to Learning," January 30, 1961.

122 W.B.T. Radio, Charlotte, N. C., presented James C. Davis's "Thomas Wolfe: The Legend and the Man," May 12, 1961. This included taped interviews with Fred Wolfe, Paul Green, Corydon Spruill, Richard L. Young, and others.

123 The West German Radio, Cologne, presented selections from Wolfe in its program, "English for Seniors," Summer, 1965.

RECORDINGS

124 David Reid Hodgin, of Hendersonville, N. C., has recorded his "Ballad of Tall Tom Wolfe."

125 The Library of Congress recorded conversations with Mabel Wolfe Wheaton (February 23, 1947), Mrs. Julia Elizabeth Wolfe (December 20, 1948), and Fred Wolfe (July 14, 1949), and these talks about Thomas Wolfe are available on both discs and tapes.

126 Kenneth Allan Robinson discusses Wolfe in "Books and the Bad Life," Record No. 300-94 of the Educational Audio-Visual, Inc., Pleasantville, N. Y.

I27 Alexander Scourby has recorded "Circus at Dawn,"
in the Adventures in American Literature Series,
Side I, Harcourt, Brace & Co., 1963.

THEATRICAL PRESENTATIONS

I28 Ketti Fring's play adapted from *LHA* ran a successful
season on Broadway in 1957-1959, and won both the
Pulitzer Prize and the Theatre Critics Award. It has since
been performed by road groups, college dramatic
groups, and little theatre groups both in the United States
and in Europe.

I29 The Marblehead, Mass., Play House presented a dramatic
adaptation from *TWATR*, starring Kay Francis,
on August 21-26, 1950.

I30 *Mannerhouse* was produced at Yale University on
May 5-7, 1949.

I31 *Herrenhaus*, the German translation of *Mannerhouse*,
by Peter Sandberg, was produced at the Deutsche
Schauspielhaus in Hamburg in 1953. It was
later played in Dusseldorf and other German cities by a
touring company.

I32 "Le Manoir," Georges Sion's French translation of
Mannerhouse, was produced by the Theatre National de
Belgique, Brussels, in its 1957-1958 season.

I33 "The Return of Buck Gavin," a one-act play, was produced
by the Carolina Playmakers, Chapel Hill, N. C.,
March 14 and 15, 1919.

134 "The Third Night," another one-act play, was produced by the Carolina Playmakers, December 12 and 13, 1919.

135 The 47 Workshop at Harvard University produced "The Mountains" and "Welcome to Our City," two longer Wolfe plays, in October, 1921, and May, 1923, respectively.

136 Motion pictures based on Wolfe's novels have been several times considered. In 1948, Arthur Ripley wrote a screenplay based on *LHA* for Paramount Pictures, and some scenes were actually shot in Asheville and Chapel Hill. Donald Wayne prepared another script for *LHA*, but neither of them was ever completed. Charles Laughton and Paul Gregory at one time owned screen rights to Wolfe's novels, but so far they have defied successful production.

Supplement

(These are entries recently published or
brought to the compiler's attention after the
final preparation of the bibliography.)

SA1 *Thomas Wolfe: Death the Proud Brother*, edited and
annotated by Heinz Ludwig. Frankfurt am Main: Verlag
Moritz Diesterweg, 1964. 64 p., 18 cm. This is an
English text with notes for German students.

SA2 *The Notebooks of Thomas Wolfe*, edited by Richard S.
Kennedy and Paschal Reeves. Chapel Hill: University
of North Carolina Press, 1970. 2v.

SA3 *Thomas Wolfe: Schau Heimwärts, Engel*. Berlin: Verlag
Volk und Welt, 1962. 646 p., 21 cm. This is the
Schiebelhuth translation, with a "Nachwort"
by Joachim Krehayn, 641-646.

SB1 "The Company," *Mainstream*, XI (January 1956), 25-37.
From *YCGHA*, 129-140.

SC1 "Eugene Writes a Paper," in Herbert R. Moyes, ed.,
An Editor's Treasury (1968), 1515-1516. From
LHA, 207-209.

SC2 "From a Train Window," in Bernard Smith and Philip
Van Doren Stern, eds., *The Holiday Reader* (1947),
357-362. From *OTATR*, 30-35.

250

SC3 "Letters," Digest of *Letters* in Frank Magill, ed., *Masterpieces of World Literature*, 4th ser. (1968), 538-541.

SE1 Blake, Pauline. "Thomas Wolfe: Death's Chosen Son." M.A. thesis, Wichita State University, 1957.

SE2 Daniels, Thomas E. "Eliza Gant: Thomas Wolfe's Symbol of 1920's America." Ph.D. dissertation, Washington State University, 1968.

SE3 Robinson, Walter Ray. "Thomas Wolfe: His Mother and and Eliza Gant." M.A. thesis, Virginia Polytechnic Institute, 1968.

SE4 Rubin, Louis D. "The Weather of His Youth." Ph.D. dissertation, Johns Hopkins University, 1954.

SE5 Singh, Hari. "Time and Man in the Novels of Thomas Wolfe," Ph.D. dissertation, Osmania University (India), 1968.

SF1 Allen, G. W. (Review of Reeves), *Saturday Review*, LII (June 21, 1969) 54.

SF2 Anderson, Patrick. (Review of Nowell), *Observer* (London), March 26, 1961, p.31.

SF3 Anonymous. (Review of Field), *Publishers' Weekly*, February 19, 1968, p. 104.

SF4 Anonymous. (Reviews of *FDTM* and *OTATR*), *Book Buyer*, I (December 1935), 14.

SF5 (Review of Revised *LTHM*), *American Literature*, XL (January 1969), 595.

SF6 Anonymous. (Review of Holman), *Choice*, III
(January 1967), 1015.

SF7 Anonymous. (Review of *Mannerhouse*), *U.S. Quarterly
Book Review*, V (1949), 152.

SF8 Anonymous. (Review of Turnbull), *Kirkus Review Service*,
January 1, 1968, 45. See also January 15, 1968, 63.

SF9 Anonymous. (Review of Revised *LTHM*), *Times*
(London) *Literary Supplement*, January 2, 1969, 5.

SF10 Appel, Benjamin. (Review of Turnbull), *Carleton
Review*, IX (Summer 1968), 104.

SF11 Belman, Samuel I. "Hemingway, Faulkner, and
Wolfe . . . and the Common Reader," *Southern Review*,
2nd ser., III (Summer 1968), 834-849.

SF12 Bledsoe, Jerry. "Wolfe's Dixieland: Tom's Home Broods
in Silence," *Greensboro* (N.C.) *Daily News*,
March 10, 1968, C1.

SF13 Bradbury, Malcolm (Review of Field),
New Statesman, LXXVIII (July 18, 1969), 86.

SF14 ———. (Review of Turnbull), *New Statesman*, LXXV
(May 31, 1968), 729.

SF15 Butwin, David. "A Climate Fit for a Weatherman,"
Saturday Review, LII (May 31, 1969), 32, 37.
On a visit to Asheville and Wolfe's home.

SF16 Cargill, Oscar. (Review of Turnbull), *American
Literature*, XL (November, 1968), 412-413.

SF17 Comino, Ionna. "Thomas Wolfe," *Contemporanul*, May 31, 1968, p.2.

SF18 Corrington, John W. "Three Books about a Southern Romantic," *Southern Literary Journal*, I (Autumn 1968), 98-104. (Reviews of Field, Turnbull and the Revised *LTHM*).

SF19 Dressel, John, and Gross, Sol. "The Lost Boy of Thomas Wolfe," *St. Louis Magazine*, October 1965, 7-8.

SF20 Fisher, Roscoe B. "Kitty Sue Talks about Tom," *Greensboro Daily News*, April 21, 1969, p. A7. Brief reminiscences of Mrs. Dave Parish of Badin, N.C., who knew Wolfe as a child.

SF21 Hillman, S. (Review of Turnbull), *Saturday Night*, CXXXIII (May 1968), 38.

SF22 Hovde, A. J. (Review of *Purdue Speech*), *College English*, XXVII (January 1966), 335-336.

SF23 Hynds, Reed. "Thomas Wolfe Visits City—says he'll write a 'really great' book," *Star-Times* [*St. Louis*], September 20, 1935, p. 17.

SF24 Johnson, Elmer D. (Review of Field), *Library Journal*, XCIII (February 1, 1968), 553.

SF25 Malin, I. (Review of Turnbull), *Catholic World*, (April 1968), 46.

SF26 Misiego, Micaela. "Thomas Wolfe, poeta da solidade," *Grial* [Vigo, Spain], XIX (1968), 1-29.

SF27 Mitchell, John B. "Thomas Wolfe on the Peninsula," *Daily Press*, (Newport News-Hampton, Va.), October 26, 1969, p. 3-5, illus.

SF28 Reeves, Paschal. "Gleam From the Forge: Thomas Wolfe's Emerging Idea of Brotherhood," *Georgia Review*, XXII (Summer 1968), 247-253.

SF29 Rubin, L. D. Jr. (Review of Holman), *American Literature*, XXXVIII (January 1967), 574-575.

SF30 Sakamoto, Masayuki. "The Discovery of One's Other Self: *YCGHA* Reconsidered," *Studies in English Literature* (English number), (1968), 17-35.

SF31 Schneider, D. B. (Review of Reeves), *Library Journal*, XCIV (May 1, 1969), 1878.

SF32 Seymour-Smith, M. (Review of Turnbull), *Times* (London) *Literary Supplement*, July 5, 1968, p. 13. See also September 12, 1968, p. 968.

SF33 ———. (Review of *YCGHA*), *Times* (London) *Literary Supplement*, November 22, 1968, p. 734.

SF34 Singh, Hari. "Thomas Wolfe: The Idea of Eternity," *South Carolina Review*, I (May 1969), 40-47.

SF35 Snider, William D. "Three Tar Heels at Harvard," *Greensboro Daily News*, February 11, 1968, p. C5. The three were Wolfe, Albert Coates and William Polk.

SF36 Spitz, Leon. "Was Wolfe an Anti-Semite?" *American Hebrew*, CLVIII (November 19, 1948), 5.

SF37 Sutton, Horace. "Wolfe Wouln't Know Asheville with Urban Renewal Changes," *Times* [Roanoke, Va.], June 1, 1969, p. B13.

SF38 Toynbee, P. (Review of Turnbull), *Observer* [London], IX, (June 1968), 29.

SF39 Untermeyer, Louis. (Review of *SLD*), *Yale Review*, XXXV (Winter 1946), 337.

SF40 Walser, Richard. (Review of Rubin), *South Atlantic Quarterly*, LIV (October 1955), 567-568.

SF41 Witonski, P. P. (Review of Turnbull), *National Review*, XX (June 18, 1968), 616-617.

SF42 Yoder, Edwin M., Jr. "Thomas Wolfe: A Life of Suffering and Achievement," *Daily News* [Greensboro], February 4, 1968, p. D3.

SG1 Danielson, Eric. "Thomas Wolfe," Sven M. Kristensen, ed. *Fremmede Digtere in det 20 Arhundrede* (1968), III, 13-23.

SG2 Davis, Burton. "Thomas Wolfe: An Obituary," *New York Post, A Century of Journalism Panorama* (1943), III, 126-134.

SG3 Gardiner, Harold C. *Fifty Years of the American Novel* (1959), viii, xi, 102, 197-215, 283.

SG4 Hilfer, Anthony. *Revolt from the Village* (1969), 27-28, 32, 194, 202-219, 222, 237, 239, 245-249, 253.

SG5 Murray, Henry. "Personality and Creative Imagination,"
English Institute Annual (1942), 143-144,
150-152, 154-156, 158, 160.

SG6 Reaver, J. R., and Strozier, R. I. "Thomas Wolfe and
Death," M. R. Westbrook, ed., *The Modern
American Novel* (1968), 79-89.

SG7 Russell, Frank A. (Ted Malone). "Thomas Wolfe,"
Mansions of Imagination Album (1940).

SG8 Schoenberner, Franz. "Wolfe's Genius Seen Afresh,"
New York Times, Books of the Times (1965), 14.

SG9 Van Nostrand, Albert. *Every Man His Own Poet*
(1968), 2, 8, 9-18, 86-87.

SG10 Vogel, Stanley, and Murphy, Ella. *An Outline of
American Literature* (1961), II, 289-294, 319.

SG11 Wallace, Margaret. (Review of *LHA*), *New York
Times, Books of the Times* (1965), 13; Also in
New York Times, America's Taste. . . . (1960), 216.

SG12 Witham, W. T., ed. *Panorama of American Literature*
(1947), 337-340.

Index

258

LeRoy, Gaylord C.   G264
Lessing, Doris   F547
Letters of Thomas Wolfe
   A138-A140, B43, B62-B68,
   B72, B109, B116, B118,
   C117-C120, C123-C127, C129,
   F32, F38, F40, F41, F48, F204,
   F213, F215, F271, F362, F369,
   F384, F442, F468, F491, F547,
   F602, F650, F653, F683, F704,
   F743, F798, SC3
Letters to His Mother   A69, A78,
   A134-A136, A141, B44, C121,
   C122, C128, E105, F54,
   F64-F66, F243, F331, F349,
   F420, F465, F601, F654, F741,
   F749, F752, F758, F780, F823,
   F872, SF5, SF9, SF18
Levine, Harry   G265
Lewis, Sinclair   G175, G266,
   G365
Lewisohn, Alice   C123, C127
Lewisohn, Ludwig   G267
Lichtinhagen, Leo   F548
Lieber, Maxim   F549
Lindell, Börje   A161
Linder, Wolfgang   E77
Lindroth, Colette   D25
Lindroth, James   D25
Liss, Joseph   C68
Little, Thomas   F550
Littlejohn, Daniel   F551
Logan, Susan H.   E78
Loggins, Vernon   G269
Lomax, Elizabeth   C68
Lombardo, Agostino   G270

Longley, Marjorie   G271
Longstreet, Stephen   G272
Look Homeward, Angel
   A1-A38, A142-A147, B5,
   B61, B70, E9, E41, E55, E104,
   F9, F10, F27, F67-F71, F144,
   F220, F229, F277, F279, F347,
   F357, F366, F388, F401, F415,
   F426, F431, F500, F517, F541,
   F543, F563, F567, F591, F659,
   F662, F667, F688, F727, F736,
   F782, F802, F808, F811, F814,
   F817, F829, F852, F870, G18,
   G91, G120, G224, G239, G279,
   G305, G319, I36, SA3, SG11
   See also Frings, Ketti.
The Lost Boy   A126, A130,
   B73, C139, G262, G393, SF19
   See also THB.
Luccock, Halford E.   C243,
   C264, G273
Luce, Robert B.   C106
Lucignani, Luciano   F522
Ludwig, Heinz   F553, SA1
Ludwig, Richard M.   G274
Luedecke, Henry   G275
Lynch, W.J.   F554
Lynn, Kenneth S.   F555
Lyons, John Ormsby   E79, G276

McAfee, Helen   F556
Macauley, Thurston   F557
McClain, John   F558
McClennen, Joshua   C37
McCole, Camille   F559, G277
McCormick, John   G278

276